WHAT MARX REALLY MEANT

G. D. H. COLE

WHAT MARX REALLY MEANT

GREENWOOD PRESS, PUBLISHERS
WESTPORT, CONNECTICUT

335.4
C689w

Originally published in 1934
by Alfred A. Knopf, New York

Reprinted from an original copy in the collections
of the Brooklyn Public Library

First Greenwood Reprinting 1970

Library of Congress Catalogue Card Number 79-90489

SBN 8371-3082-4

Printed in the United States of America

CONTENTS

WHAT MARX REALLY MEANT

CHAPTER I

THE FOUNDATIONS OF MARXISM

THIS BOOK of mine requires at the outset a few words of explanation; for otherwise there is a danger that some readers may search in it for what they will certainly fail to find. It is not meant primarily, or to any considerable extent, either as an exposition or as a criticism of Marx's doctrines, here paraphrasing, condensing and expounding the words of the master, or there seeking to set him right where I believe him to have been wrong. There exist plenty of expositions and abridgements of Marx by followers of his doctrine; and criticisms and refutations of him are as the sands of the sea-shore. There are even competent judicial essays upon his work, with which I have no desire to set up this book in rivalry.

My object is something different. It is to disentangle in his teaching, from what is dead or no longer appropriate, what remains alive and capable of that process of growth and adaptation which is the prerogative of living things. I am conscious that my own thought has been deeply influenced by Marx—the more perhaps because I came to him after I had first received, and then repelled, the influence of the Hegelian doctrine. I am no Marxist, if to be one involves, as many of his followers seem to suppose, unquestioning acceptance of all his doctrines, and even a belief in the literal inspiration of all the Marxian scriptures. But I am Marxist, to the extent that I have found in certain of his doctrines, and above all in his methods of social analysis, clearer light than anywhere else by which to seek an understanding of the fundamental economic and political problems of to-day.

In this sense alone, I claim, has anyone a sound Marxian title to call himself Marxist in 1934. For it is the rankest injustice to Marx to suppose that he would have written exactly as he wrote in 1848, or 1859, or 1867, or even 1883, if he had been alive and writing to-day. No sense was stronger in Marx than the sense of change; and how much has changed almost out of recognition since Marx died more than half a century ago! Only idiots learn *The Communist Manifesto* and the key passages of *Das Kapital* by heart, and conceive themselves thereby to have unlocked the secrets of the capitalist system as it now exists. Only disciples who utterly misunderstand both the meaning and the method of their master can think that an analysis of the economic development of the first half of the nineteenth century, primarily in a single country, will serve in lieu of fresh thinking about the world-bestriding capitalism of a century later. No thinker thinks beyond his time, in the sense that his thought can be adequate for any generation later than his own. He may lay lasting foundations, good for later generations to build upon; but woe betide those who seek to save themselves the pain of mental building by inhabiting dead men's minds.

If Marx is to be of any service to us, we must not parrot his phrases or repeat his doctrines by rote, but let him help us to do afresh for our day and generation what he sought to do for his own. For this task we are likely, I believe, to find his method more directly helpful than his doctrine. For if we begin with Marx's doctrines, and set out to discover where and how far they are still applicable to the world of to-day, we shall be in danger of producing either an apologia or a criticism, without throwing any real light upon our own problems. We shall run the risk of assuming that precisely the questions Marx asked are the questions that need asking now, and that the answers will be merely modifications, or perhaps negations, of the answers which he found. But in fact the questions that it is important for us to ask may be different questions, and the answers may have to be stated in radically different terms.

Yet, of course, the world we have to study has grown directly out of the world Marx studied. Our world is continuous with his; and to some extent he was able to foresee aright how the one would develop out of the other. We shall doubtless find after all that many of his questions are our questions too, and derive from them answers of the same order as his own. But we must not, at our peril, assume in advance that this is so of any particular question. We must look closely at our own world, not only for the answers to our questions but equally for the questions themselves.

That is why, if Marx helps us at all, his method is likely to help us more than his conclusions. For a method of study and analysis is likely to remain valid for longer than any set of conclusions arrived at by its use. This is not to say that method can remain static in a changing world; but it is reasonable to suppose that the general forms of thought will change more slowly than their particular content.

Of course, it is possible that Marx's method will not help us.

There are, I know, some Marxists who hold his method to have been an unfortunate philosophical aberration, in despite of which he hit on a number of important truths. But these are either the parrots of Marxism, who learn diligently without reflection, or its mere hangers-on, in search of comfortable crumbs of congenial doctrine. Marx's method is integral, not only to his conclusions, but to the entire basis of historical study on which his conclusions rest. His method will fail to help us only if his whole analysis was from beginning to end upon the wrong lines. It may have been so; and those who hold *a priori* that it was so will be indisposed to attempt its use for an analysis of the world to-day. I have not found it so, when I have tried to use it; and all I ask of the readers of this book is that they should follow me in the experiment of seeking to read the signs of our times by a method which is largely that of Marx, ready to discard the method if, after making due allowance for my shortcomings as a guide, they find it unhelpful, but also ready, if it does help, to carry the analysis further for themselves by the same method. For no one who has once made Marx's method his own need ever be at a loss for fresh fields in which to apply it, though he may often be in danger of seeking to apply it where it does not belong.

THE DIALECTICAL METHOD

Having said this, I feel I shall be expected to proceed at once to explain what this wonderful Marxian method is, in order that my readers may be in a position to follow the analysis of the world of to-day with full knowledge of the method by which it is being made. This, however, is not what I propose to do; for the Marxian method is best understood not by reading a theoretical exposition of it, but in the first instance by seeing it at work. Later in this book, I shall attempt to state what I believe its essential qualities to be; but at this stage I shall say but a few words about it.

In the first place, all living things are subject to constant change, which arises partly from their environment and partly from within themselves. This is true of societies no less than of individuals; for societies are constantly changing collections of individual men and women. In order to understand any human society, we must study it not as something static, but as a continually changing thing, subject to an unceasing process of development, growth and decay. It is intelligible only in relation to its entire past history, as well as its present condition, which is indeed only a cross-section of its history. Even if our aim is to understand the present, we have to think of the present as a constantly moving point; for even while we are making our analysis to-morrow is becoming to-day.

It follows that, even if our aim were only to understand, and not to use our understanding as a basis for action, the method of static analysis could not, in the field of the social studies, yield us satisfactory results. For if a thing is in fact in constant motion, it is fatally misleading to analyse it on the assumption that it is standing still. For a thing which has change as the very essence of its nature will not stand still for the student's convenience: it can be grasped only in and through its changes, and by an understanding of its processes of change. That is the fundamental mistake of orthodox economics, which sets out to analyse capitalist society on the assumption that it is standing still, and then tries to introduce the dynamic factors at a later stage, as modifications of a static analysis. But this method is radically wrong; for if the vital factor of change is left out of the original analysis, it cannot be successfully reintroduced. Man cannot breathe the breath of life into a dead body, or give concreteness to what is admittedly an abstraction.

The falsification inherent in static analysis of living and changing things becomes still more evident as soon as we ask ourselves what the purpose of our analysis is. For in our study of such things we are assuredly seeking not only to understand, but also to make our understanding a basis for action. Being men and members of a society of men, we cannot escape the necessity of acting, or dissociate our desire to understand society from our desire to act aright as members of it. We can, of course, seek to make our analysis as objective as possible, in order to avoid falsifying facts to suit our personal wishes and ideals; and it is of vital importance that we should do this to the fullest extent of which we are capable. But, however objective we try to be, we cannot possibly even wish to stop our understanding influencing our action, or exclude considerations of practice from our attempts to understand. All social studies, however objective they may seek to be, have a practical aspect; and, if it is disastrous to allow our wishes to distort our observation of the facts, it is no less so to forget, or deny, that understanding of the facts is bound to influence action, and thereby modify the facts themselves. For actions are facts, and men's understanding is a fact, which becomes a social fact as soon as it is diffused by speech or writing, or even as soon as it affects the actions of him who understands.

A sound method of social analysis must therefore be dynamic, in the sense that it must set out from things as they are, in continual change and growth, and not from dead abstractions from which the quality of change and the power to change have been carefully removed. It is above all at this point that Marx's method diverges at the very outset from that of the "orthodox" economists. For they, from the time of Ricardo up to the present, have one and all, with varying degrees of consciousness, begun by making an abstract and static economic world as a field for their analysis, and have allowed change to intrude into this world of theirs only when they have completed its equipment with a full set of static institutions, and studied down to the last detail the hypothetical "behaviour" of these institutions in the absence of all changes which could operate as disturbing factors. This is the celebrated "equilibrium analysis," carried to its barren perfection above all by Pareto and the economists of the Austrian school, but used less consciously as a method by all their predecessors of the classical schools after Adam Smith.

For example, in this abstract world of the economists, there is no room for technical changes which affect the productivity of industry, the balance of machine and human power, the structure of the productive system, the character of the labour process, the supply of and demand for the various kinds of commodities—in fact, every aspect and element of economic life. Not, of course, that the economists are unmindful of these things. They are not; but they treat them as disturbing factors which cause conditions in the real world to diverge from the pattern of the abstract world which they have made. They fall in love with this creature of their minds, until they come readily to believe that man's chief task in society should be to make conditions in the real world resemble as closely as possible this abstract world, in which things always work themselves out with the precision of mathematical equations, and nothing unexpected can ever happen. But, for this to be achieved, all possibility of progress would have to be emptied out of the world; for progress is essentially and inevitably a disturbing force, upsetting current adjustments and existing relationships, and changing the very nature of things as well as their relative positions.

Our first precept, then, is to begin with the real concrete world of things as they are, and not with a simplified abstract world of our imagination. But we must think of things as they are, not as standing still, so as to be reproducible by timeless portraiture, but as changing and growing while we regard them, and as carrying about in all their ceaseless movements and interactions the whole living history of their growth. It is often said that the origin of a thing can never explain it; and that is true enough. Its origin is but one fragment of its history, even as its present activity is another fragment. To study things historically is to set out to interpret them, not by their origins, but by the whole active force of which their entire history is the expression.

But that is not all. If we are setting out to understand a thing, we must look directly at the thing itself, and not primarily at men's ideas about it. This is not because ideas are unimportant, or uninfluential in shaping the world's history, as some Marxists seem to suppose, but because in the last resort ideas are about things, and not things about ideas. The thing is prior to the idea men form of it, though the ideas, once formed, can exert a profound influence in changing the shape of things, and in bringing new things into existence. Throughout human history, things and ideas ceaselessly interact, but never so as to upset the primacy of things. For, in order to become a force in history, the idea must be made flesh, and become a thing.

THE CONCEPTION OF HISTORY

This, and neither more nor less than this, is the basis of the "Materialist Conception of History"—a name so misunderstood and so overlaid with wrong associations as to make clear explanation of it a terribly difficult task, not because the conception itself is unclear, but because its name is apt to conjure up a wrong picture which it is a labour of Sisyphus to remove. For most people think instinctively of materialism as asserting the supremacy of matter over mind, or even as denying the existence of mind save as a derivative quality of matter, whereas no such doctrine is involved in, or even reconcilable with, the "Materialist Conception of History." What this conception does assert is that mind, as a formative force in history, works by embodying itself in things, changing their shape and potency, and combining them into relations and systems whose changing phases are the basis of the history of mankind.

For what are the "material" things that Marx conceived to be the active determinants of social change? They are not, though they include, mere natural objects, offered to man for his use apart from any activity of his own. They include, more and more as civilisation advances, things which men have made by changing the form of natural objects, directing the labour of their hands with the informing power of the human mind. Moreover, even natural objects make their contribution to human history largely, though not exclusively, through men's knowledge of their use. The sea is barrier, and not highway, till men learn to make vessels that will carry them upon it. Coal becomes a productive power only when men have discovered that it will burn, and have learnt the art of mining. Storms and earthquakes may destroy, and climate may cause vegetation to grow or perish, or may influence men's bodies and minds without positive collaboration of men's minds with nature. But the advance of civilisation consists above all else in the growth of men's knowledge of the ways to make natural objects serve their ends, and to fashion out of them things that exist and work not by nature, but by art bending nature to man's will.

The things, then, that Marx calls "material" and regards as the agents of social evolution are more and more products of the human mind. Not nature, as in Buckle's conception, but man's power over nature lies at the root of history. Why call such a conception "materialist," when it in fact embodies the fullest recognition of the conscious determining power of mind?

Marx called his conception of history "materialist," because he was determined to mark it off sharply from the metaphysical Idealism of Hegel and his followers. Where he wrote "materialist," it would be natural in our day to write "realist"; for it is Realism, and not Materialism, that we are accustomed to contrast with Idealism as a philosophical point of view. In this book, I shall write "realist" in place of "materialist," wherever "realist" will convey better to the modern reader the meaning of Marx's doctrine. For I can see no point at all in that form of servility which clings obstinately to a name, even when it has been proved again and again to be a source of needless confusion and misunderstanding. This irreverence will doubtless annoy the theological parrots that screech about the Marxian temple. Let them squawk. Our business is to understand.

According to the Idealists, ideas and not things are the ultimate substance of being. The world we seem to know, the world of fact and event, is but a shadowing of a more real world of pure idea. The thing is nothing, save as a pale and unsubstantial reflection of the idea. Mind not merely shapes matter to its will, but makes it out of nothing save itself. Real things, or rather the appearances that masquerade as real things, owe such half-reality as is conceded to them solely to being emanations of mind or spirit. Consciousness, which is the attribute of mind, is therefore prior to existence in space and time, which is the attribute of things. There are no things: there are only thoughts thinking them.

But now even these thoughts begin to dissolve. For how shall thought subsist without a thinker? How shall many thoughts exist save in the substance of a unifying mind? But the minds of mere men will not serve; for they dwell in bodies which, being things, are but the unsubstantial wrack of thought. The Idealist proceeds at last to the One Universal Mind, wherein all thought has its source and ultimate substance, so that no thought is finally real, except it exist in the Universal Mind. Thus Idealism, which begins by upholding the claims of mind against matter, ends by annihilating minds equally with material things, leaving in substantial existence only the Universal One who bears the same suspiciously close resemblance to the Absolute Nothing as a perfectly empty circle bears to the figure O.

Absolute Idealism is conceived most naturally in static terms; for how can the Absolute, which includes all, change? Change must be out of one form into another; but can the Absolute ever discard, or add to itself, even a single characteristic? It was left for Hegel to re-think Idealism in dynamic terms, so as to make of the Absolute, not a One existing from all time, but an immanent reality gradually achieving actual existence by the evolutionary process of its own thought, discarding ceaselessly the dross of partially conceived and incomplete truths, so as to draw nearer in actual as well as in immanent reality to the ultimate Oneness of the completely coherent and rational self-realisation of the Idea. This process was the Hegelian dialectic, on which Marx built a "materialist"—say rather a "realist"—dialectic of his own.

For Hegel, human history was merely a phase in the dialectical self-realisation of the "Idea." Things were not, save in and for the developing Idea. Minds were not, save as stuff to be burned up to nothing more than the infinitesimal speck of reality distilled out of them in the fierce heat of the crucible of universal history.

In that fierce heat only the rational can live; and therefore only the rational is deemed to possess reality. But as everything of which we have direct experience falls short of rationality, all our experience must be deemed to be an experience of unreal things. All Idealism before Hegel resolved itself into this flat denial of the reality of things experienced. It was Hegel's achievement, by invoking the conception of degrees of reality, and by re-stating Idealism in evolutionary terms, to put back an element of reality into our everyday experience. But in the Hegelian universe of becoming, the stigma upon common experience remained; for things possessed such imperfect reality as they had only as the embodiment of the developing idea.

To this Idealist conception Marx opposed an uncompromising Realism. Seizing upon Hegel's evolutionary conception of being, he applied it directly to the substance of the world of actual experience. The things we see and feel and experience directly with our minds and senses are real, but they are not static. They are constantly changing, becoming, waxing and waning, passing into something other than themselves, even as Hegel said; but their mutations are their own, and not reflections of anything external to themselves. The Hegelian dialectic is the right method of apprehending reality; but it needs to be applied directly to the world of things, and used directly as a clue to the interpretation of ordinary human experience.

In Hegel's universe, the evolution of the Idea is accomplished by a ceaseless succession of ideological conflicts. Every idea that embodies a partial truth meets in the world its opposite and contradiction, which is also the embodiment of a partial truth. Between the two there follows a conflict, out of which at length a new and higher idea, embodying new but still partial truth, emerges—to generate in its turn a new opposite and a new conflict. The struggle of ideas is fought out again and again in the dialectical form of thesis, antithesis, and synthesis; and each synthesis becomes, in the moment of its victory, a thesis in terms of which a fresh struggle is to be fought. This process must go on until finally the goal is reached in that complete and insuperable synthesis which embodies in itself the whole truth and nothing but the truth.

Marx takes over, and applies directly to the world of human affairs, all the Hegelian paraphernalia of conflict—of theses, antitheses and syntheses succeeding one another in a ceaseless ascent of mankind towards more developed forms of social and economic organisation. But what he sees evolving in this way is not the Idea, but life itself—the multifarious life men embody in the patterns of the successive epochs of human civilisation. There is no need to go outside the world of men and things for the clue to the evolutionary process. For men and things are themselves the subject-matter of evolution.

In this conflict of Marx and Hegel, the issue is not whether the dominant power is mind or matter; for the Hegelian conception subordinates both alike to the supposed Idea, and makes men into things in order the more to exalt the Absolute. Marx's so-called Materialism, which was in fact Realism, upheld actual mind equally with actual matter against the Absolute which was greedy to engulf them both. He did not pose the question of mind *versus* matter at all, because he conceived it to be wholly without meaning for the world of men. For in the world of men and things, mind and matter are so interpenetrated and at one that it is futile to ask which counts for more. Mind cannot exist save in the material substance of the brain, or receive impressions save through the material avenues of the sense-organs; and the material objects external to man amid which he lives and works, from the soil itself to the steam-engine and the electrical generator, owe their form and nature and productive power so largely to man's activity as to be essentially products of mind, constantly evolving and changing under the influence of man's inventive power.

When therefore we speak, in Marxian terms, of the "powers of production" as the fundamental forces responsible for social evolution, the phrase has no meaning unless it applies not only to the natural forces which are at man's disposal, but also to the artificial forces which men have made by their use, and not only to all these forces, natural and artificial, taken together, but also to men's knowledge of how to apply them. The Realist Conception of History is so far from representing men as merely the sport of things that it stresses more than any other theory the creative function of men in making the world after the pattern of their own knowledge. The outcome of the Realist Conception is not to dethrone the mind of man, but on the contrary to assert that men make their own history against those who hold that God or the Absolute makes it for them, or that the whole course of human events is no more than a stream of undirected chance.

Men make their own history; but they make it primarily in the economic sphere. The great history-makers are those who by invention or experiment, or by enlarging the boundaries of human knowledge, alter the character of the powers of production, and therewith the ways in which men get their living and organise themselves for economic ends, or those who by destroying civilisations and sweeping away the works and knowledge accumulated by generations of toil and experiment, drive men back to painful new beginnings of economic and cultural activity. This is not to say that the dominant rôle in history belongs to great scientists and inventors on the one hand, and to great captains of destruction upon the other; for often the great invention arises as the cumulative result of the work of many innovators, and the most destructive warfare in history has often arisen not from one man's ambition or military genius, but from the migrations of entire peoples, or the clash of rival groups within a common civilisation. Emphatically, the "great man" theory of history does not hold good; but to deny its validity is not to deny that great men do count, for both good and ill. There is no warrant for the view that the Russian Revolution would have followed the same course without Lenin, or the French Revolution without Napoleon, or that someone else would have been bound to hit on just the same inventions as Watt and Siemens and Marconi at just the same time even if these particular individuals had never been born.

Great men do count; but they count because their greatness fits in with the opportunities of their time. Nor do they count exclusively; for it is not in the least true that in their absence the world would stand still, or that they are the only, or the principal, formative force in world history. What forms world history above all else is the continual interaction between what is given to men as their social inheritance, natural or acquired, and the minds of men in each generation.

In considering how men's social heritage acts upon them, and how men act upon it, in any particular epoch, it is irrelevant how much of this heritage is natural and how much the product of the activity of earlier generations of men. For our own generation, the steam-engine and the electrical generator are just as much parts of the objective situation which confronts mankind as the climate, or the minerals that are found near the earth's surface. It is, of course, true that there will soon be no steam-engines unless men go on making new ones, whereas there will be a climate (but not necessarily quite the same climate) even if men suspend all activity in relation to it. But that is not the point, which is rather that each generation finds itself presented with a certain objective situation including both natural and artificial elements, and that it is upon this situation that each generation of men has to build, within the limits imposed by this situation, and with the materials which this situation affords.

This view of history does not, as many people appear to suppose, imply any sort of fatalism. It does not say that, given a certain objective situation *apart from the human beings who have to handle it,* there is only one possible outcome, so that the next phase of human history is utterly predestined however human beings may behave. It does insist that, as history is a chain of connected development, the next phase must be of such a nature that it can be developed out of its predecessor, and that men's power of influencing the course of history is limited to a choice between alternatives which are possible in face of the objective situation. It follows that, when the historian looks back on past phases of development, he will be likely to find in the objective situations of the past sufficient apparent reasons for history having followed the course which it has actually followed, rather than any other. But this will be because his view of the objective situations of the past will include the actions in them of the human beings who shaped their growth. This is only the familiar dilemma of free will and determinism in its sociological aspect. Every event that has happened must have had sufficient cause, and must therefore have been determined; but it does not follow that events which have not yet happened are predestined apart from the influence of those who have still to act in relation to them. For the causes are not complete until the human beings whose action makes history have done their part. The free wills of men form part of the chain of causality; and those wills are limited only by the conditions within which they have to act.

Marxism is determinist, but not fatalist. No one who reads Marx's political writings, or his elaborate plannings of Socialist strategy, can reasonably suppose that he considered the victory of Socialism to be predestined as to both time and place, and the behaviour of men in the objective situations which faced them to be limited to an inevitable reaction to economic circumstances. He clearly held that it made a quite vitally significant difference to the prospects of Socialism how Socialists behaved, and that their behaviour was capable of being influenced by instruction and exhortation and example.

THE COMING OF SOCIALISM

It is, however, sometimes suggested, with more plausibility, that Marx did believe the coming of Socialism to be inevitable, and held that men could, by their conduct, only advance or delay its coming, or cause it to come in a more or less satisfactory form. It is quite possible that Marx did hold this; but, whether or no, it does not follow as an inexorable deduction from his conception of history. If he held it, his case would be that the objective conditions facing the modern world were of such a nature as to make some form of Socialism the only possible next stage in the development of Western civilisation. On this view, nothing except Socialism would be compatible with the limiting conditions of objective possibility, and men's power of influencing history would be restricted to making Socialism well or ill, and in this or that of its variant possible forms. Such a judgment, whether correct or not, does not form part of the Realist Theory of History in the strict sense: it is a deduction from that theory when it has been brought into contact with the available facts of a particular historical situation, and its validity depends not on the soundness of the theory alone, but also on the observer's skill in selecting and interpreting this particular set of facts. If something other than Socialism should succeed to Capitalism as the next historical form of social organisation, that would not at all prove the Realist Conception of History to be wrong. It would at most only show that Marx had made a mistake in interpreting a particular set of facts in the light of his theory.

It is no doubt possible to hold, as an integral element in a theory of history, that historical epochs do succeed one another in a predestined order, so that there *can* never be more than one possible successor to any given system. But what conceivable ground can there be for such a view? If it is held at all, it must be held simply *a priori;* for it is by its nature incapable of verification or even of plausible demonstration in the light of the facts. It is, in effect, a piece of mysticism, wholly out of keeping with the realistic temper of the theory we have been discussing. Hegel could plausibly hold such a view, because for him all history was the logical unfolding of the Idea, and freedom consisted in furthering this cosmic process. But nothing can square it with Realism; for to the realist there is no logical obstacle to a given objective situation, considered apart from those who are to handle it, having more than one possible outcome.

It is of course fully possible for a realist to consider that Socialism is both by far the best and by far the most probable successor to Capitalism as a form of social organisation, and even to reach, on the basis of his study of the facts, the conclusion that there is no *positive* alternative. But by this he can mean only that he can see or imagine no positive alternative, and that in his judgment there is none. He cannot rationally mean that in the very nature of things there *can be* no alternative, even of a positive kind.

Moreover, even if his judgment is objectively right, the possibility of a *negative* alternative remains. It may be a case of Socialism or—chaos. The only alternative to the building up of some sort of Socialist system may be the sheer dissolution of the civilisation that has reached this critical stage. And, in such a situation, the behaviour of men in facing it may make just the vital difference between the collapse of a civilisation and its advance to a new phase of development. Men's choice is confined to the objectively possible; but how vital that choice may be when the alternatives are delicately poised!

Undoubtedly, Marx did think that Socialism would be the next phase in the history of Western civilisation. Undoubtedly, he often spoke as if he regarded the coming of Socialism as inevitable, and only the time and manner of its coming as open to doubt. But this judgment of his, based upon his observation of the objective situation of his own day, must not be confused with his theory of history, or erected into a dogma to challenge which is to put the whole Realist Conception into jeopardy. Marx's rightness or wrongness on this point does not in any way affect the validity of his general theory.

There is, then, ample scope within the Realist Conception of History for the constructive influence of the minds of men. Indeed, its practical value as a guide to method lies largely in the warning which it gives men against banging their heads uselessly against brick walls. It directs the mind away from the Utopian and unrealisable save in fancy towards the real possibilities of the objective situations in which they are placed, and teaches them, by thinking and acting realistically, to control the course of history far more than they could if they were content with Utopias of the mind. For it is no less indispensable for the social than for the mechanical engineer to accept the qualities and limitations of the forces and materials with which he has to work.

THE CLASS-STRUGGLE

The Marxian method, however, involves something further, which in this analysis I have so far stressed hardly at all; and it is at this point that the method and the theory come closest together. We have seen that, in the Hegelian dialectic, development takes place always and essentially by means of conflict. In the realm of ideas, antithesis joins battle with thesis, till out of their conflict a new synthesis is born; and this struggle is mirrored in the phenomenal history of men and things. Marx, in turning the Hegelian conception upside down, takes over from it the central importance assigned in it to the notion of conflict, and equally with Hegel makes conflict the necessary dynamic of social change. But of what nature is the inverted conflict to be? It is easy to master the notion of a conflict of ideas leading to the discovery of a new idea based on both the contestants; but in Marx's inverted Hegelian world, who are the contestants to be? If Marxism were truly "Materialism," as most people understand that term, they could be only material things apart from the minds of men. Social evolution would have to take the form of the non-human powers of production fighting one another—a process which it would be exceedingly difficult to express in dialectical form. But in Marx's view the combatants in social conflict are not things but men, or rather groups of men ordered in economic classes in accordance with their differing relations to the non-human powers of production and to one another.

This is the theory of the class-struggle, repeated in changing forms through human history till its end is reached with the final abolition of classes and the institution of a classless Society. There will be much to say about this theory in later chapters, when we come to discuss the class structures and loyalties of the world of to-day. Here we are concerned with the theory only as an element in the Marxian method.

In reading Marx's writings, above all *Das Kapital,* one often feels that he regards the class as somehow more deeply real than the individuals who make it up—certainly as a more important influence on historical evolution. Especially does he tend to speak in this way of the modern world; for he conceives that, under the capitalist system of large-scale machine production, the individual workman has lost the status and character of an individual producer, and become merely a "detail-labourer" whose work has meaning only in relation to the work of numerous other labourers working at the same or at related processes within a complex productive unit. Even the individual capitalist has largely lost his independence, and become a contributor to a chain of related processes linking one commodity to another from the first raw material to the final output of consumers' or of capital goods. This rapidly developing interrelation of the entire economic system is the process of economic "socialisation," to which political Socialism is the appropriate counterpart. Capitalism is becoming "socialised," and is above all "socialising" the workers whom it employs as elements in a growingly social productive process; and this indispensable "socialisation" of the productive powers of society is laying the necessary foundations for the socialisation of the ownership of the means of production, of the control of the political machine, and of the economic classes which it will merge into the social solidarity of the coming classless Society.

It is of vital importance to state our conception of the reality of classes aright. Marx sometimes seems to be playing dangerously—all the more so because but half-consciously—with the Hegelian conception of degrees of reality, as if the reality and historical influence of classes somehow condemned their individual members to a subordinate order of real existence. But it is quite unnecessary to entertain any such metaphysical view. For groups can be real, and exert a real influence, without derogating at all from the reality of the individuals of whom they are made up; and a man may be a "detail-labourer" in a factory, with no isolable individual product of his own, without losing his individuality as a person, however much he acts and thinks as a member of a group.

At this point we are confronted once more with the same question as we met with in the discussion of man's freedom to make his own history within a system of economic necessity. For here again the status and implications of membership of a group or class set limits within which the individual is compelled to work. All action is in the last resort individual action, but the individual who occupies a defined place within an established social system can act effectively either to uphold or to change it only if he acts appropriately in relation to the objective conditions. This means, in social matters, acting in association with others who are similarly placed, or whose circumstances, even if they differ, are such as to afford a basis for co-operative action. It is of course always possible for an individual to dissociate himself from those who are similarly placed with himself, and to act in opposition to his own group or class. But, even in this case, he will be able to act effectively only if he transfers his allegiance to some other group or class, within which he can find like-minded collaborators. In any Society of men, collaboration is the prerequisite of effective social activity. There has never been a human Society in which each individual acted by himself, without group loyalty or collaboration. Such a Society can be imagined by mad philosophers or *laissez faire* economists; but it is quite out of the question that any real Society of men should ever bear a significant resemblance to it.

This collaboration among men is by no means based exclusively either on a rational calculation of self-interest, or on a merely passive acceptance of the implications of a common status. It is neither Benthamite nor sheerly determined apart from men's wills and desires. Based largely on community of needs, experiences and purposes, it is informed by a spirit of loyalty and fellowship. It affects men in their altruistic as well as their egoistic impulses; and the strength with which it is felt differs greatly from man to man, quite apart from differences in their economic and social experience. For this reason a class cannot be defined, when it is regarded as an active agent of social change, simply in terms of the common economic experience. It becomes fully a class, in this positive sense, only to the extent to which it is permeated by a spirit of loyalty.

It is sometimes suggested that a class becomes a class, in this positive sense, only to the extent to which its members become "class-conscious." But this is not wholly so, if class-consciousness is held to imply a clear formulation of the notion of class-solidarity in the members' minds. Class loyalty can be very strong, at any rate in its negative reactions, without the notion of class-solidarity being clearly present in the minds of most of the members. But class-consciousness, through which loyalty becomes a reasoned conception of solidarity without losing its emotional content, is a powerful agent in strengthening the ties of the class-group. The sense of loyalty becomes the stronger for being made the basis of a rational idea; and classes become powerful instruments of social change when the instinctive class-loyalty of the majority passes under the leadership of a rationally class-conscious minority. Marxian Socialism, which could have no wide appeal if there were no foundation of class-loyalty for it to build upon, has been a means of equipping large sections of the working classes in the industrial countries with this reasoning class-conscious leadership. For if Marxism is essentially rationalistic in its methods and doctrines, it has its roots deep down in the simple sense of a common fellowship among the oppressed.

That class-loyalty need not imply class-consciousness in the individual is seen far more clearly among the upper than in the lower strata of human Societies. For those whom the existing social and economic arrangements suit best are often least conscious of acting together on a class basis. They feel themselves to be acting in defence, not of a single class, but of the whole Society, as it is actually constituted; and they repudiate angrily, and often quite sincerely, the suggestion that their attitude is influenced by considerations of class. Yet such people have usually a very high degree of class-loyalty and of solidarity one with another, as we can see by their eagerness to sustain common and exclusive cultural and social standards of their own; by their intermarriages one with another, their care in preserving from invasion their own educational institutions and their monopoly of certain professions and callings, as well as by their skill in assimilating such outsiders as do penetrate from above or below inside the circle of their class. To classes in this position, class-consciousness of a reasoned and explicit kind is unnecessary: it is a positive danger. For they are the stronger if they, and even their leaders, can believe that they are acting, not in any narrow spirit of class-egoism, but as the protagonists of the community as a whole. The British middle-class in the generation following the Reform Act of 1832 possessed this spirit almost to perfection; and until only the other day a large section of the American middle classes had it too.

On the other hand, for a class which has still to win power, in order to become a controlling agent of social change, a considerable degree of positive class-consciousness is essential. For a far higher degree of deliberately organised co-operation is needed for changing the face of Society than for preserving the *status quo* under conditions which make its continuance easy. A governing class comes to need class-consciousness only when the onslaught upon it is already being pressed hard, and it has been forced into a posture of defence. For in such circumstances the only hopeful line of defence is prompt and vigorous counter-attack; and class-loyalty without class-consciousness is incapable of taking the offensive.

Class-consciousness is, however, essentially a matter of degree. Any class contains some members who possess it in a high degree, some who possess it not at all, and some at every intermediate stage between the extremes. The objective conditions are, of course, the most important determinants of the strength and diffusion of class-consciousness. But they are not the only determinants; for the turning of class-loyalty into class-consciousness is largely a matter of propaganda and organisation. Trade Unions spring up everywhere as capitalist production develops; but both the numbers of their adherents and the degree in which they are animated by a class-conscious point of view depend greatly on the character of their leadership. It takes a highly organised class-conscious minority to imbue the collective organisations based on common interests and loyalties with any high degree of class-consciousness.

We begin to see now what is meant by Marx's insistence on the reality and efficacy of economic classes. They are real in and through their capacity for organised collective action. The creation of Trade Unions, of Co-operative Societies, of rudimentary political organisations formed largely on a class basis is the first step towards the collective self-expression of the working class. But it is only the first step; for such bodies are formed first sporadically, among groups here and there, under the impulsion of immediate needs and experiences. They are not class-organisations, but group-organisations formed on such a basis as to have the potentiality of cohering at a second stage into larger units and associations, under the influence partly of developments in the objective situation— the growth of larger-scale Capitalism, for example—and partly of constructive leadership using the opportunities which the developing situation presents. But, though they have this potentiality, there is no certainty of it being realised; for the objective situation by itself will not suffice to create a consciously organised class. That is the work of men—of leaders; and, while the developing situation is a powerful agency in calling latent leadership into active life, the successful conscious organisation of a class is no more inevitable than the advent of a Lenin or a Napoleon.

Indeed, even when class-organisation has been brought to

a high pitch of mechanical efficiency, under the inspiration of leaders possessing a reasoned class-conscious point of view, success is not assured. For, if the leadership subsequently fails, the imposing mass-organisation may rot away inwardly, preserving the semblance only of the class-solidarity and class-consciousness which gave it its original driving-force. Nothing in human history is ever inevitable until it has happened, not because things happen without a cause, but because no chain of causation is ever complete until it has actually produced its effect.

Leadership, then, is essential to make a class an effective agent of social development. But if classes need constructive leadership, leaders are nothing unless they are able to place themselves at the head of forces upon which the objective situation confers the opportunity of real power. Marx's point is not merely that effective action in the sphere of world history is always collective action, involving the collaboration of a group, but also that these groups must be of a particular kind. A man may collect a group of followers round him on the basis of an idea, or groups may arise on a foundation of neighbourhood, race, nationality, or religion; but in Marx's view no group plays a dominant rôle in world history unless it appears as the representative of a class. This does not mean that the part played by other groups is unimportant or ineffective, but only that it is secondary, and is never the main agent of transition from one stage of social evolution to another. A group which is not also the embodiment of a class can make history within the framework of a given social system, and can exert a powerful secondary influence on the character of the change from one system to another; but it cannot itself effect a change of system.

Why does Marx hold this? Because each social system, that is, each stage in social development, corresponds to a particular arrangement of the powers of production, and therefore involves a particular set of class-relationships. But a group which is not the embodiment of a class does not stand for any particular way of arranging the powers of production. It does not stand for a particular social system based on a particular stage in the development of man's power over nature, and expressing itself in a set of economic class-relationships calculated to secure the most effective use of this power. It cannot therefore stand as the representative of an existing social system, or as the protagonist in the struggle to replace it by a new one. For as soon as it came to be either of these things, it would have become the representative of a particular economic class.

Be it clearly understood that Marx does not suggest that the groups which stand as the representatives of classes must always be consciously aiming chiefly at economic ends, or must express their aspirations always in economic terms. On the contrary, he affirms that class-struggles are often fought out in terms which have apparently little or nothing to do with economic questions or with class-relationships. A group may become the representative of a class even if it begins and develops without any conscious reference to class issues. Men have often fought out essentially economic struggles in religious and ideological terms, making the will of God or the dictates of universal justice in the image of their own class-needs, or taking over and turning to a class-purpose an institution or a doctrine which had no class-implications in the minds of its original makers. Everyone is familiar in these days with the view that there has been an intimate connection between the growth of Protestantism and Puritanism and the rise of the capitalist system, not because Protestants and Puritans were conscious hypocrites, eager to throw a veil of religion over their economic rapacity, but because the developing class of traders and industrial *entrepreneurs* seized avidly on an ethic which fitted in admirably with the economic practices appropriate to the objective situation with which they had to deal. Similarly, in eighteenth-century England, Wesleyanism exactly suited the needs of the new class of abstinent capitalists because it not merely strengthened them for money-making by encouraging their abstinence, but also gave them the satisfying sense that they could make money to the glory of God. This glorification of money-making, on the ground that money made and saved is the outward and visible sign that a man has wrought hard in this world of tribulation, runs as a strange thread of self-deception through one early Wesleyan apologia after another.

Groups and associations are not classes, but they can and do become in varying degrees the representatives of class aspirations and points of view. To this power they owe their ultimate efficacy as agents of social transformation. But this is not to say that any group can become an agent of social transformation by coming to represent a class. For not all classes at all times are either the protagonists in the defence of an existing social order, or the leaders of a crusade against it. There are classes to which, at least at a particular stage of social evolution, a rôle of dominance is necessarily denied—for example, the class of landlords in a situation already dominated by large-scale industrial Capitalism. A class only plays the leading rôle in defence or attack if its class point of view coincides with the requirements of the existing arrangement of the conditions of

production or with those of an alternative arrangement calculated to advance the development of production to a higher
stage. The class stands between the active groups which represent it and the economic foundations on which it rests.

How, then, does a class come into existence? It arises out of
the requirements of the objective situation of the powers of production. At any stage, men possess certain natural and acquired
resources of things and knowledge of the use of things, which
together form their equipment for carrying on the work of
production. But this work can be carried on only if there arises
in fact, or by conscious adoption, an arrangement for its conduct. There must be laws or conventions or customs regulating
the right of use, or ownership, of the instruments of production;
and there must be operative relationships between men as producers, whether these relationships arise out of force or by consent. Someone must dig, fetch and carry, organise and give
orders: there must be some way of dividing the products of
associative labour; and finally there must be some way of en-
forcing conformity with the rules and conventions of the established system, whatever it may be, and some way of assigning
to each man his place and function. In other words, every arrangement of the powers of production necessarily implies a
social system—an ordering of the relationships between men
and things and between men and men, on a basis consistent
with the development of the available productive resources.
But this in its turn has involved, at every stage of human history up to the present, a set of class-relationships; for the
arrangement of men into groups with different economic
functions and claims has been at every stage an arrangement of
them into economic classes.

Observe that I say "has been," and not "must be"; for it is not suggested that the division of Society into economic classes is inevitable for all time. What is suggested is that the class-systems of the past and present, however much evil they may seem to embody when they are judged by ideal standards, have been, at the time of their origin, instruments for organising the advance of man's power over nature, and therefore for the increase of human wealth and the enlargement of the opportunities for welfare. They have not been necessarily the best instruments possible at the time of their advent to power—to believe that would be to relapse into fatalism—but they have been the means of improving, economically, on what went before.

Or rather, they have been so, subject to one qualification of outstanding importance, the omission of which has vitiated much Marxist thinking. This qualification is that the entire process with which we have been dealing relates to the internal development of a given civilisation, and not to the impact of one civilisation upon another. For, where a whole civilisation is overthrown, as happened at the decline and fall of the Roman Empire as a world system, the course of development follows the lines made possible by the economic power and knowledge of the conquerors, and not of the defeated civilisation—so that in such a case a higher stage of economic evolution and knowledge may be displaced by a lower. But where this happens some part at least of the civilisation of the conquered will usually be mastered in time by the conquerors, and so preserved and caught up into a fresh advance. Moreover, what is from one point of view a regression may be from another the basis for an advance. The fall of the Western Roman Empire opened the "Dark Ages"; but it also got rid of slavery as the basis of the productive system, and replaced it by serfdom, which is undoubtedly a higher economic form.

THE HISTORICAL PROCESS

This question of the impact of one civilisation on another presents for the pedantic adherents of the "Materialist Conception of History," in precisely the form in which it was originally enunciated by "the master," the most difficult and perplexing problem. The *Communist Manifesto,* in which the doctrine is first plainly set out, appears to treat all human history from beginning to end, and with no limitations of either space or time, as a continuous process of world development from one all-embracing primitive Communism through a series of world class systems to a world system of advanced Communism, or Socialism. But is there really any warrant for this view? Is not Marx in reality beginning with an analysis of the social development of Western Europe and the countries brought from time to time within its orbit from the Dark Ages to the growth of an advanced system of Capitalism, and then trying to apply the results achieved by this analysis to human history as a whole? May not the first of these steps be valid, and the second invalid, in the form in which it is made in the *Communist Manifesto*?

I hold this to be so. I believe that the Realist Conception of History is universally valid, but that it is wrong and absurd to attempt to interpret all history by it as the growth of a single civilisation. The civilisation in which we are living to-day has no doubt been immensely influenced by the civilisation which culminated and fell in the Roman Empire; but it is in no sense continuous with that civilisation, or merely developed out of it in accordance with the internal rhythm of social evolution within a single system. The roots of our civilisation are to be sought not in Imperial Rome, but in the tribal institutions of the barbarians whom Tacitus described, and of all those mingled racial and cultural elements which swept down upon the Western Empire and destroyed it. What we owe to Rome is to be explained in terms not of the internal rhythm of economic development, but of the impact of one civilisation upon another.

To envisage the matter in this way is to remove the greatest obstacle to the acceptance of the Marxian analysis. For the puzzle for those who have regarded all human history as a continuous process has always been to explain why, in order to advance from a slave-economy to a serf-economy—an admitted economic advance—mankind had, in so many respects, to fall back so far. Were the Dark Ages really an advance on the Roman Empire? Civilisation for civilisation, can anyone possibly believe that they were? But, if they were not, what becomes of mankind's continuous advance to higher stages of social development?

The difficulty disappears if it is accepted, on the one hand, that all human history is not the history of a single civilisation, and on the other that human progress is not inevitable, but has to be struggled for by men at every stage of development. Why, historians have often asked, did not the Roman Empire emancipate itself from slavery, and advance to a higher stage of economic organisation, without the need for men to undergo the searing experience of the Dark Ages? I should answer that this happened because the Roman Empire decayed internally through failure to use its opportunities. It could have survived and continued to advance, if the forces subordinated within it had been able to find leadership and organisation strong and

intelligent enough at once to readjust its conditions of economic life from within and to resist the disintegrating forces
pressing upon it from outside. In default of this, its culture fed
upon its body till, like the ill-fated heroines of Victorian ro-
mances, it fell into a decline and died.

It has often been said that this fate overtook the Roman Empire because the plenty and cheapness of inefficient slave labour
deprived it of all incentive to improve its productive power. The
slaves themselves were too weak, scattered and disorganised
to achieve more than a few sporadic revolts; and on a basis of
slave labour there could arise no active class of industrial *entrepreneurs* powerful enough to make a bid for the control of
the political machine. Slave labour is indeed antithetical to the
growth of machine-production because in general the mass of
slaves cannot be trusted to operate the machines. This may be
in part the explanation of the ancient world's failure to apply
to economic uses the inventions of Alexandria, or to make, except in the unique field of civil engineering, any significant
advance in the arts of production. But what they did achieve
in the erection of buildings and aqueducts shows that they could
develop in the economic field when they gave their minds to
it; and the customary explanation of their failure seems to be
inadequate. It would be more plausible if they had tried to
apply machinery and failed; but in fact they did not try. It
is a far more plausible view that tribute and extension, rather
than slavery, killed Imperial Rome. For the Empire was too
large to be held together under centralised control except by
vast military and administrative expenditure; and the magnitude of the tribute levied on the provinces for these and other
purposes and the centralisation of the entire system prevented

them from accumulating the resources needed as the basis of economic advance.

My point here, however, is not that the Western Roman Empire fell from this or that cause, but that its fall was the end of a civilisation in Western Europe, so that the social development of Western Europe since then is to be regarded as belonging to the history of a distinct, though of course a related civilisation. To recognise this is to escape the fantastic error of trying to squeeze all classical history within the confines of a shape made to explain the development of modern Europe, instead of working out a distinct pattern, on the basis of the same Realist Conception, for the interpretation of the Ancient World in terms of its own problems and productive powers. No one who looks at the matter in this light will be tempted to equate the slaves of the Roman Empire with the modern proletariat, or to ransack ancient history for isolated events in which he can trace a fanciful resemblance to the class-struggles of to-day.

World history has to be written in terms not only of the internal evolution of a number of distinct civilisations, but also of their impact one on another. The conception of class suffices to explain the internal development of a civilisation from stage to stage, or at any rate that of the particular civilisation with which we are practically concerned in the world to-day; but it does not suffice to explain the action of one civilisation upon another.

It does not follow that for the explanation of other civilisations, or of the impact of one civilisation upon another, we have to go outside the economic field. For a distinction needs to be drawn between the theory that economic forces are the final determinants of social change, and the secondary theory that these economic forces are in all cases necessarily personified by economic classes. Mass migrations of hungry peoples in search of the means of living are assuredly due to economic causes; but they are not class-movements. Yet they are capable of determining the fate of an entire civilisation, of checking or turning aside its internal course of development, or of bringing its growth abruptly to an end. War and conquest have played in human history a part which can by no means be explained as a mere by-product of class-struggles, even though they may admit fully of explanation in economic terms. Similarly, the explanation of the internal history of some civilisations—China and India, for example—may be economic, and yet quite incapable of being brought within a formula designed to explain the history of Western Europe since the fall of Rome.

It is a sound principle of theoretical method never unnecessarily to extend a generalisation. There is always a temptation for him who hits on a truth to see in it the philosopher's stone that turns the whole universe into a blaze of light. But the light of reasoning is apt to become feebler as it proceeds from its centre to the circumference; and what may be a convincing explanation of the facts which originally suggested it may fail to be even plausible when it is stretched to cover a wider ground. Or, at best, even where the central truth is all pervasive, it may need to be quite differently stated in relation to different groups of facts. Marx's Realist Conception of History may be universally valid without his statement of it in terms of class-struggles possessing the same universality. There are other possible dialectical forms besides the class-struggle.

But if, at one extreme, it is dangerous to claim too much extension for Marx's statement of his theory, at the other extreme it is at least as dangerous to apply it too intensively even nearer home. There are some Marxists who cannot see a flapper use her lipstick without producing pat an explanation of her conduct in terms of the powers of production and the class-struggle. It is, of course, undeniable that the prevalence of lipstick at a price within the normal flapper's purse is a by-product of capitalist mass-production, and has therefore an economic cause; but in relation to world history it is a phenomenon completely irrelevant to the class-struggle, and of no significance at all. Nor is there any sound reason for tracing all important and historically influential events to economic causes, much less for regarding them all as manifestations of the class-struggle, whatever outward form they may assume. For no one in his senses doubts that men are constantly acting on grounds that are non-economic, or that non-economic actions and organisations can and do influence history. All that the most rigid Marxist needs to claim is that the influences which are not manifestations of the class-struggle are of a secondary order, and exert their effects, however important they may be, within limiting conditions set by the evolution of the powers of production.

Thus, to take a few modern examples, if two countries go to war, it is not necessary to prove that their conflict is the outcome of a rivalry inherent in the development of modern Capitalism. It may be; but it may also be due to some quite different cause. If a particular people, or section of a people, manifests a spirit of violent Nationalism, it is not necessary to prove that this Nationalism is really but a perverted form of class-feeling, or that it depends finally on economic grounds. Possibly it is, and does: possibly not. Or again, if a particular body of men is strongly Catholic or Protestant, it does not follow that their creed is merely a cloak for their pursuit of their economic ends. Perhaps it may be so, or half so. But assuredly war and national-

ism and religion, greatly as they have been affected by economic forces, are not to be explained away as purely economic
things.

There are many causes at work in history, even if one set
of causes dominates the rest and shapes the general course of
social development within a particular civilisation. Moreover,
as Marx and Engels again and again insisted, what is originally
derivative has the power of becoming an independent cause.
Thus Marx holds, as we saw, that the need of mankind to organise for the use of the developing powers of production gives
rise to legal and political systems for the enforcement of the
class and property relationships required at any given stage of
economic development. These legal and political powers are
thus in the first instance derivatives of the powers of production
at the stage which has been reached when they are set up; but,
once established, they become independent forces with a power
to influence history and to react upon the course of economic
development, as the feudal State held back for a time the growing strength of Capitalism, and as the capitalist States of to-day
are damming up the overflowing forces of man's productive
power. Any institution, whether it be economic or not in its
origin, and whether or not it is or has become an embodiment of
the standpoint of a class, can act upon men's minds, and upon
other institutions, and can therefore influence the course of history. The only question that is at issue between Marxists and
non-Marxists is whether class-institutions, based on the changing
powers and conditions of production, play the dominant part
in social evolution, and set limits within which the other forces
have to act. The independent and important influence of these
other forces is not denied.

The worst enemies of Marxism are those who harden it into

a universal dogma, and thus conceal its value as a flexible
method of social analysis. For the Realist Conception of History is a clue to the understanding of social realities, and not
a complete explanation of them. Nor is it meant primarily as
a theory; for Marx's object in formulating it was not simply to
understand, but by understanding to gain the power to control.
He sought a theory, not for a theory's sake, but because he
wanted to find a guide to action, and did not believe that men
could hope to act aright unless they could gain a correct appreciation of the objective facts. But a theory which is to serve as a
guide to action can afford least of all to decline into a dogma,
or to be formulated rigidly on mechanistic lines. For the first
essential of successful action is flexibility in the application of
principles—a quality often confused with opportunism, but in
truth its very opposite. For the opportunist does not apply
principles: he flouts them. But the successful man of action
holds fast to his principle, but at the same time understands
the need of restating it constantly in relation to changes in the
objective situation. In this opening chapter, I have tried to
state Marxism not as dogma, but primarily as method and
way of approach, embodying in its method principles which are
too realistic to harden into dogmas, and too closely related to
the objective situation for it to be possible to state them to-day
in the same terms as Marx used in stating them from fifty to
ninety years ago. Some Marxists will say that what I have been
stating is not Marxism at all, but a radically different doctrine.
Even if that were so, it would not matter, provided that mine
was the better doctrine for to-day. But I think what I have
written is in essence Marxist, in that sense in which Marxism
is to-day a living force, and not the opium of the Socialist
orthodox.

CHAPTER II

THE GROWTH OF CAPITALISM

A GREAT DEAL of unprofitable discussion has taken place about the date at which the capitalist system came into being. Some writers refuse to speak of Capitalism as existing before the machine age which began, broadly, towards the end of the eighteenth century, and thus regard Capitalism as the child of the "Industrial Revolution." Others, tracing back its development from the nineteenth century, find it already in existence in a rudimentary form at the latter end of the Middle Ages, gradually superseding and pushing out of existence the localised economy of the medieval city and the manorial system. Yet others, connecting it with the wars of religion, credit it with a birthday somewhere in the sixteenth century; and another school of thought, working back from the great age of mechanical inventions and discovering that the "Industrial Revolution" did not, after all, begin in 1760, land up somewhere in the seventeenth century—perhaps about the date of the foundation of the Bank of England.

These discussions are of little real value. Obviously Capi-

talism was not born, as a child is born, at any precise moment
of time. It did not come into existence at any definite period.
It grew gradually, out of capitalistic elements which had existed
in previous stages of economic development. There were
plenty of capitalistic features in the economic life of the
Middle Ages in their prime, and not merely at their latter
end. What happened was that these elements developed, ousting
stage by stage and bit by bit the other characteristics of the
medieval system. The so-called "domestic system," widespread
but never anything like universal in the seventeenth and eighteenth centuries, was a development of these earlier capitalistic
qualities, based especially on the growth of the capitalist merchant. The advent of power-driven machinery on a large scale
enabled Capitalism to spread directly from the sphere of commerce to that of industrial production over a growing number
of its branches. It is a matter of definition, and not of knowledge, to say when the Age of Capitalism began. What can be
said with assurance is that Merchant Capitalism rose to a position of economic predominance in the seventeenth and eighteenth centuries, and Industrial Capitalism in the nineteenth.
Some would proclaim a new age of "Finance Capitalism" in
the twentieth century; but that is a point which we can for
the moment leave aside.

Some of the most forcible chapters of Marx's *Capital* are
devoted to an account of the development of the capitalist
system. For by "Capital" Marx means not merely the existence
of an accumulation of resources or instruments of production,
but a particular form of social organisation in which the ownership of these resources, at a certain stage of their development,
assumes a particular character and involves a particular set of
relationships between men and men. The essence of "Capital,"

as Marx sees it, lies in the ownership of the resources of production by a class of persons distinct from those who perform the bulk of the productive labour of Society, in such a way that the personally "free" possessors of labour-power and the "free" possessors of accumulated productive resources confront each other as two distinct and opposite economic classes, one of which must employ the other before production can take place. "Capital," in this sense, comes into being as a corollary to the divorce of the main body of producers from the instruments of production; and the value of capital to its owners depends on the existence of a supply of labourers available for employment at a wage. In other words, "Capital" is monopolistic ownership of the resources of production other than labour-power; and the value of capital is simply the power of exploiting labour which this monopoly confers.

This thesis is often stated as if it involved the view that the coming of Capitalism carried with it the degradation of labour, and a fall in the workers' standards of life. So it did, for particular groups of skilled artisans whom it deprived of their craft independence, and for particular bodies of peasants whom it displaced from their holdings in the interests of capitalist farming. At every stage, the advance of Capitalism has involved, as it still involves to-day, the displacement and degradation of particular bodies of persons whose traditional methods of living it supersedes. But this does not at all imply that its historical effect has been to lower the standard of living for the poorer classes as a whole. Any such view would be quite un-Marxian, and indeed plainly nonsensical. For obviously the advance of capitalist methods of production took place precisely because they were far more efficient in the creation of wealth than the methods they superseded. By whatever injustices and oppressions the rise of Capitalism was accompanied, it did undoubtedly lead not only to a large positive increase in total wealth, but also to a wider diffusion of consuming power. It would be sheer nonsense to contend that the poor became in the mass poorer under Capitalism than they were under the systems which it displaced. This was not even true of the period which was chiefly in Marx's mind as he wrote; for even in the earlier decades of the nineteenth century, when the abuses of the Industrial Revolution were at their worst, it is scarcely possible to argue that there was more material poverty in England than there had been in the eighteenth century, or, to go back further, when the medieval economic system was in its most flourishing phase.

For it is quite misleading to compare the lot of the general body of workmen under Capitalism, at any stage of its development, with that of, say, the very limited groups of skilled craftsmen in the medieval towns, or the small minority of peasants who possessed adequate holdings of their own, without taking into account the mass of sheer poverty which existed in the medieval villages as well. Nor can such instances of the tragedy of a craft as the decline of the handloom weavers in the course of the Industrial Revolution, or such special cases as the wrongs wrought under the Enclosure Acts during the same period, be taken as representative of the effects of advancing Capitalism upon the living standards of the poorer classes as a whole. It is practically certain that at any time after the first decades of the Industrial Revolution the average real income of the poorer classes was higher than it had ever been before; and it is utterly beyond question that the further development of Capitalism in the nineteenth century was accompanied in every capitalist country by a real and rapid advance in working-class standards of life.

Moreover, the rise of Capitalism, apart from the improvement in the standards of living for the wage-earners which has marked its successive phases, has also at every stage increased the relative as well as the absolute numbers of the middle classes, and of all those who are better off than the manual workers. It created, in its earlier phases, a large new middle class of self-made men who rose from relative poverty to affluence or comfort by the exploitation of the new powers of production. It has, at every stage, swollen the numbers of the professional classes; and it has, in its later phases, created a new class of well-paid salary-earners—technicians, managers and administrators—who enjoy a high economic standard as the servants of joint stock enterprise. The creation of this great middle class is the characteristic social achievement of Capitalism; but it cannot possibly be argued that this achievement was purchased by a positive lowering of the standards of life of the poor below what they had been under earlier systems.

Nor did Marx ever attempt to argue in this way. His contention was that Capitalism routed the earlier systems precisely because it was a superior way of exploiting the developing resources of production. It destroyed in its coming many vested interests among the privileged bodies of workers as well as among the higher privileged classes of landlords and ecclesiastics. It did lower the standard of life for groups of small masters who found themselves degraded into the wage-earning class, or of peasant farmers whom it deprived of their land, as well as of some skilled workers whose craftsmanship was superseded by new methods of production. But it also brought with it a higher standard, not only for the new industrial employers and the rising professional groups, but also for large bodies of workers who exchanged the status of serfs, or virtual serfs, or of very poor peasants and cottagers in the rural areas, for that of wage-workers able to sell their labour to the highest bidder, and to move far more freely from place to place in search of employment. It is safe to say dogmatically that Capitalism, wherever it came, raised the standard of living for far more persons than it drove downwards in the scale of material comfort. The age of the Industrial Revolution was insanitary and unhealthy enough, in all conscience, as Marx and Engels, drawing on the reports prepared by Chadwick and his fellow-reformers, were able to show with a wealth of graphic example. But was it, taken as a whole, as insanitary or unhealthy as the centuries before? Save in exceptional areas, where new factory towns were run up at top speed, so as to dwarf the feeble efforts of the sanitary reformer, there is no sufficient evidence that it was.

Of course, it is open to argue that the workers under Capitalism, though they had on the average larger real incomes than the generations before them, suffered spiritual degradation in the loss of craftsmanship and independence. But this view also is suspect; for does it not rest on comparing the spiritual condition of a privileged minority of craftsmen and substantial peasants with that of the worst-placed bodies of workers under the new system? How much spiritual independence or pride of craft had the typical peasant of the Middle Ages, or the typical English villager of the eighteenth century under the rule of the squires, or again the typical worker under the domestic system? The view that Capitalism degraded the general condition of the poor in the advancing industrial countries is based on sentimentalism, and not on an objective study of the facts.

This attitude is in no wise inconsistent with the doctrine that Capitalism is based upon the exploitation of labour. For so were the systems which preceded it, in an even higher degree. The exploitation of the wage-workers is not disproved by arguing that serfs, or slaves, were exploited even worse. The conception of exploitation is relative, not to the absolute standard of living, but to the discrepancy between the standard actually achieved and the standard attainable at any particular stage in the development of the powers of production. The labourer under Capitalism may live absolutely much better than the medieval serf—as he obviously does—and yet be exploited if the full use of the available resources of production and a more even distribution of the product would enable him to live much better still. His exploitation is to be measured, not by what he receives, but rather by what he fails to receive.

In a later chapter, this question of the exploitation of labour will have to be argued out in its theoretical aspect, as it arises in connection with the Marxian theory of value. Here the purpose of mentioning it is only to make clear that Marx's theory of exploitation does not involve, but explicitly contradicts, the view that the rise of Capitalism has made the lot of the labouring class as a whole absolutely worse. The manual workers' share in the total product of the economic system may possibly have fallen under Capitalism—it is difficult to say—but their absolute standard of living has assuredly risen.

THE EXPLOITATION OF LABOUR

The sense of riches or poverty is, however, essentially relative. Men feel rich or poor, not absolutely, but in relation one to another and to the available supply of wealth. Consequently,

a rise in the absolute standard of living in a Society does not
carry with it a corresponding increase in the sense of material
well-being unless it comes about in such a way as to reduce
economic disparities between class and class and, where such
disparities exist, to give men the sense that their wealth has
risen in relation to the total available supply. Increases in the
absolute standard of life which do not satisfy these conditions
are speedily absorbed into the current conception of the minimum required to support a reasonably tolerable way of living.
This is what both Marx and Ricardo have in mind when they
estimate "real" incomes in terms, not of the goods they will
buy, but of the amounts of effort the production of these goods
has cost—or, in other words, as shares in the social income.
Wages, says Ricardo, have fallen, even if they will buy more
goods, when they absorb a smaller proportion than before of
the total value of production. Exploitation, says Marx, has increased, even if the standard of living has risen, when the
labourer's proportionate share in the total product is less than
before.

Now, Marx envisaged the process of capitalist production as
involving a constant struggle between capitalists and labourers
over the sharing-out of the product of industry. On the one
hand, the labourers are pressing constantly for improved conditions, in the form both of higher wages and of shorter hours
and better working conditions, and, through their Trade
Unions as well as through their power to change their jobs,
are becoming more alert to take advantage of favourable conditions in the labour market. And on the other hand the capitalists are constantly revolutionising the methods of production,
and trying to make labour more intensive within the hours of
work, so as to secure a larger return upon their capital, and

to have more left for themselves after meeting such claims from the workers as they are compelled to concede.

The competitive character of capitalist industry, even apart from the pressure of the workers for improved conditions, forces upon the capitalist *entrepreneurs* the necessity constantly to revolutionise the processes of production, so as to keep down costs and make industry more productive. This competitive pressure ought to make possible a steadily rising standard of life; for it involves a constant advance in the productivity of the economic system as a whole. But the increased productivity of each hour of direct labour applied to industry is secured only with the aid of an enlarged mass of capital, involved not only in the provision of more expensive machines, but also in the growing roundaboutness and complexity of the business of production and marketing. In order to keep up the rate of profit on this increasing mass of capital, the *entrepreneur* has to decrease the share of labour in the final product of industry; and he is constantly fighting against a tendency for the rate of profit on capital to fall, as the mass of capital grows larger in proportion to the total costs of production. He is aided in this struggle by the fact that the progressive substitution of machinery for labour diminishes the pressure of demand on the labour market, and thus makes it harder for the Trade Unions to insist on better terms of employment. Nevertheless Marx held, in common with the classical economists, that the rate of profit on capital would tend to fall, even while the total amount of profit was rapidly increasing; for the increased profit would have to be spread over a still more rapidly growing mass of invested capital. This tendency would strengthen the capitalist resistance to working-class claims; for any attempt to press these claims to a point at which they would seriously lower the rate of profit would lead to a fall in the volume of capital investment, and this would react in turn on the demand for labour and so bring about a situation favourable to wage-reductions, or to the more intensive exploitation of labour.

Even so, the rapidly growing productivity of industry ought to lead to a rising standard of life, on account of the greater volume of goods available. Indeed, Capitalism has a strong incentive to aim at a rising standard, because of the tendency of most machine industries to a law of increasing return, or decreasing cost, as the amount produced increases. Capitalism, as it is under the necessity of continually raising productivity, requires a constantly expanding market for its wares; and where is it to find such a market save in the growing demand of the general body of consumers? For the commodities which most obey the law of increasing return are chiefly those which cater for mass-demand.

Capitalism, however, because of its competitive character, cannot set out to increase the incomes of the general body of consumers up to the limits of productive capacity. For all the incomes paid as wages and salaries, and also incidentally those paid as rent and interest, appear to it in the guise of costs of production, which each *entrepreneur* must keep down if his margin of profit is not to disappear. In the early stages of capitalist development, this pressure arises out of the competition of individual capitalists, or businesses, within the same economic Society. But even when, at a later stage, combination has largely replaced competition in each leading industry within each advanced country, the necessity to keep costs down remains, both because the integrated capitalist groups continue to a great extent to compete internationally, and because each trade group is in rivalry with every other in trying to persuade the consumers to spend on its products as large a fraction as possible of their total incomes. It is possible, in theory, to imagine a completely combined capitalist world, from which both these remaining forms of competition have been eliminated; but, despite the growth of international cartels and combines in certain trades, there is no sign of this happening in practice. In fact, international competition, and perhaps also the competition between trade and trade for a share in the consumers' total incomes, come to be much more intense in the later phases of capitalist development.

Marx explains this tendency by reference both to the increasing advantages of expanding the scale of output under the conditions of modern machine-production, and to the growing pressure upon the world market as the number of highly industrialised countries becomes greater. When only one or two countries are industrialised, it is relatively easy for them to find foreign markets for a large part of their expanding output, by displacing in the less advanced countries the more expensively produced commodities of craft and peasant industry, and, at a slightly later stage, by setting out to equip these countries with machinery and modern transport services with the aid of the export of capital. This export of capital is indispensable; for the less developed countries cannot afford to pay at once for the expensive equipment which the advanced countries are eager to sell. The conditions required for the export of capital are, however, in being; for the large mass of profit made in the advanced countries is seeking outlets for profitable investment. It is clogging the home market for new capital, and threatening to force the rate of profit down. But the less developed countries offer a field in which invested capital is likely to find even more profitable, though perhaps more hazardous, outlets than at home; for with an abundance of cheap labour to draw upon it should be possible to produce many types of goods at lower cost in the more backward than in the more advanced countries.

Consequently, capital emigrates in search of higher profits; and its emigration, by creating a demand for goods which the advanced countries are well equipped to produce, keeps up the rate of profit in these countries. But this process involves a patent contradiction. For, broadly, the capital invested abroad will be profitable to its owners only in proportion as the goods made with its help enter subsequently into competition with the goods produced in the more advanced countries, where their competition will have the effect of keeping down wages and thus restricting home demand.

As long as the number of countries carrying on advanced industrial production remains small, and the number of new countries to which the expansive process of foreign investment and supersession of native industries can be applied remains relatively large, the effect of this contradiction is not seriously felt. It was not seriously felt in Marx's own day; but he predicted that it was bound to become serious in the next phase of capitalist growth. For he foresaw that the application in a number of countries of an advanced technique of capitalist production was bound to lead to a rapidly increasing rivalry between these countries for the right to exploit and develop the less advanced areas, with a view both to securing markets for their products and to assuring themselves of adequate supplies of such foodstuffs, raw materials and tropical products as the conditions of their own territories compelled them to import. Marx foresaw the advent of the age of Economic Imperialism, dominated by the rivalries of the advanced countries over markets, spheres of influence, territorial expansion, and the building up of alliances and groupings designed to foster their several economic interests. He foresaw—and his successors, above all Lenin, have elaborated the theme in the light of later events—that these rivalries would inevitably lead to wars of colonial conquest, and finally to wars between the great Imperialist Powers, and that these wars, and the huge economic losses and piling up of debts which they would involve, would endanger the stability of the capitalist order, and afford an opportunity for the forces of social revolution. In these internecine wars between capitalist countries Marx held that the capitalist system was destined to perish.

THE CONTRADICTIONS OF CAPITALISM

But imperialist wars would be, not the ultimate cause of the fall of Capitalism, but themselves the consequence of the inherent contradictions of the system. For the wars would arise out of the sheer necessity for each national capitalist State to develop markets and spheres of influence outside its own frontiers, owing to its inability, under the exigencies of the profit-making system, to find at home an outlet for its expanding productivity. Marx undoubtedly held that a time would come when, by reason of its internal contradictions, Capitalism would no longer be able to meet the expanding claims of the working class for an improved standard of life. It could meet them, as long as it was able to press on with the development of the resources of production and to find an outlet in the world market for the growing product of industry. But there would come a time when this resource would fail it, and thereupon the increasing pressure of international capitalist competition in the limited world market would force the capitalists in each country into an attack on wages. For each national group of capitalists would be set on reducing the costs of production in order to secure a larger share in the limited market; and any group which failed to do this would find itself left behind in the race. The result of being left behind would be a rise in unemployment, which would be equally effective with a fall in wages in reducing consumers' demand, and would, moreover, soon bring about a fall in wages by reducing the power of the Trade Unions to resist.

This process of reducing costs in face of international competition is, however, fatally self-contradictory. For reduction of costs, at the expense of wages, leads also to a restriction in the volume of demand. Capitalism, therefore, when it once embarks upon this process, condemns itself to an inability to make use of the advancing powers of production; for it can no longer find a market for the increased supply of goods which it is in a position to produce. At this point, according to the Marxian theory, Capitalism becomes ripe for supersession by an alternative system.

For, whereas the capitalist method of production has been hitherto a means of promoting the development of the productive powers of Society, it turns at this stage of its history, and by an inherent tendency which it cannot escape, into a fetter upon the effective use of the available resources. At this stage, but not until this stage has been reached, Marx holds that the capitalist system involves, by virtue of its essential nature, a fall in the working-class standard of life.

The contradiction which thus becomes manifest in the capitalist order is simply the consequence of the commodity status of labour. For a system under which labour-power is bought by private *entrepreneurs* at a price, just like the materials and implements of production, and therefore ranks as a cost of production, is inevitably committed to regarding the incomes distributed as wages as a necessary evil, to be kept down to the lowest possible point. Even when individual capitalists preach the doctrine of high wages, they cannot escape the net of this contradiction. For, save to the extent to which they are able, by securing more efficient production than their competitors, to reconcile high wages with low wage-costs per unit of output—and to this there must be quite narrow limits—they cannot afford to pay higher wages than their competitors at home and abroad. As we have seen, a perfectly combined world Capitalism might in theory transcend these limits; but no such system is within the bound of practical possibility. For Capitalism is essentially competitive, despite the growth of combinations within it; and if it became completely combined it would cease to be Capitalism at all. Such complete combination would imply the unified control of all the powers of production by a single world authority; but who supposes that Capitalism is consistent with the creation of such an authority, or could survive its establishment?

As long as Capitalism retains its competitive character—that is to say, as long as it continues to exist—there are narrow limits to the application within it of the policy of high wages. For, while an individual *entrepreneur* who is far-sighted enough to pay higher wages than his rivals, and clever enough to make good use of the high-quality labour which his offer of higher wages will secure, may find that high wages pay, the "economy" of these high wages depends mainly, not on their absolute level, but on their superiority to the wages offered by other employers. As soon as they become general, they lose most of their effect, because they can no longer be effective in attracting the best workers. They retain, of course, their effect in expanding home demand; but unless a country is able to isolate itself from international competition under a regime of Economic Nationalism this advantage will be speedily offset by the pressure of foreign competition. The lower costs of foreign producers who pay lower wages will enable them to capture the external markets of the high-wage country, and, unless it adopts a high protective system, to invade its home market as well.

It may be answered that Capitalism in a particular country can escape this dilemma by resort to Economic Nationalism. But only under very rare conditions can Economic Nationalism be a way of escape. For it involves a deliberate refusal to take advantage of the economies of international specialisation, and the production at home of goods which could be produced with less expenditure of effort elsewhere. If therefore lowers to a serious extent the productive capacity of the country which adopts it; for it means that productive resources must be diverted from more to less efficient uses. A country which has so wide a diversity of natural resources and so large a population that it can produce, without serious economic sacrifice, nearly everything it needs for an advancing standard of life is in a position, by adopting Economic Nationalism, to escape the fatal barrier to a high-wage policy which international competition sets up. But in all the world to-day there are at most only two countries which can possibly be regarded as approaching nearly enough to satisfying these conditions—the United States and the U.S.S.R. One of these countries has already thrown Capitalism over. The other is, as I write, heading uncertainly towards an experiment in controlled Capitalism on a basis of Economic Nationalism, and with a deliberate endeavour to apply a high-wage policy as a necessary element in its success.

But the degree of central control which is indispensable for the carrying-through of a high-wage policy is exceedingly great. In the first place, the natural tendency of each *entrepreneur* to desire to keep his wage-costs, like his other costs, down to the lowest possible point must be successfully overcome by a control which will give him the assurance that all his competitors in the same trade will raise wages at least as much as he is compelled to raise them. But this is not enough. For, if costs rise more in one trade than in others, the higher-cost trade will be at a disadvantage in selling its products. Demand for its products will fall off, and consumers will transfer their purchases to other goods. There must therefore be, in the second place, a sufficient assurance that the rise in wages will be spread, with approximate evenness, over all industries that are competitive in this wider sense.

But even this is not all. The policy of high money wages in all trades will, if manufacturers are left to their own devices, be likely to be speedily counteracted by the raising of prices on response to the expansion of demand, until the higher wages will purchase little if any more than the wages previously paid. Indeed, they may purchase less, if the initial expansion of demand is seized on as an opportunity for speculative activity, and gives rise to an uncontrolled inflationary movement of bank credit. In order, therefore, to give its policy of high wages a chance of success, the controlling authority of the experiment must take effective steps to regulate prices of commodities, and also to control the expansion of bank credit.

In effect, then, a policy of high wages, designed to enable Capitalism to escape from its inherent tendency to a failure to employ the resources of production to the full, involves, even in a single country, however well placed for its adoption, a completely centralised control of all the vital factors in the economic system. It means the abdication of the private capitalists as controlling agents, and their supersession by a unifying authority which, even if they begin by dominating it, is bound to have a political rather than an economic character. It is, however, impossible, when once this authority does assume a political character, to prevent it from responding to the will, not of the capitalists alone, but of the entire electorate, which will, under such conditions, be certain to convert it before long from State-controlled Capitalism into a form of Socialism. Therefore, finally, the maintenance of controlled Capitalism of the sort under discussion must depend on the destruction of the democratic-parliamentary form of government, and its supersession by an unconcealed political autocracy under capitalist control. Either Fascism or Socialism is the logical end of the attempt to establish a planned and unified capitalist regime.

But if the end is naked capitalist autocracy rather than Socialism, what will happen next? Will the capitalist autocrats be able so to overcome their instinctive opposition to working-class claims as, even after they have destroyed for their own security the independent organisations of the working class, to persist in handing over to the defeated workers the higher and higher incomes required to afford an adequate outlet for the expanding product of industry? If they do not, the old capitalist contradiction will recur, with a renewal of unemployment and business losses and stagnation, and a consequent re-emergence of the forces of discontent, to threaten and in the end to cast down their autocracy. If they do, the rising standard of the workers will strengthen their feeling of power, and make them less ready to submit to the continuance of an autocratic regime. For why, they will ask, should not they control the system on democratic lines? That way, too, the autocracy will break in the end, and give place to Socialism. But it is more likely to break in the other way; for it is most improbable that a capitalist autocracy could deliberately set out to raise the working-class standard of life.

All this relates only to a policy of high wages and Economic Nationalism pursued by a country well situated for its adoption. It does not apply to any capitalist country in Europe, because no such country could embark on a thorough-going policy of Economic Nationalism without such economic loss as to lower, and not raise, the standard of life. In Western Europe at any rate, Economic Nationalism is irreconcilable with high wages; and there is not even a temporary way of escape by this method from the contradictions of the capitalist economy. For European Capitalism is irrevocably dependent on the world market, and cannot therefore evade the limitations imposed upon it by international competition. Capitalist autocracy in Germany, working on lines of Economic Nationalism, will not be able to choose between high and low wages. Low wages will be forced upon it, whatever expedients it may adopt.

It is undeniable that, in this matter of the inherent contradictions of capitalist economy, the present situation of Capitalism fully bears out all the essentials of the Marxian analysis. A generation ago, it was common to laugh Marx's predictions to scorn, and to point, in refutation of them, to the advancing standard of life which Capitalism was able to offer to the workers in all the advanced countries. But no one can dismiss Marx's contentions in this facile fashion to-day. World Capitalism does stand convicted of a lamentable failure to make use of the rapidly increasing productivity which the progress of knowledge and invention has put within men's power; and world unemployment and the cry about "over-production" are sufficient witnesses to its failure. World Capitalism has reached a point at which, so far from being able to promise confidently a progressive advance in the standard of life, it is busy cutting wages on the plea of international competition, and endeavouring to retrench upon the social services on the ground that high taxation is strangling business enterprise. Finally, instead of relying confidently on a popular electorate to keep it in power because it does "deliver the goods," it is turning in one country after another to the forcible suppression of its critics, and the establishment in one form or another of Fascist systems as means of preserving its economic authority.

THE DECLINE OF CAPITALISM

The Marxist contention is that this situation arises because the capitalist system has lost its appropriateness as a method of developing the resources of production. As the scale of production expands and machine-technique improves, the economies arising out of the large-scale organisation of the productive processes continually increase, both in the sphere of actual manufacture and in those of marketing and the purchase of raw materials. Consequently, in the more developed industries, each enterprise has a powerful incentive to expand output, in order to lower costs. But the expansion of output is limited by the extent of the available market; and this factor makes strongly against any system of Economic Nationalism save in vast countries. It leads rather to Economic Imperialism; for in each great country the larger producers are eager not only to absorb their smaller rivals, but also to secure the largest possible market outside their own territory. They are, however, save to the extent to which they can make themselves positively more efficient than their competitors, unable to expand their foreign markets without unfavourable reactions on the home market. For, except where they can build up closed markets for their products by the method of Imperialist expansion, their share of the world market depends on the prices at which they are prepared to sell, and therefore upon the wages they are compelled to pay. But in face of the increasing number of highly industrialised countries, the possibilities of an expanding world market for any one of them may dwindle; and the contraction of the home market—or at least the failure to expand it in proportion to the advance in productive power—causes a disuse or underuse of available productive resources, manifested in a growth of unemployment, which is further swelled by the efforts of the producers to reduce their costs by further mechanisation of industry.

In this dilemma, the capitalist world turns to the use of combination as a means, not of promoting efficiency, but of holding up prices by the systematic restriction of output. Factories are bought up in order that they may be put out of action, so as to ease the pressure on the remaining firms; and differential prices are introduced, according to what the market will bear. This usually means the charging of higher prices to home than to foreign buyers, in an intensive effort to sell abroad by methods of "export dumping." It reacts further on the home market, by reducing the purchasing power of the wages and other incomes distributed to the producers. It may benefit one group of *entrepreneurs* as against another or as against their employees; but it is bound to react disastrously on the total volume of wealth produced. It amounts to a positive confession of the failure of Capitalism to fulfil any longer its function of developing the powers of production.

But clearly this situation does not arise out of any real satiation of human needs or desires. For not only are vast communities, including the majority of the human race, still in a condition of primary poverty which contrasts tragically with mankind's expanded productive power: there is also, even within the most advanced economic Societies, a mass of destitution and a standard of living, even for the main body of the wage-earners, far below what is necessary to satisfy those current aspirations which are embodied in the contemporary conception of a reasonable standard. There is no lack of wants, but only of what economists call "effective demand"—that is, of wants which capitalist producers can see their way to supplying at a profit.

Now, clearly the satisfaction of human wants ought not to stop short of the point at which all the available resources of production are fully employed in meeting them, up to the limit at which the cry for more leisure becomes more insistent than the cry for more goods. It is the indictment of Capitalism in its present phase that it finds itself impotent to apply this elementary rule of commonsense to the working of the economic system. It fails, as we have seen, because instead of setting out to produce as much as possible, subject to the demand for reasonable leisure, and to distribute incomes sufficient to ensure a market for all it can produce, it is based on treating only one particular form of income—profit—as the end to be aimed at in production, and all others, above all wages, as evils, or costs, to be kept down to the lowest possible point.

As soon as this contradiction becomes manifest in the actual working of the capitalist system, the general character of the requisite remedy irresistibly suggests itself. It can be only the institution of a system which will aim at the distribution of the largest total income consistent with the available resources of production, in such a way as to create a demand corresponding to the magnitude and the nature of these resources. But this can be brought about only if a single authority is responsible both for the planning of the social production as a whole and for the distribution of the incomes which will be used in buying it. In other words, the remedy is Socialism—the socialisation of the means of production, distribution and exchange.

The tendencies which exist in growing strength within the capitalist system point the way towards this solution. For, whereas. Capitalism in its early stages was a system of unrestricted individual competition between rival *entrepreneurs,* it has been compelled in its later stages more and more to deny its own premises, and to resort to combination as a way out of the difficulties which the competitive system involves. Trusts and combines, and more recently what is called "rationalisation," embody this denial of the validity of the competitive principle, and point the way towards the positive socialisation of forms of enterprise which have already taken on a social, as opposed to an individualistic, character. Moreover, the growth of the joint stock system, with its growing divorce between the ownership of industrial shares and any constructive contribution to, or responsibility for, the conduct of industry, has made sheer nonsense of the old view that business can be successfully carried on only by enterprising capitalists who stake their personal fortunes upon a concern that is their private property. The capitalists as a class do not personally conduct business enterprise to-day; for the most part they only see to it that business shall be conducted in their interest. There are, of course, still capitalists who personally run businesses which are largely their own; but they are less and less typical. The typical *entrepreneur* of to-day is far less a capitalist than a salaried nominee of the capitalist interest.

THE CONDITIONS FOR SOCIALISATION

Under these conditions industry becomes ripe for socialisation. For the capitalists as a class become functionless; and there is no valid economic reason why the salaried conductors of business should continue to be appointed at their bidding, as the servants of their interest. The right way of appointing those who are to be responsible for the conduct of business operations is the way that will ensure that industry shall be so conducted as to use all the available productive resources for the satisfaction of human needs. This implies a control constituted in the interests, not of a limited class, but of the entire body of consumers whose needs are to be met. It implies not merely the socialisation of each industry or the co-ordination of all industries in accordance with a socially devised and controlled Economic Plan, but also Socialism as a political system, organising the national economy in accordance with a democratic conception of welfare; for no conception of welfare which stops short of seeking the means of good living for all the members of Society is any longer consistent with the full use of the available resources of production. Industrialism has become too productive to be consistent with oligarchy: Socialism is the indispensable system for the age of plenty.

For a working model of the new socialised system of production and distribution of incomes we have only to turn to

Russia, having over Marx the inestimable advantage as theorists that we can watch the system which resolves capitalist contradictions in actual process of growth. The Russian system, of course, still falls far short of being Socialism, in any completed sense. It is transitional; and even the essential institutions have by no means yet taken on a final form. But it is already evident that, under the new Russian system, it is utterly impossible for the characteristic dilemma of Capitalism ever to arise. There can be no question at all, however much Russian production may increase, of the inability of the Soviet system to ensure a market for as much as can possibly be produced. For the Russians begin by discovering how much their resources will enable them to produce, decide how much of the available productive capacity to devote to the accumulation of means of production for the future and how much to the provision of free collective services, and then distribute to the consumers enough income to buy the entire remaining product. A system organised on these lines can never suffer from the disease of being unable to use its productive resources for lack of buyers.

Of course, this does not mean that the Russian system is proof against errors of judgment. No system is. It is possible for the controllers to make mistakes about the proportions of their incomes people will want to spend on different things, so as to produce relatively too much of one thing and too little of another; and it is possible for them to anticipate wrongly the future course of demand, so as to accumulate new means of production in the wrong proportions. It is also quite possible both for the controllers and for the workers to be inefficient in actually carrying out the plan, as undoubtedly is the case over a large part of Russian industry to-day. It is not contended that the Russian system ensures the Russian people a high standard of life—obviously it is at present very far from doing this—but only that it does ensure that as much as they can possibly produce will readily find a market, so that overproduction and underconsumption, and also unemployment, save as a temporary consequence of friction in the process of industrial change, simply cannot arise.

In effect, the Russians, despite their present inefficiency as producers and their low standard of life, have solved the dilemma which Capitalism had found insoluble, and have ensured that every advance in technical efficiency shall be passed on to the consumers in the form of a rising standard of life. If other countries, far ahead of Russia in their mastery of productive technique, were to apply the same method of planned socialisation, they would be able promptly to secure results which can come in Russia only at the end of a long and painful process of learning the new technique.

For Socialism is, as we have said, the only appropriate economic system for an age of plenty. While scarcity continued to be the law dictated to men by the condition of the powers of production, the development of these powers to a higher point could most easily be secured under a system based upon the exploitation of the majority and on the private accumulation of wealth. For, in order to ensure an advance in productivity, it was necessary to provide for the withholding of a large part of the scanty productive resources of Society from use in supplying current needs, and their application to the building up of additional productive resources for the future. Capitalism provided the readiest means of achieving this accumulation at a time when there was no means to hand of securing it by collective action, as there is to-day in Russia. The private capitalist, spurred on by the incentive of the profit or interest to be earned on his accumulated capital, was prepared to abstain from reckless consumption in order to increase his future wealth and his power. He was prepared to keep down the standard of life of his employees in order to swell his profits, and thus to get more capital for accumulation. In doing this, he caused much misery; but he did also add to the productive power of Society, and make possible improved standards of living for the future.

This system, despite all the miseries and injustices which it involved, and despite its effect on the minds of the accumulators, was defensible as long as the primary need of Society was to ensure a sufficient accumulation of capital, and no better means of accomplishing this end could be found. But it was defensible only on condition that it did put all the available productive resources to the fullest possible use in supplying either consumers' goods or instruments of production for the future. For as soon as it began to leave productive resources unused, its claim to be an efficient system for the accumulation of capital was fatally undermined. The accumulation of capital is not an end in itself, but only a means to increased consumption in the future. It is of no conceivable advantage to expand the instrument of production, except as a means to an increased provision of consumers' goods. The entire process of capital accumulation has meaning and justification only if it does actually issue in a higher standard of living; and, if it does not, the accumulation is sheer waste.

When, therefore, Capitalism reaches a point at which it can no longer guarantee a rising standard of life as a result of increasing productivity, that means either that it has ceased to make adequate provision for the accumulation of wealth, or that it is allowing its accumulations to run to waste by failing to put them to proper use. It is then due for supersession by a different system. In fact, the present troubles of Capitalism are not due to its failure to save enough, but to its inability to find outlets for the savings which it makes. The root problem for Society to-day is no longer that of ensuring adequate accumulation, but that of providing a sufficient outlet for what can be produced.

This does not mean, of course, that accumulation is no longer necessary. It is; but in the advanced countries at any rate it presents no serious difficulty. It used to be argued, against any form of Socialism or economic democracy, that if the poor controlled the economic system they would always prefer immediate to future satisfactions, and would therefore never consent to a sufficient accumulation of wealth. It is a significant comment upon this view that the one Socialist economy which exists to-day is that in which by far the largest proportion of the productive resources is being applied to the increase of future rather than present wealth, despite the extreme poverty of the country. Accumulation on the scale on which it is now being practised in Russia would be utterly self-destructive for any capitalist country. It is not so for Russia, because under a Socialist system there is no obstacle to the increased productive capacity issuing in a higher standard of living. But a more advanced industrial country, even if it became Socialist and thus removed the limits of useful accumulation, would not need to save on anything like the Russian scale. For it would set out with an established industrial equipment, whereas the Russians have to build up their economic system from the very foundations.

In the next stage of economic development the accumulation

of capital, like the conduct of industry—of which indeed it forms a part—is due to become a social function under collective control. Fundamentally, capital accumulation consists not in saving money, but in directing a certain part of the available resources of production to the making of capital goods rather than goods for direct consumption. Money, except in the form of hard cash, cannot be really saved or accumulated: it can only be used to promote accumulation by being spent on capital goods. Money that is saved, and not spent, is wasted: it has no real existence. For money is only a token of spending power, and realises itself only in being spent. Accordingly, the real accumulation is done, not when money is saved, but when productive resources are directed to the making of capital goods. This direction of productive resources is clearly a function of the control of industry, which will fall to any authority which undertakes the planning of production. A Socialist economy connotes the socialisation of the process of accumulation: it is wholly inconsistent with the maintenance of the practice of relying on individual saving to provide the capital needed for economic development.

But if the private capitalist is no longer necessary in order to ensure the adequate accumulation of capital, the last economic defence of Capitalism goes by the board. For, as we have seen, the capitalist has already ceased to be necessary as an active agent in the conduct of industry. He has become, *qua* owner of capital, a passive recipient of a share in the proceeds, who contributes nothing to the efficiency of the productive process.

The overwhelming strength of the economic case for Socialism is, however, obviously in itself no guarantee of its coming; for systems are created not by logical arguments but by men.

The logic of the case may help the coming of Socialism, but only to the extent to which it works on men's minds so as to strengthen the movement of those who are seeking to institute a Socialist system. But the strength of a movement depends not only, or even mainly, on the cogency of its arguments, but also on the forces behind it. Marx believed that Socialism would supersede Capitalism not only because it was the system best fitted further to develop the resources of production, but also because it was the creed of a growing movement, based on the working class, which would in due course become powerful enough to overthrow the capitalist autocracy. He believed that this would come about because he held that Capitalism, by the very necessities of its own development, was bound to lead to a polarisation of economic classes and to the creation of a more and more powerful and class-conscious movement among the exploited. For large-scale production requires the aggregation of the workers into large masses subject to common conditions and a common discipline, and thereby makes easier the task of organising them in Trade Unions; and the growing interrelation of capitalist industries and the growing pressure of international competition drive home the lessons of class-solidarity on both a national and an international scale. This is an aspect of the Marxian doctrine, vital to Marx's faith in the coming triumph of Socialism, that we have so far left unexamined. We must go on now to ask how far he was right about this increasing polarisation of classes, or about the consequent growth of national and international working-class solidarity. In fact, we must consider Marx's doctrine of the class-struggle, in the light of the actual development of class-relationships in advanced economic Societies during the most recent period of capitalist evolution.

CHAPTER III

THE REALIST CONCEPTION OF HISTORY

ALL ECONOMIC SYSTEMS are ways of applying the power of human labour, by hand and brain, to the available instruments and materials of production. These instruments and materials —the means of production apart from human labour—consist for any Society of the resources afforded by nature in the condition to which they have been brought by the labour of past generations. They include, that is to say, in addition to the sheer gifts of nature, all usable instruments of production accumulated in the past, and all stores of usable things that are available as a result of past labour. The power of human labour, which is to be applied to these means of production, includes all forms of active work, by hand or brain, that is capable of being applied to the making of useful things or the rendering of useful services; and in it are embodied the acquired knowledge and skill which are the legacy of the labours of previous generations of men. The economic problem for any Society is that of establishing the right relations between men and the things upon which they are to labour, so as to make the most advantageous use of the available resources of production, including both men and things.

Any relationship between men and things involves also a relationship between men and men. For men, in arranging for the social exploitation of the means of production by their own labour, must of necessity establish certain corresponding relationships among themselves. There must be some form, rudimentary or advanced, of the division of labour between man and man; and there must be some defined relationship between men and things to regulate the rights of men to the use of the available means of production. These relationships between men and men, involving the definition of rights of property and personal freedom and obligation, have in the past been embodied in various class systems, so that each class system has corresponded to a particular stage in the development of the social use of the resources of production, including both things and men.

The question "What is the right relationship between men and things, and between men and men, for the exploitation of the resources of production?" can therefore be answered only in relation to a particular stage of economic development, and not absolutely. For the answer must depend on the character of the available means of production, and on the stage reached by men's knowledge of their use. There can therefore be no absolutely best economic system, desirable for all time; for different economic systems best meet the needs of mankind at different stages of historic development.

The system which is economically best for any particular period is that which is best adapted to improve the use of the available resources of production, both by advancing the efficiency of production itself and by affording an outlet for the distribution of the largest possible amount of real wealth, or material welfare. This holds good for any stage of social evolution in which the scarcity of real wealth is the dominant economic consideration, in the sense that there is not enough produced to ensure everyone a standard of life which is regarded as adequate by the consciousness of Society. But it does not hold good for a stage at which the problem of producing and distributing enough real wealth for everybody has already been solved.

No system of organising the resources of production can hold good for all time. For, as these resources are constantly being altered by changes in men's skill and knowledge of their use, the appropriate forms of economic organisation must be constantly changing as well. Economic systems therefore need to be reconstructed from time to time if they are not to be calamitously out of adjustment with the developing resources of production. The study of social evolution, from the economic point of view, is the study of the changing phases of the resources of production and of the adjustment to them of the economic systems which men construct for their use.

Any economic system, involving as it does a particular set of relationships between men and things and between men and men, needs the support of a corresponding system of political and social relationships. It cannot function successfully unless the individuals and classes who are its active agents are protected in, or compelled to, the rights and duties assigned to them under it. In other words, any economic system requires a legal system whose concepts and precepts correspond to the needs of the economic situation. The economic purpose of the legal system is to secure the appropriate conditions for the effective use of the resources of production, and to repress any claims or activities likely to interfere with these conditions. No economic system can develop its full potentialities except with the aid of a legal system in harmony with its needs. This is why economic revolutions always carry with them the necessity for corresponding political and legal revolutions.

For the form and content of the law, and the political structure of the Society which upholds it, are intimately connected with the underlying needs of the economic system. A Society of hunters or fishers is bound to organise itself, politically, after a different fashion from a Society of men who live by agriculture or by industrial production, or depend on international commerce for the means of life. It is easy to trace broad correspondences between the underlying economic structures of different Societies and their political organisation, and to see how, in the past, political systems have been adapted to changes in the fundamental economic conditions. This can be seen most plainly of all in the different forms which the institution of property assumes in different civilisations, or phases in the growth of civilisation, and in the changing status of the human beings who perform the ordinary labour required. Slavery corresponds to one phase, serfdom to another, and "free" wage-labour to a third; and slavery, serfdom and wage-labour are all legal and political as well as economic concepts, expressed in different systems of law and in different political institutions.

In the Marxian view, political and legal systems, and the theories which men frame in explanation and justification of them, are derived from the necessities of the economic order. They embody in laws, political institutions, and theories of jurisprudence and politics, the precepts required to uphold particular economic systems which arise out of the development of the powers, or resources, of production; and they are subject to change, in face of whatever resistance, in response to changes in the economic conditions of Society. For economic changes, by forcing upon men new methods of exploiting the available resources of production, compel them to modify the relations of men to things and of men to men, and accordingly to readjust the political systems which uphold such relations. It is inconceivable that a modern Society, employing the resources of large-scale machine production, should continue for long to be organised politically after the fashion of a feudal monarchy, or that the localism of the medieval system of city government should survive the impact of the world market. At every stage of civilisation, there must be a sufficient degree of correspondence between the conditions of production and the political and social system embodied in law and custom; for otherwise there will develop a conflict between the rising economic forces and the established political system, and the latter, so far from upholding the conditions required for further economic advance, will be found to stand perilously in the way of the effective use of the available productive resources.

ECONOMICS AND POLITICS

According to Marxism, economic forces play throughout history the creative and dynamic part. The resources of production are in constant evolution as men's knowledge and command over nature increase, and consequently there is a constant need for changes in the political structure of Society. But political systems do not change constantly and gradually in step with the development of the powers of production. For any system of government, once established, embodies the authority of a particular class; and this class, having seated itself in political power, is by no means willing to yield up its privileges without a struggle merely because the economic conditions have so changed as to make its supersession desirable. Its authority is the guardian of countless vested interests and claims, for the defence of which it exists. The entire system of law which has grown up within it is the expression of these claims in the form of rights and prohibitions; and the government itself is the political representative of the dominant class. Accordingly, while the political system does change gradually in response to changing economic needs, it changes slowly and against the will of those who control it; and its adaptation usually both lags behind the changes which occur in the economic sphere, and is limited to what can be done without departing from its essential class character, or admitting claims inconsistent with the vested rights of the dominant class.

This resistance to necessary changes causes major change, when it does come, to take a revolutionary form. The need for change accumulates, in face of increasing resistance, as the proposed modifications threaten more deeply the essential institutions of the dominant order, until at length the forces making for a change of system grow too powerful to be resisted, and the old political system is broken by revolution and superseded by a new system embodying a different set of class ideas and claims. The class struggle, which has been in progress within the dying system, enters on a revolutionary phase; and a new class, previously held in subjection, assumes in its turn the powers and responsibilities of making a new State.

We shall have to examine more fully later on this Marxian concept of revolution. Here the point is that the political institutions of Society are regarded as a superstructure raised upon economic foundations, and embodying the rule of the class which is predominant in the economic field.

This, however, does not mean that all political developments are capable of explanation in purely economic terms. For, even if the roots of political systems are in the economic order, any set of institutions which men create is bound to acquire a life and potency of its own. A system of government, when once it has been established, has therefore a secondary power of influencing the movement of history, and of reacting on the course of economic development. Human history does not proceed solely under the impulsion of economic forces, but is affected profoundly by the forms which the social and political life of Society assumes. What is itself mainly the outcome of economic forces is capable of becoming an independent, though still a secondary cause.

What is true of political institutions is no less true of other forms of social organisation. Any underlying economic condition of Society, embodied in a particular system of production, involves a corresponding set of values, not only in an economic but also in an ethical sense. Things and forms of conduct are regarded as good or bad at different stages of civilisation according as they further or hamper the carrying on of production in accordance with the requirements of the predominant economic system. This involves, in ethics as well as law, a system of values which reflects the ideas and interests of the controlling economic class, that is, of the class upon which devolves the responsibility for the successful management of production.

These ethical ideas, appropriate to a particular phase of social evolution, acquire, like the political institutions of Society, a sanctity of their own, and become highly resistant to change. Equally with the law, they help to uphold and sanction conduct in harmony with the needs of the established economic order; and, equally with law, they become, when once established in men's minds, independent causes, capable of influencing the further development of Society. For men think within a social framework, and the shape of thought on political and economic matters is derived from, and corresponds to, the shape of the Society within which the thinking is done. The forces which arise within a given social system, as a challenge to its economic and political institutions, have perforce to challenge also those elements in the established morality which reflect the needs and notions of the system that is to be attacked. But it is often harder to get the attacking forces to attack ideas than institutions; for every dominant class teaches the absoluteness of moral precepts with even more fervour and assurance than the finality of the established type of State and of the existing class-relationships. Besides, morals are entangled with religion, and men are less accessible to reasonings about morality than about politics or economics.

It is nevertheless clear, and affirmed by all sociologists, that moral ideas about social relationships are not absolute, but relative to the needs and conditions of different types of Society. Even if there is an absolute moral law, it can have, in such matters, no absolute and timeless content. There is no positive individual human action that can be pronounced *a priori* to be absolutely right or wrong, wholly without regard to the circumstances in which it is performed. When once this is recognised, it is easy to accept the view that positive precepts of social morality must change with changes in the economic and political conditions of Society, and that current codes of conduct are profoundly influenced by the character of the contemporary economic and political system.

Nor does this apply only within the field of moral ideas and precepts. Men's entire way of thinking is obviously conditioned by the nature of the Society in which they live. This is not so much because social conditions affect the answers men make to the questions which they ask themselves—though of course this is the case—as because social conditions affect the framing of the questions. Each age has its own problem, dictated to it by the conditions in which it lives, and imperatively demanding solution: and the philosophies and sciences of every age, while they are built upon the legacies of the past, are essentially attempts to find answers to contemporary problems.

Of course, this does not mean that every individual is limited to thinking only in terms of the problems of his own age. No one, indeed, can help being influenced by his age, however much he may try to escape from it; but subject to this thought is free, and can range at will over all questions that men can frame. A man can live in a past age, and think in terms of its problems; or he can construct a dream-world of his own, and do his thinking in terms of the imaginary concepts appropriate to his dream. A scientific enquirer can pursue his researches without caring a whit about their practical results, in a spirit of disinterested curiosity.

THOUGHT AND ACTION

But out of all the welter of contemporary thought, the age will select. More thinkers and enquirers will be attracted to those problems which peculiarly vex the age than to others; and thinkers, no matter how subtle or profound, who have no message for their age, will be passed over—to be rediscovered, perhaps, centuries later, when their thought has become appropriate to the problems of a different stage of social development. The Marxian contention is not that men can think only in terms dictated by current economic conditions, but that out of men's thoughts those alone will influence the course of social evolution which are relevant to contemporary problems.

Clearly, then, human thought is not a mere mechanical product of the economic conditions of Society. It is an independent force, itself powerful in the shaping of the economic conditions. But it is a force which builds upon what it finds in being, and takes its form and direction from the problems which the objective situation presents. Marx's point is not that thought is impotent in the shaping of man's destiny, but that it is neither arbitrary nor capricious in its working, but is, in its social aspect, fundamentally a seeking of answers to questions set by the conditions of contemporary Society, which is itself a product of men's past thought as applied to similar objective problems.

There is in this view of thought, as in the entire Realist Conception of History, nothing derogatory to the powers of the human mind. What is emphasised is that the thought which makes history is not a "pure" thought, divorced from the material and substantial things of the workaday world, but thought applying itself to these things, and acting upon them so as to develop their latent powers. Marx, true to his principle that being is logically prior to thought, exalts thought by enlisting it in the service of being.

Nevertheless, the Marxian view shocks many people because it exalts the thinker who keeps his nose to the grindstone of fact above the pure contemplator beloved of the Idealist philosophers. If that is shocking, then Marxism is shocking in the fullest sense; for his view emphatically is that the thought that counts is thought which bears a close relation to the practical problems of mankind.

But what, it will be asked, of mankind's theoretical problems, which have nothing to do with current political or economic affairs, but arise out of a disinterested desire to understand, or out of a wish to solve the purely personal problem of a man's own place in the universe? Marx says nothing to deny the value of disinterested curiosity, or its power to discover vitally important truth, and to react upon social development; but he is impatient of that type of thinking which seeks, apart from society, a purely personal interpretation of man's place in the world of being. For he is profoundly convinced that ideas are social products, and lose their meaning when they are cut away from a social context. The problem of man's place in the universe is for him a social problem, to be asked and answered afresh by each generation in social terms, and in close relation to the objective conditions of Society. He does not deny that men can think in abstraction from their social environment; but he holds that such purely individualistic thinking will be abstract, and therefore barren. Real and creative thought must be about real things; and abstractions are never real. Thought divorced from being is an abstraction: thought divorced from social being is no less an abstraction. It ends in a futile Solipsism, or in a no less futile denial of all reality save the Universal that annihilates the universe.

What shocks most in Marx, however, is not his aversion to this type of thinking, but his insistence that when men think they are thinking of one thing, they are in fact often thinking of something else. It is above all his contention that the great struggles of history have all been at bottom economic, even when men have fought them out consciously in religious or ethico-political terms. It infuriates a religious man to be told that the form and substance of his religion are really at bottom expressions of his economic interests and desires, or a philosopher to be told that his philosophy is really a thought-projection of the conditions appropriate to a particular class-structure of Society. No wonder it infuriates him; for he is conscious of having thought out his position in religious or philosophical terms, without having been deflected from the process of thought by any consideration of personal economic interest.

It is important, if we are to regard Marxism objectively, to get as clear a view as possible of Marx's meaning at this point. He is not accusing the religious or philosophical thinker of hypocrisy or deliberate mystification, though of course both these things do often occur—as when infidel prelates in the eighteenth century defended their position by urging that religion was good for the poor, or when a religious person makes his observances a cloak for living an immoral life. These abuses, however, are accidental, and beside the present point. For what Marx holds is that men holding certain religious or philosophic beliefs in full honesty may in fact be fighting under their banner in a struggle which has at bottom an essentially economic content.

RELIGION AND HISTORY

In advancing this doctrine, Marx had doubtless most of all in mind the circumstances of the Reformation. Since his time, numerous writers have attempted to show the intimate connection between the spirit of Protestantism and the needs of the commercial classes which were beginning in the sixteenth century to claim emancipation from the restrictions imposed on capitalist enterprise by the ethical code of the Catholic Church. It is significant that Calvin broke away from the medieval tradition concerning usury by authorising the receipt of interest, and that the Protestant communities were everywhere those which broke most easily with the old codes of business ethics. But the argument goes much deeper than this. It is, fundamentally, that the new Capitalism was in its essence individualistic, and therefore found itself in strong hostility to the social doctrines and atmosphere of medieval Christendom. The rising merchants and manufacturers wanted to go their own way, untrammelled by codes of conduct which had been framed to suit the localised and regulated economy of the Middle Ages. They were emancipating themselves from the control of the Gilds and corporations which had dominated medieval economic life, and from the conception of status and limited gild fellowship which went with them. They were getting away from the notion of a "just price," based on the conditions of production, to the rival idea that the right price for a thing, or a worker, was what it, or he, would fetch in the market—neither more nor less. Ethics and Economics were being torn apart by the rapid changes in the conditions of manufacture and exchange; and the Catholic Church, conservative in social doctrine, stood in the way of the fuller development of the new powers of production.

Accordingly, when Protestantism, in some one of its many forms, presented itself to a community of traders or manufacturers, it came reinforced not so much by conscious considerations of economic interest as by an appeal which fitted in admirably with the new conditions of life. The trader became a Protestant, not because he put it to himself that Protestantism squared better than Catholicism with his business interest, but because he was already thinking individualistically in connection with the everyday problems of life, and a religion which emphasised his individual relation and responsibility to his Maker gave him the kind of spiritual attitude that he wanted. It was not in the least that his religion was insincere: he was but following the example of men in all ages by re-making his religion after the model of his desires and values.

Only in this sense can the religious struggles of the sixteenth and seventeenth centuries be held to have had an economic basis. The underlying forces which broke up the Catholic Church and set in its place a number of Churches were by no means all economic; but the new Churches which based themselves on Protestantism did to a great extent develop a doctrine and outlook well adapted to the needs of the rising capitalist system, and the forms which the various Protestant Churches assumed were profoundly influenced by the economic conditions of the countries in which they grew up.

THE RISE OF NATIONALISM

The break-up of Catholicism is, however, obviously connected with the rise, not only of the capitalist system, but also of the new national States. It was fully as much a "nationalisation" of religion as a change in doctrine. It cannot therefore be explained satisfactorily in economic terms unless the rise of the Nation-State admits of a similar explanation.

This undoubtedly raises a very difficult question. It is of course beyond doubt that the movement towards political nationalism found stout supporters in the majority of the commercial classes, and that Kings owed much, in their struggles both with feudal barons and with the claims of the Universal

Church, to the support of burghers and craftsmen. For the traders and producers wanted above all things order, and saw the chief hope of this in strengthening the hands of the King's Government against both feudal potentates and the overriding authority of Pope and Holy Roman Emperor alike. They were opposed too to Church exactions destined to go to the support of a central Church organisation at Rome; and this led them to support monarchs who were prepared to set up a National Church as the auxiliary of the National State.

Almost everywhere, the main body of the commercial classes was on the side of the new Nationalism. But it does not, of course, follow from this that the rise of the Nation-State can be explained in wholly, or even mainly, economic terms. Certainly there were other forces, as no one who has read Machiavelli can doubt, besides those of economic change that made in the direction of a strengthening of national consciousness and national control. What above all marks off Machiavelli from earlier political thinkers is the completely secular character of his conception of politics and the State. Order is his political objective, as it was that of the traders; but he brings home the truth that order could be ardently desired for other than economic ends. The Nation-State, based on secular principles, triumphed because, amid the collapse of the medieval system, it provided not for the traders alone, but for everyone who was frightened or beggared by the confusions of the times, the best available guarantee of order and personal security.

To admit this, however, is only to push the question a stage further back. For the root cause of the rise of political Nationalism must be sought in the forces which led to the dissolution of the medieval system. These forces were undoubtedly economic. Medievalism broke up in face of the alterations in

the economic condition of Europe which followed the taking
of Constantinople by the Turks and the discovery of the New
World. Shut off from traditional contacts with the East, and
offered instead the vast opportunities of the New World in
the West, European civilisation rapidly ceased to base itself
upon the Mediterranean. The countries whose seaboards lay
along the Atlantic Ocean ceased to be at the world's circumference, and found themselves at its centre. Spain, France,
Great Britain and the Low Countries became the strategic
points for the next advance of European civilisation; and the
rivalries between their adventurers and monarchs for a share
in the new opportunities for wealth provided the most powerful incentive to strengthen the national State, and to cast off
the outworn allegiance to a civilisation based upon the Mediterranean Sea. Only strong national States could hope to claim a
part in the riches of the great new world that was being opened
up; and among national States that which was least power-
fully organised for backing up its claims was certain to lose
the prize.

The rise of political Nationalism does in this way go back
to economic causes. But it cannot be regarded as the creature
of a coherent economic class. For, while the commercial classes
gave it their support, and were powerful allies of the monarchs
in their struggle against the medieval system, these classes
were not nearly strong enough to carry the day by themselves;
and most of their power came after the battle for the Nation-
State had been decisively won. Kings needed burgher help;
but the new national States were real monarchies and not dis-
guised commercial oligarchies such as they became later on.
In this first struggle associated with the rise of Capitalism,
the growing capitalist class won, not power over the State,

but the conditions necessary to their subsequent rise to dominance. Social evolution need not proceed by the simple and immediate substitution of one form of class-power for another. There are hybrid forms and transitions which may take centuries to work out before a new class-system is thoroughly and completely established.

Moreover, the rise of strong, centralised Nation-States was largely the consequence of the growing need for the enforcement of law and order over a wider area. With the extension of the market and the breakdown of local isolation, there came a more pressing demand for a strong hand wielding a wider justice, both to keep turbulent local barons and freebooters in order, and to supplement and co-ordinate the local jurisdiction of city and manorial courts. The traders, as the chief journeyers from place to place, compelled by the nature of their calling to carry about with them large values in merchandise or money, were especially urgent for protection that would enable them to go their ways in peace and security. The growth of agriculture and of settled systems of manufacture created a lively demand for the suppression of internal disorder and destructive civil warfare, including the abolition of private armies of retainers living on the neighbourhood. Strong States, with fairly extensive territories and high centralisation of armed force, alone could meet these claims; and consequently the weight of the developing economic forces was usually thrown on the side of the Crown against the barons, as the readiest way of creating the conditions required.

This brief discussion of one particular critical phase in social development has been designed to clarify the meaning of the Marxian contention that political and ideological struggles which appear to exert a dominant influence in shaping the general course of history are in the last resort the outcome of changing economic forces and conditions. Given the economic situation of Europe at the close of the fifteenth century, it was necessary, Marx would argue, that the loose unity of medieval Christendom should be broken up, that the claims of the universal Church should be repudiated, that strong Nation-States should be brought into existence, and that the capitalist *entrepreneur* should escape from the restrictions imposed on him by Gild and Church, and should take to himself an ethic and a religious outlook in harmony with his changed economic needs. For the alternative to these developments would have been, not the continuance of the medieval system, but its sheer dissolution with nothing to take its place—the death of a civilisation instead of its rebirth into a new phase. These things may not have been inevitable, any more than the coming of Socialism is inevitable to-day—for nothing is built except men build it—but they were the only alternative to a chaos which could only have ushered in a new Dark Age.

HOW MEN MAKE THEIR HISTORY

For the point is this. Men make their own history; but they can make it, in any constructive sense, only by accepting the limitations and opportunities of the age in which they live. This implies, not only that they must act in ways appropriate to their age, but equally that they must think and feel in terms appropriate to it. For men's thoughts and feelings are the foundations of their actions; and it is only by thinking and feeling appropriately to the needs and opportunities of their time that men can become the constructive agents of social development.

It is in this sense that men's social ideas, as well as their political and social institutions, rest upon an economic basis. Thoughts and feelings are man's weapons in his struggle to make the best of things. Their biological purpose is practical— to make man more at home in his environment, and to help him adapt his environment to his needs. He has, of course, a private as well as a social environment; and the use which he makes of his mind has reference to this private environment as well as to its wider social context. But when we speak of the thought or mind or spirit of an age we are referring to those ideas and feelings which are characteristic of it, and enter, as the product of many individual minds, into its collective consciousness. These are the social ideas and feelings which, arising out of the common factors in the objective situation, find lodgment in the minds of many different individuals, and form the substance of current intellectual intercourse. It is to these alone that the Marxian doctrine refers, when it asserts that social ideas and attitudes are ultimately traceable to economic causes.

If, however, the major movements of history are unintelligible except in relation to the development of the powers of production, it is disastrous to ignore the fact that any institution, or any form of thought, when it has once come into being, is capable of exerting an independent influence of its own. While the fundamental forces behind historical development may be economic, the actual course of events is being continually affected by forces of any and every kind—political, ideological and religious as well as economic. For an institution, or an idea present in the minds of men, is part of the objective situation, whatever its origin and whatever the forces that have shaped its development. Thus, the State, as it is shaped at any

particular stage in the history of a Society, may be the outcome of a special phase in the evolution of the powers of production. But it is also, since it exists, a force not without influence on the course of economic development. It reacts on the
very conditions which brought it into being; and, still more,
it can delay and obstruct the readjustment of social relationships so as to make them correspond to a new phase in the development of the productive powers. Similarly, if an idea once
finds lodgment in the minds of men, the fact that its acceptance
may have been due to its original harmony with the economic
needs of the time will not prevent it from persisting after this
harmony has disappeared, or from reacting upon the ways in
which men reorganise their social relationships in face of
economic change.

No one who appreciates this vital point will make the absurd
mistake of trying to interpret all history in exclusively economic terms. To do this is to empty out the human content of
historical development, and to represent men as mere automata
responding blindly to stimuli from the world of experience. No
such denial of personality is implied in, or consistent with,
the Realist Conception. For according to that conception men
act in the light of the entire objective situation; and this situation includes not only the economic factors in the environment, but all the factors. It is ridiculous to argue that in every
case the economic factors are bound to prevail over the rest;
for how is it possible to say that men's minds will always act
in one particular way in evaluating the relative importance of
the factors concerned? It is the judgment of men that co-
ordinates the several factors, so as to arrive at a basis for pur-
posive activity; and in making such judgments men are free
to make their own estimates of value. Only the crudest pseudo-

Benthamite psychology can support the conclusion that always and in all circumstances they will be swayed by the economic factors in preference to the others.

What can be argued is that, however men decide to act, the economic forces will in the long run make their action ineffective unless it is in sufficient harmony with the requirements of the economic situation. The economic conditions circumscribe, but by no means abrogate, human freedom; and, in a given situation, there may be many alternative courses open, none of which is impossible on economic grounds. Within this wide range of choices the non-economic forces are free to operate, inducing men to do this in preference to that on whatever grounds may appeal to them, and thus vitally influencing the movement of historical events. Only when men try to pass beyond the limits set by the absolute possibilities of the economic situation are they sharply pulled back into a path consistent with the requirements of economic development.

It remains, however, true that, while non-economic forces can be of great importance in the shaping of history, their influence is in fact mainly negative. For they are powerful to the extent to which they have already become embodied in strongly entrenched social institutions, or in ideas widely received as axiomatic. But nothing becomes embodied in an institution, or a received idea, or dogma, until it is already old; for it takes time for ideas and institutions alike to grow and acquire the sanctity of being past question. The established ideas and institutions of an age, unless it be an age that has accomplished a successful revolution, are the legacy of the age that preceded it. They are not creative, but conservative of existing values. They are, to be sure, challenged and contradicted by rival ideas and institutions; but these rivals are power-

less against them unless they can stand up against the authority
of the established order. In other words, the ideas and institutions which appear to play a creative rôle in history are those
which are identified with living and growing social forces.

These social forces, which are the exponents and embodi-
ments of new ideas, arise primarily in the economic field. They
are the ideas, selected out of the welter of contemporary
thought, which meet the needs of groups and classes created
or enlarged by the development of the economic forces. Thus
ideas are powerful in history in two ways. They can add
strength and resisting power to groups and classes which are
threatened by the development of the powers of production.
That is their negative and obstructive rôle, in which they serve
as the allies of the established order, whatever it may be. But
they can also lend consciousness and attacking power to the
rival groups and classes which the development of the powers
of production has called into being; and this second is their constructive rôle in history, whereby they become the slogans and
premonitions of the future. In both these ways they exert a
vital influence on human affairs. For no established order can
effectively resist change unless it believes in itself and possesses a code of ideas justifying its own authority; and equally
no movement challenging the established order can succeed
unless it is able to equip itself with a philosophy corresponding
to its own needs and aspirations.

The rôle of ideas in history is thus vitally important, but also
secondary. For ideas have their influence, not as disembodied
notions, but as the creeds of bodies of men whom they inspire
to action. The idea is nothing without a thinker: the social
idea is nothing unless it is embodied in a social movement.
Even as there can be no mind without a body, there can be

no socially influential conception without a movement to make it real.

Class is itself an economic phenomenon; but the conception of class is a social idea. There can be a working-class, or a capitalist class, without the persons who compose it being conscious of themselves as a class. But only as they become conscious of themselves as a class, at least to the extent of accepting a leadership which possesses this consciousness, do they become capable of acting effectively as a class. The fact of class comes first, and the consciousness of class is secondary to it; for always and everywhere a thing must exist before men can become conscious of it. But the existence of a thing, among conscious beings, provides the essential condition for the growth of consciousness about it. Given the existence of a class, some degree of class-consciousness necessarily follows.

But no particular degree of class-consciousness has this logical necessity. For an idea, vaguely present in men's minds, can remain indefinitely inchoate and unclearly formulated, as a feeling undeveloped into a positive conception. The creative function of thought is to give clarity and distinctness to vague feelings presented to men by the crude experience of events. Without this added clarity, the members of a class may act, under stimulus, as a class—as has happened again and again in history, whenever men have shown an instinctive solidarity unexpressed in any common creative purpose. The rising capitalist class fought its early battles in this way, holding together by instinct even before there had been any clear formulation of capitalist objectives or philosophy. Strikes among the workers have repeatedly revealed the same instinctive solidarity, among men who could certainly not have formulated with any clarity the foundations of their loyalty. The General Strike of 1926 in Great Britain evoked a response far transcending the consciousness of the British working-class. But a class that fights by instinct alone fights with feeble weapons; for instinct may help it to resist, but not to construct. As long as its action remains on the plane of instinct or feeling, and does not rise to the height of the conscious idea, it cannot win more than sectional and occasional victories; for it cannot formulate a plan of campaign, or define the objectives of its action. It must rise to the stage of class-consciousness, at least to the extent of accepting a class-conscious leadership, before it can be fit for the exercise of authority, or hope to remake Society after the image of its own desires.

Thus, on the basis of our Realist Conception, ideas, while they are secondary to economic forces, are nevertheless the direct agents of historical evolution. Where there is no idea, no consciousness expressing itself in a positive policy, there can be no effective historical movement. That there can be no such idea without a movement in which it can be embodied goes without saying: the complementary, and no less important, truth is that there can be no successful movement without an idea.

But, whereas the economic forces, however much they are themselves the result of human activity, are necessarily always there—for there must always be an objective economic situation—there is no corresponding necessity in the development of ideas. Ideas arise out of situations: there is no other way in which they can arise. But they do not arise of necessity, or of necessity attain in men's minds the strength of social convictions. To express in clear-cut ideas the needs and desires appropriate to the objective situation is the task of great thinkers: to impose these ideas upon the minds of those whose needs and desires they are fitted to express is the function of education and propaganda. But neither thinkers nor propagandists of the required calibre are produced automatically by the objective situation alone. The situation acts as a stimulus; for it suggests the problems, and arouses the sense of need. But a stimulus does not necessitate a response. The universe is full of abortive stimuli.

The social thinker and the social propagandist arise in response to the objective situation; but they arise not of necessity, but of their own motion. The needs of a situation may fail to be met because no one thinks and articulates the thoughts required to give coherence and direction to an instinctive social movement, or because the propagandists and educators fail to use the thoughts that the thinkers and planners have placed at their disposal. There is no inevitability in history, because there is no inevitability in men's response to a given objective situation. They cannot act outside the possibilities which it presents; but they can, and often do, fail to take full advantage of these possibilities. That is what is meant by saying that mankind makes its own history; but let us add that mankind can fail to make it well.

CHAPTER IV

ECONOMIC CLASSES

MARX'S THEORY of the class-struggle was first explicitly formulated in the *Communist Manifesto* of 1848. Marx never restated it in a similar full and explicit form, though of course it underlay the whole of his thought. Actually, the unfinished final chapter of the third volume of *Capital,* edited from Marx's papers by Engels after his death, is the beginning of what promises to be a thorough discussion of the nature of economic classes and of their relationships. But this chapter remains the merest fragment, broken off before the exposition has fairly begun, and highly provocative in the wonder which it arouses. Would Marx, if he had expounded the nature of classes towards the close of his life, have written of them in the same terms as he had used more than thirty years before? Or would he have recognised that there had been, in the interval, vitally important changes in the class-structure of advanced industrial Societies, and that these changes were, to some extent, different from the anticipations which he had entertained? The question is probably unanswerable; but let us at any rate remember that the familiar Marxian account of the class-struggle was written near the beginning of Marx's public life, and reflects the capitalist conditions of the first half of the nineteenth century, and not of Marx's later years.

This is of great importance; for the *Communist Manifesto* was written before joint stock enterprise had become the accepted form of developed capitalist production over the greater part of industry, and before the middle-classes had assumed the new character given to them by the increased wealth of modern Societies, and the greater complexity of modern technical processes. The middle-classes, that is, the classes between the governing groups of the *bourgeoisie* and the wage-earners, have increased markedly as a percentage of the entire population with the more recent developments of capitalist enterprise, and have assumed, under the joint stock system, new relations to the processes of production. Any modern theory of classes must take full account of these changes: it is merely beside the point to repeat without modification a statement of the basis of class-divisions conceived in terms of the very different economic conditions of a century ago.

Let us begin by outlining the theory, in the form in which it is stated in the *Communist Manifesto*. We are there presented with a theory of world-history as a succession of class-struggles for economic and political power. We are concerned in this chapter only with Marx's picture of the most recent of these struggles—the conflict between the exploiting *bourgeoisie* and the exploited proletariat, which is conceived to be the dominant theme of contemporary Western Society. These two classes are represented as so dominating the Society of to-day that the admitted existence of other classes, or of groups which cannot be adequately classified as either *bourgeois* or proletarian, is conceived of as, not indeed unimportant from the standpoint of the day-to-day political struggle, but irrelevant to a consideration of the general historical movement. These other groups may exert here and there, or now and then, a temporarily decisive influence on a particular phase of the struggle; but it is inconceivable, in Marx's view, that they should finally determine the issue, or play a truly creative part. For they have in them, he believes, no power to create an alternative social pattern of their own; and accordingly they can act only so as to obstruct or fog the issue, or as secondary allies of one or the other of the major classes.

Moreover, Marx undoubtedly speaks as if these secondary class-groups were already in process of disappearance, or destined to disappear with the further advance of Capitalism. He thinks of the two great classes of *bourgeois* and proletarians as destined, for all practical purposes, to become in the final phase of the struggle between them co-extensive with the whole of Society, or at least so nearly co-extensive as to reduce any remaining groups outside them to the rôle of impotent spectators or obviously subordinate assistants. From the standpoint of the broad process of social evolution, only the proletariat and the *bourgeoisie* are held to count.

We must ask, then, first of all in what terms Marx seeks to define these outstanding classes. He admits that their precise limits are unclear, and that there are, in capitalist Society, many border-line cases. But he holds that both proletariat and *bourgeoisie* can be sufficiently defined by the places which they occupy in the existing economic system. The proletariat is that class which consists of persons who depend for their living on the sale of their labour-power, and are unable to secure an income except by resigning all claim to the product of their labour. They are workers who are shut off from direct access to the means of production, and live by the alienation of the only commodity they possess—their power to produce wealth by labouring upon machines and materials which are not their own. The distinctive characteristic of this class is not so much that its labour is paid for by a wage—though it is—as that its product belongs, not to its members, but to the purchasers of their labour-power.

The proletariat must, of course, be held to include not only those who in this way alienate their labour-power but also their dependents, who, equally with them, live out of the proceeds of the sale of labour-power as a commodity. It includes, obviously, the employed wage-workers in agriculture as well as industry and commerce; but it does not, by the terms of its definition, include anyone who is not either an employed worker or the dependent of an employed worker. How far it can be held to include employed workers who receive not a wage but what is called a salary we had best leave over for consideration at a later stage. Whatever limits may be assigned to the proletariat as a class, obviously its central mass consists of the general body of manual wage-earners, and it is predominantly a manual-working and wage-earning group.

Marx, however, warns his readers against attempting to define economic classes by the forms in which they receive their incomes. For there are, he holds, far more distinct forms of income than there are separate economic classes. The distinctive characteristic of the proletariat is not the receipt of a wage, however important that aspect of the status of the majority of its actively working members may be, but the alienation of its labour-power, based on its divorce from ownership of, and direct access to, the means of production on which it is required to work.

This warning becomes far more important when we turn

to consider the character of the *bourgeoisie*. For the class which Marx calls *bourgeois* receives its income not in a single form, but in many different forms. It is the class which predominantly lives by the receipt of profit, interest and rent—all three of these, and not any one or two of them. Marx states this by saying that the *bourgeoisie* lives by the receipt of "surplus value," which he conceives of as a fund, arising out of the exploitation of labour, out of which rent, interest and profits are all paid. The *bourgeoisie* lives out of surplus value to much the same extent as the proletariat lives out of the proceeds of the sale of labour-power. But the *bourgeoisie* as a class must be defined strictly, not as the recipients of surplus value, but as the owners of those resources of production upon which the proletariat is employed to work. The *bourgeoisie* is essentially a class of owners of the means of production; the proletariat is essentially a class of employed persons who do not own the means of production, apart from their own labour-power.

The power to labour is merely useless and abstract without access to the means of production; and accordingly the proletariat as a class has, under Capitalism, no power to produce wealth unless the capitalists are prepared to employ it. But the means of production are also useless and unproductive unless labour is applied to them. The labourer has to find an employer, in order to get the means of life. But it is also true that the employer, or capitalist, has to find labourers whom he can employ if his capital is to possess any value. Marx again and again stresses this point, insisting that Capitalism is fundamentally a relationship among men, and that its essence consists not in the accumulation of a stock of goods or instruments of production, but in the availability of a proletariat from which surplus value can be extracted. This is the point of the argument of the closing sections of the first volume of *Capital,* in which the rise of the capitalist system is discussed and traced to the emergence of a propertyless class of free labourers compelled to live by the sale of their labour-power.

THE PETITE BOURGEOISIE

This, however, takes us beyond the *Communist Manifesto* to a later formulation of Marx's doctrine. In the *Manifesto,* there is only a brief historical section of which the sole purpose is to bring into relief the dominant importance of the class-struggle and of the two great classes between which it is carried on. There is much said of the rôle of the *petite bourgeoisie,* as well as of the two outstanding classes, but always on the assumption that the *petite bourgeoisie* is a dying or decaying class, because its very existence is bound up with the survival of the small-scale forms of production which are being remorselessly crushed out by the advance of capitalist industry. The *petite bourgeoisie,* as it appears in the *Communist Manifesto,* consists chiefly of small master craftsmen and independent artisans, small traders, and small farmers, who are being driven from one position after another by the development of large-scale methods of production. It is thus, in Marx's view, essentially a threatened and obsolescent class, attempting to retain for itself a status and economic position which the advancing powers of production are rapidly making untenable.

This decaying class is represented as standing, in the contemporary phase of the class-struggle, between the protagonists, hovering doubtfully in its allegiance, but unable to stand by itself or to formulate a policy of its own. It hates and fears the advance of large-scale Capitalism, which threatens

it with submergence; and it is animated by democratic sentiments on account of its hostility to the greater *bourgeoisie,* and
its desire for equality with the class above it and for a share
in the formulation of policy. But it is also fearful of the class
below it, towards which it stands commonly in the relation of
employer; and it desires not social and economic equality, but
the maintenance of its own position of petty economic privi-
lege. Consequently, while it is willing to accept the support of
the workers for an attack on the *bourgeoisie,* it will do this
only on condition that the attack is directed to the realisation of its own limited objectives, and not to the overthrow
of *bourgeois* Society as a whole. It wants to clip the wings of
large-scale Capitalism; but even more it wants to preserve the
decaying system of small-scale Capitalism. Its attitude is therefore, even when it appears to be radical and democratic, in
reality always reactionary; for its supreme desire is to preserve conditions which are inconsistent with economic progress.
In a serious crisis, while it may begin by siding with the proletariat against the *bourgeoisie,* it will always change sides
as soon as the *anti-bourgeois* movement threatens to develop
into a fundamental attack upon the capitalist system. For, in
the last resort, it will always prefer gradual erosion by the
further development of large-scale industrialism to complete
supersession as the consequence of a proletarian victory.

   This analysis of the attitude of the *petite bourgeoisie,* set out
in general terms in the *Communist Manifesto,* is applied with
much more detail by Marx and Engels in their occasional writings commenting upon current affairs, especially in their
studies of the actual events of 1848 and the following years.
*Revolution and Counter-Revolution in Germany, The Class
Struggle in France,* and other writings of this sort amplify and

illustrate with a wealth of example the teaching of the *Communist Manifesto* concerning the historic rôle of the *petite bourgeoisie.* Nor is there any doubt that Marx and Engels were essentially right in their diagnosis both of the economic position of the *petite bourgeoisie* of 1848, and of its political attitude. It was, in the economic sense, a decaying and reactionary class; and politically it did seek to use the proletariat to help it to increase its own power in relation to the greater *bourgeoisie,* but did at once rally to the side of the *bourgeoisie* when there was any risk of the proletariat getting out of hand, and attempting to fight its own battles, or to deliver a frontal attack upon the capitalist system.

The essential struggle, as Marx conceived it, could be obfuscated or temporarily sidetracked by the attitude of the *petite bourgeoisie,* but could not be prevented from dominating the situation in the long run, precisely because the preservation of small-scale industry and trade, in face of the advance in the powers of production, had ceased to be a possible policy. The *petit bourgeois* might be a long time dying; but his doom was certain, and his power even to cloud the fundamental issue destined to become inevitably less.

What then of the proletariat, of which Marx thought as essentially the rising class destined to accomplish the overthrow and suppression of the capitalist system? The position of this class was contrasted by Marx and Engels with that of previous subject classes which had accomplished their emancipation and risen to a position of economic and social dominance. For, whereas the embryonic capitalist had managed, under feudalism, to prosper and to develop into a full-blown *bourgeois* on his road to power, the modern labourer was faced with the prospect of an increasing exploitation which, as Capitalism developed further, would cause him to sink deeper and deeper into misery and distress. The capitalists had conquered political and economic power by becoming prosperous enough to assert their claims with success; but the modern proletariat was to force its way to power along the road of "increasing misery."

THE THEORY OF "INCREASING MISERY"

That this is the doctrine of the *Manifesto,* and that it remained Marx's doctrine in his later writings, there is simply no doubt at all. But it is never explained why increasing misery should be the means to the conquest of power by the proletariat, whereas increasing prosperity was the weapon of the *bourgeoisie.* Yet the view is plainly paradoxical; for, on the face of the matter, the increase of misery is far more likely to weaken and dispirit a class than to aid it in the prosecution of the class-struggle. There are in fact, at this point, two unresolved and imperfectly co-ordinated elements in the Marxian doctrine. On the one hand it is argued that the capitalist system will in its development reach at a certain point, because of its inherent contradictions, a position in which it will be unable to carry further the evolution of the powers of production, or even to carry on at all, and will be plunged into a series of economic crises of growing amplitude and severity which will in the end involve its destruction. On the other hand it is argued that this destruction will come to it at the hands of a proletariat forced into misery by the growing difficulties of the capitalist system, and powerful enough, in its misery, to set manfully about the construction of an alternative system.

If, however, the further development of Capitalism seemed

to promise both a laying bare of the inherent contradictions of capitalist production and the increasing misery of the working classes, what was the outcome likely to be? The first of these developments would threaten Capitalism with destruction; but the second would make less likely its supersession at the hands of the proletariat. In effect, the probable outcome would be the collapse of Capitalism under conditions in which the proletariat would be too weakened by its misery successfully to establish an alternative system. In these circumstances, a collapsing Capitalism would be likeliest to be succeeded, not by Socialism, but by sheer chaos and the dissolution of the entire civilisation of which Capitalism had been a phase.

It can be objected to this view that the proletariat might get both more miserable and stronger, because its misery would make it more revolutionary. But surely the essence of the Marxian conception is that revolutions are made by economically advancing, and not by decaying economic classes?

One answer is that domination comes, in the evolution of the historical process, to that class which is best adapted to further the development of the powers of production, and that this law designates the proletariat as the successor of the capitalist class. But does it? Marx's economic analysis, which is at this point essentially sound, leads to the conclusion that the further development of the powers of production will be best advanced by the institution of a classless Society, which will make the satisfaction of the individual and collective needs of all its members the guiding principle of its economic organisation. The solution of Society's present difficulties is to be sought, not in the domination of a new class, but in the abolition of classes and the complete socialisation of the economic system to serve the needs of a classless Society. The dictatorship of the proletariat is advocated only as a necessary means of bringing about the transition to the classless Society. The "proletarian State" stands not for a new epoch in social evolution, but only as an instrument for effecting the change from Capitalism to Socialism.

There are, however, in this doctrine two distinct elements— the assertion that the contradictions of Capitalism can be re- solved only by the institution of a classless Society, and the assertion that a temporary dictatorship of the proletarian class is necessary in order to bring this Society into being. These two assertions are quite independent, and acceptance of the one does not carry with it the acceptance of the other. It may be true that the proletariat is the only agency through which Socialism can be brought into being; but this conclusion does not follow immediately from the demonstration that Socialism is the appropriate method of resolving the contradictions of Capitalism.

Marxists, however, hold that the instrument of this trans- formation of Society cannot be anything other than a class, and that, in the present phase of history, the proletariat is the only class that can possibly fulfil this revolutionary function. To Marx, surveying the actual conditions of 1848, this conclu- sion seemed obvious, because there was no other serious claimant to the rôle of revolutionary leadership. The *petite bourgeoisie* was ruled out of court because it was a decaying class, whose powers and conceptions were bound up with a decaying and obsolescent method of small-scale production. The proletariat, on the other hand, seemed clearly designed for the rôle of revolutionary saviour; for it was a rising class, developing with the advance of Capitalism, and growingly disposed to advance claims inconsistent with the maintenance

of the capitalist system. But it has to be considered to-day
whether these views still hold good nearly a century later,
in face of large changes both in the class-structure of advanced
industrial Societies and in the workings of Capitalism. Moreover, even if Marx's thesis concerning the dominant rôle of the
proletariat is reaffirmed, it has to be considered whether Marx
envisaged correctly the actual method of the rise of the proletariat to power.

This last point is obviously bound up with the question
whether Marx was right in holding that, with the advance of
Capitalism, the proletariat was destined to fall into a period
of increasing misery. The doctrine of "increasing misery"
seems to have been interpreted by Marxists in a number of
different ways. One interpretation is that the proletariat is
destined to become more miserable only in a relative sense,
in that, while the working-class standard of living may rise
in terms of goods, the degree of exploitation is destined to increase and the capitalist to pocket a growing *proportion* of the
total product of industry. This interpretation is, however,
plainly inconsistent with Marx's own words. He does quite
explicitly prophesy for the poor a fall in the standard of living, and not merely a failure to improve it in proportion to
the increase in capitalist wealth. The second interpretation,
which seems the most natural for some of the passages, especially for the *Communist Manifesto,* is that the tendency of
Capitalism to force down working-class standards is already
in action, and may be expected to become more marked with
every stage in the further development of capitalist production. This view, consistent with what Marx wrote, is plainly
wrong in relation to the facts. For undoubtedly for half a century after the *Communist Manifesto* was written, working-

class standards of life were rising, and rising most of all in the most rapidly developing capitalist countries.

Accordingly, resort was had to a third interpretation. Working-class standards could continue to rise as long as Capitalism continued to be a developing system, consistent with the further advancement of the powers of production. The tendency to increasing misery would come into force only as this condition ceased to be satisfied, and Capitalism turned into a fetter on the development of these powers. Only as the inherent contradictions of Capitalism were brought into actual operation by the growth of the system, would the pressure of capitalist competition begin actually to force down the working-class standard of life.

This interpretation alone is consistent both with what Marx said and with the subsequent evolution of Capitalism. On this view, the first foreshadowings of increasing misery appeared in the first decade of the twentieth century, when, at any rate in Great Britain, the most advanced industrial country, the increase of international competition began seriously to check the rise of wages, and to cause some actual fall in the purchasing power of money wages in face of a rising cost of living. But the strength of the new forces was not plainly manifested until well after the war, when it appeared first in the slump and working-class setbacks of 1921 and the following years, and then, far more plainly, in the world depression which set in late in 1929. Even then, the tendency to depress working-class standards manifested itself very unequally as between trade and trade, hitting hardest the workers engaged in the industries most subject to international competition, including that of the developing capitalist economies of the Far East.

The result of this pressure was, not an even fall in working-class standards, but a pressing down of certain sections of the working class, whereas other sections were relatively well able to maintain their position. Thus, the German workers suffered far more than the British; and coal-miners and textile workers suffered far more than workers engaged in the services or in production for a less competitive market. Pockets of working-class misery were the consequence, rather than a general depression of standards for the working class as a whole. This caused cleavages in the working-class ranks, because it made the hardest-hit sections far more amenable than the rest to extreme types of propagandist appeal.

But the interruption of capitalist competition and the growing difficulties of the capitalist system reacted not only so as to depress working-class standards in this way, but also so as to decrease the organised power of the workers. Unemployment lessened, or even undermined, the authority of Trade Unionism in the industries in which the pressure was greatest; and these were precisely the industries in which capitalist expansion had been greatest, and working-class organisation strongest and most effective. Moreover, the new phase of Capitalism carried with it the adoption of a new technique of rapidly growing mechanisation and standardisation of industrial processes, and a new complexity of organisation. These developments diminished the proportion of workers engaged in productive industry—the stronghold of Trade Unionism— and increased the proportion in the less easily organised and less class-conscious services, such as distribution and clerical occupations. It also diminished, in productive industry, the proportion of skilled to less skilled workers; and this too tended to weaken the organised Labour Movement, which had rested largely upon the strength of organisation among the more highly skilled workers.

Thus, as the contradictions of Capitalism grew more obvious and menacing, the *industrial* strength of the working-class movement, instead of increasing, tended to decline; and the "proletariat" of wage-workers came to form a smaller proportion of the total population in the most advanced industrial countries. This decline in industrial power, it may be argued, was more than offset by an advance in class-consciousness and in *political* strength. Trade Unionism might grow weaker in consequence of unemployment and technical change; but the inevitable pressing-down of the working-class standard of life would create in its place a class-conscious and militant Socialist Movement.

This would, indeed, be likely to happen, first among the sections hardest hit by the decay of capitalist industry, and later over industry as a whole, as the pressure to cut down wages became generalised—if there were no alternative open. That it has happened is shown by the advance of Socialist and Communist doctrines among the workers. But has it happened, or is it certain to happen, to the extent necessary to compensate for the decline in the proletariat's industrial power, and to enable the proletariat to establish itself as the master of Society? If there is no alternative way of resolving capitalist contradictions, even for a time, it is reasonable to conclude that the decay of Capitalism will drive the proletariat solidly to Socialism. But is there no alternative? And, even if there is not, is the proletariat by itself capable of the strength required to overthrow Capitalism and install Socialism in its stead?

These questions are answerable only on the basis of a careful study of the actual class-structure of the capitalist Society of to-day. We cannot assume that this structure is the same as that which Marx studied in 1848: indeed, we know that it is not. We must try to look at it objectively, as Marx tried to study objectively the conditions of his own day. What, then, are the salient classes, and class-divisions, in the highly developed industrial countries of to-day?

THE CAPITALIST CLASS

First, what of the capitalist class? Evidently there has been, during the past century, a profound change in its character and economic position. Marx began writing at a time when, above all in England, the new type of industrial capitalist created by the development of power-driven machinery and the factory system was rapidly supplanting the older type of merchant capitalist who made his money by trade rather than by the direct exploitation of the productive process. The great capitalists of the seventeenth and eighteenth centuries had been predominantly merchants rather than industrial employers, though even under the domestic system of manufacture the rich merchant was tending to become virtually a large-scale employer as well. This tendency foreshadowed the coming of the phase of Capitalism which Marx saw developing fast in his own day. With the advent of power-driven machinery, capital had to be aggregated into large masses for the actual carrying on of production; and the factory-owner began to displace the merchant as the typical representative of the capitalist system. This rise of a new and numerous section of industrial capitalists who could not be readily assimilated to the old order was accompanied by the struggle for reform of parliamentary institutions, and the creation of a political sys-

tem based on a suffrage wide enough to admit the *bourgeoisie*
to an effective share in political power. It led to the evolution
of the nineteenth-century *bourgeois* State, within which the
older groups of landowners and merchants were more and
more assimilated to the new industrialists, so that land came
to be a form of capital not differing greatly from other forms,
and merchant capital was more and more fused with industrial capital under the dominance of the new industrialists.

Marx foresaw the further evolution of this process, based essentially on the further development of machine technique.
He saw that the scale of production was bound to grow larger
and larger, and to call for the aggregation of capital into larger
and larger masses in the industrial field. He saw that this
growth in the scale of production would lead to an increasing
restriction of competition within each developing national
economy, both because small businesses would tend to be
crushed out, and because large businesses would grow more
and more aware of the advantages of combination. Accordingly, he envisaged, on the national scale, an increasing concentration of control in the hands of the great capitalists, accompanied by the beating down of such of the *petite bourgeoisie*
as could not become fully fledged *bourgeois* towards the proletarian class.

But Marx also looked, in two important respects, beyond the
tendency towards capitalist concentration of control, within
any national system of Capitalism, in the hands of the great
industrialists. He did not believe that this concentration would
or could assume in general a cosmopolitan form. He held
rather that each national group of capitalists, having acquired
control of its national State, would use its power to institute
an intensified and State-supported international competition

with similar capitalist concentrations in other countries. For each national capitalist group, unable to find within its own borders markets for its constantly expanding output, would be driven outwards in the search for foreign markets, as well as for raw materials necessary to keep its growing factories at work, and for concessions and openings for foreign investment that would afford profitable outlets for its growing accumulation of capital. Thus the industrialist phase of Capitalism would pass into Imperialism, which would express itself in fierce international competition between huge capitalist groups, and would lead, by way of economic rivalries, to destructive Imperialist wars.

This development of Capitalism into Imperialism could not, however, occur without bringing with it far-reaching changes in the internal characteristics of Capitalism as well. The phase of Capitalism which Marx was observing in 1848 was that in which the capitalist merchants were being superseded by the industrialists as the dominant group; but with the further evolution of the system the industrialist was destined either to be superseded by, or to develop into, the financier. The Imperialist phase of Capitalism would be also the phase of the domination of Finance Capital, as distinct from either Merchant Capital or Industrial Capital.

In this phase, the predominance would belong, no longer to the industrial employer as such, but to the owners and manipulators of huge blocks of accumulated money capital. These might be either bankers, in effective control of a mass of deposits far exceeding their own capital, and able by this means to set in motion a still vaster mass of credit created by themselves; or the heads of finance houses and investment agencies, powerful enough to swing the savings of the entire owning class in the direction they chose, and influential especially as the ministers of Imperialism in the financing of undeveloped areas; or the controllers of great industrial combines who, still remaining in form large employers of labour, would become in effect far more the manipulators of mass production for purely financial ends, and would owe their power and influence over the State rather to their financial than to their industrial pre-eminence. The dominance of Economic Imperialism and of Finance Capital would be the significant characteristics of this phase of Capitalism, and would clearly differentiate it from the preceding phases of Merchant and Industrial Capitalism.

In these two foreshadowings of the future of Capitalism, Marx was indisputably correct, and showed an astonishing prescience. In these fundamental respects he prophesied with absolute rightness the subsequent course of capitalist development. But it does not follow that he was equally correct in everything else. It has often been pointed out that, whereas Marx often speaks as if the advance of Capitalism would be bound to involve a growing concentration of the *ownership* of capital in the hands of the great capitalists, actually throughout the remainder of the nineteenth century there went on a rapid increase in the absolute and relative numbers of those who had a share in the ownership of capitalist industry, and drew "surplus value" from it in the form of rent or interest or profit. Marxists have sometimes answered that this fact is of no importance, because the diffusion of the ownership of capitalist industry over a larger section of the population has been accompanied by a steadily increasing concentration of control. The number of small owners, it is said, is irrelevant, because the small shareholder or *rentier* has in effect no con-

trol over the uses to which his capital is put, and is thus wholly
in the hands and under the control of the great capitalists.

That the smaller shareholders and *rentiers* have, economically, no real control is, of course, perfectly true. The simultaneous development of diffused ownership and concentrated
control has been made possible by the evolution of joint stock
enterprise, of which the chief advance came after Marx had
formulated his doctrines, and largely after his death. The
joint stock system did solve some of the most difficult problems
of nineteenth-century Capitalism. It made possible a far more
effective mobilisation of the money resources of the entire
bourgeoisie, including *petit* as well as *grand bourgeois* elements, for the development of industry; and at the same time,
by giving the entire *bourgeoisie* a direct stake in the capitalist
system, it greatly broadened the political basis of Capitalism,
and made the dominance of large-scale industrialism compatible with a far more extended franchise than would otherwise have been possible. It reconciled the need for concentration in the control of capital with diffused ownership, by
putting the great capitalist in a position to manipulate far larger
masses of capital than he could possibly own without provoking an overwhelming hostility from every other section of
Society.

As the joint stock system developed, it took on more and
more this property of divorcing ownership from economic
control. Small investors, unable to take large risks, and eager
to insure against them, found the great capitalists always ready
to oblige. The preference share, commonly carrying with it
either no voting right, or at most a restricted voting right in
the enterprise, gave the small investor greater security in return for the abnegation of even nominal control. But, even in

the case of ordinary shares, the control exerted by the small investors was usually quite unreal. They were many and scattered, and could have no real knowledge of the working of the enterprises to which they entrusted their money; and under the system of "one share, one vote," they could almost always be swamped by the few big holders of shares. Moreover, in pursuit of security, the small and middle investors usually "spread" their risks, entrusting their money in small doses to a number of different concerns, and so reducing their potential influence on any one of them to nothing. The growth of Stock Exchanges, which spread the excitement of gambling in stock values, meant that large numbers of shares were constantly changing hands, and caused their momentary owners to have no continuous interest at all in the businesses in which their money was placed, but to regard their shares merely as potential sources of money-income and of capital appreciation, so that it was a matter of no concern at all to know whether the company in question made rifles, or church furniture, or whiskey, or cotton goods, but only what dividends it was likely to pay and whether its shares were likely to go up or down. The consummation of this divorce of the investor from control over, or interest in, the use of his money was reached with the growth of Insurance Companies and Investment Trusts. For in both these cases the investment of the small investor's resources in actual productive enterprise was taken right out of his hands, and assumed directly by large capitalist concerns likely to be able to operate with greater skill and knowledge.

Thus, under modern conditions, the small investor and even the middle-sized investor have hardly any control at all over the economic working of Capitalism. When once they have invested their money, control of it passes right out of their hands; and even the control they can exercise over its direction to this or that form of enterprise has been increasingly surrendered by the growth of indirect investment through Insurance Companies, Investment Trusts, and other agencies of large-scale Capitalism. The ordinary investor does not control; and, what is more, he does not want to control, and cannot possibly know how to control.

Marx, then, is absolutely right in holding that Capitalism tends to a growing concentration of the control of capital; and the fact that the ownership of shares in large-scale capitalist enterprise has tended to become more diffused does not in the least invalidate this part of his argument. But the diffusion of the ownership of large-scale business enterprise over the whole of the classes above the wage-earning level—and even to a small extent over a section of the wage-earners, especially in the United States—is nevertheless a highly significant and important social phenomenon.

For this broadening of the basis of Capitalism prevents effectively the complete polarisation of classes which would result from a concentration of ownership as well as control in the hands of a shrinking class of great capitalist magnates. By diffusing the ownership of property, not over the whole of Society, but over a fraction fully large enough to offset the effects of concentration, it protects Capitalism against the massing in hostility to it of all the remaining elements in Society, and provides it with a bodyguard of retainers who feel their economic security and social status to be bound up with the continuance and prosperity of the capitalist system. Every shareholder or *rentier* who draws an appreciable part of his income from capitalist enterprise has a stake in its success, and feels himself menaced by any attack upon it. This sentiment even extends, by way of insurances, savings deposits, and the collective investments of Friendly Societies and Trade Unions, well beyond the boundaries of the investing groups and classes, and infects the attitude of leaders of working-class opinion. Meanwhile the Co-operative Movement, imitating in part the joint stock structure, albeit in a more democratic form—"one member, one vote" instead of "one share, one vote"—and compelled to work within an environment of capitalist industry, necessarily reproduces in some degree the same social attitude. Thus Capitalism, by creating a large body of dependent capitalists, averts the menace of a complete proletarianisation of all who are not able to amass enough wealth to gain an effective place in the control of the expanding process of production.

Nor is this all. The typical capitalist of 1848 was still, despite the existence here and there of large *entrepreneurs* controlling a number of separate producing plants, his own manager. But with the further growth in the scale of enterprise, there was a great differentiation of functions. The large capitalist, becoming more and more a financier, resigned the actual management of productive business increasingly to salaried officers; and round these new managers there grew up an increasing host of departmental managers, buyers and agents, technicians and professional consultants, superior clerical workers and cashiers, all in receipt of incomes intermediate between those of the large capitalists and those of the general mass of clerical and manual employees. These rising grades in large-scale industry coincided in income and social status with the grades of professional men outside industry—lawyers, doctors, teachers and a host more, whose numbers grew with the increase in total national wealth and in the size of the intermediate class as a whole. They came, indeed, to be themselves small investors out of their savings; and some of them were remunerated in part by commissions or shares in the profits of business. They thus acquired a double attachment to Capitalism, as the source both of their salaries or fees, and of the return upon their investments.

Thus, whereas the diagnosis of the *Communist Manifesto* appeared to foreshadow a narrowing of the basis on which Capitalism rested proportionate to the advance of capitalist concentration, and the flinging down of the intermediate groups, including the small capitalists, into the ranks of the proletariat, actually the basis of Capitalism grew broader with concentration, and the absolute and relative numbers of the intermediate groups increased. There was no polarisation of classes, but rather a growing difficulty in marking off one class clearly from another—a blurring of the lines of division, even if the essential characters of the outstanding classes remained plain and distinct.

I do not mean to suggest that this tendency went unnoticed by Marx. There are references in *Das Kapital* and in his writings and correspondence to show clearly that it did not. But even in his later writings Marx continued to regard the blurring of class-divisions as a matter of secondary importance, influential in shaping the course of particular phases and incidents of the fundamental class-struggle, but incapable of altering its essential character or its ultimate outcome. He regarded the middle groups in Society as incapable by their very nature of pursuing a coherent or constructive policy of their own, and as able only to get in the way of the principal combatants. Moreover, he continued to hold, even in his later writings, that in the long run the forces making for polarisation were bound to come into play more and more as the difficulties of Capital-ism increased: so that the decisive class-struggle between capi-talists and proletarians could be delayed, but by no means averted or changed in its essential character by the emergence of any new class.

It is clearly of the greatest importance, for any critique or re-statement of Marxism in twentieth-century terms, to determine whether this view is correct. Marx was right, we have seen, in predicting the growing concentration of the control of cap-ital. Was he also right in predicting, as the inevitable outcome of Capitalism, the growing polarisation of economic classes?

But before we attempt to answer this question, we must pur-sue further our description of economic classes as they exist to-day. The great capitalists, as Marx foresaw, form a small group in effective control of huge concentrated masses of capital—great bankers and financiers, the heads of great trusts, combines and concerns engaged in production or distribution, great newspaper proprietors, and a few more. These men have little to do with the day-to-day work of industrial or commer-cial management. They are great financial manipulators, con-ducting to a money tune a vast orchestra of subordinate busi-ness executants, and controlling masses of capital vastly larger than they personally own. By themselves, they clearly do not form a class: they are the leaders of a class extending far be-yond their own ranks.

Of whom, then, does the rest of the class consist? In the first place, of business *entrepreneurs* of the second rank, who are in command of large-scale businesses, but have not risen to the heights of that financial control which transcends indus-trial boundaries, and lays its commands so heavily upon the capitalist States. Secondly, of the leading officials of the great business enterprises under the joint stock system, including both those which are controlled directly by the great financiers and those which have become, like the railways, mere impersonal concentrations of capital belonging to many scattered owners. Thirdly, the men at the top of the leading non-industrial services, from Cabinet Ministers and other major politicians of the capitalist parties to the most successful lawyers, doctors, accountants, applied scientists, and even teachers.

THE NEW PETITE BOURGEOISIE

It is, of course, impossible to say where this class ends and the class below it—the *petite bourgeoisie*—begins. There are infinite gradations of wealth and social status at every point of the scale, from the greatest capitalists to the lowest-paid labourers and the chronically unemployed. But undoubtedly there is a real division, as real and important as the distinction which Marx drew in the *Communist Manifesto* between the *grande* and the *petite bourgeoisie,* but of a radically different nature.

For Marx's division between these two was based on their essentially different relations to the powers of production. The *grande bourgeoisie* was for him the class which was waxing in authority and economic strength with the development of the new powers of machine-production upon which it was based; whereas the *petite bourgeoisie* was regarded as a declining class, certain to decrease in authority and strength, because its very existence depended on the survival of methods of production and trade which were already becoming obsolete. The *petite bourgeoisie* of 1848 consisted mainly of small-scale producers and traders whose position was bound up with retail shopkeeping on an undeveloped capitalist basis and of a comparatively small group of professional men. Within it, or very closely allied to it, was the main body of farmers above the peasant level. But for the moment let us leave this section aside, as its position calls for special discussion.

To a great extent, Marx was right in predicting that the influence of the *petite bourgeoisie,* in this sense, was bound to wane. There has, indeed, been no such complete submergence of the small-scale producer—much less of the small-scale trader —as he seemed sometimes to expect. The small shopkeeper still holds on, despite the growth of the multiple stores, and, driven from one part of the field, finds new openings elsewhere, especially in new forms of supply—wireless shops, small garages, and so on. But the small shopkeepers are tied more and more by the need for credit to the large-scale producers and suppliers, as well as to the banks; and this dependence subordinates them increasingly, in the economic sphere, to the large-scale control of financial capital. The small-scale producer also survives to a considerable extent, though he has been driven more and more back to the fringes of industry. He carries on, especially in new trades not yet ready for large-scale organisation, and in supplying secondary needs of the large-scale producers, almost at times as a sub-contractor to the great firms. But he too has largely lost his independence; and while the type survives, the survival of the individuals of whom it consists is usually precarious, since they are liable at any time to be evicted by a fresh development of large-scale industry.

As far as these groups are concerned, and can be isolated, Marx was certainly right in his prophecy that their economic importance and strength would dwindle. But can they be isolated, as a factor in the class-struggle? To a great extent, they belong to the same family groups as the new *petite bourgeoisie* of small investors, senior officials, administrators and technicians employed in large-scale business, minor professional men— that is, to the same social group as sections of the population whose numerical and economic importance, so far from dwindling, increases fast with the advance of capitalist industrialism. How are we to classify a family in which the father is a local grocer, the mother the daughter of a works manager in a big factory, one of the sons a garage proprietor, another a municipal official, and a third a technician in large-scale business, while one daughter has married a schoolmaster, one a small-scale employer with a tiny workshop of his own, and another a Trade Union official? There is nothing out of the ordinary in such a case, which represents well the intermingling of the old *petite bourgeoisie* based on decaying methods of production and the new *petite bourgeoisie,* which owes its rise to the development of large-scale capitalist enterprise.

Faster than the old *petite bourgeoisie* has gone out, the new *petite bourgeoisie* has come in. Of course, the new group does not stand for the same ideas and policies as the old, any more than landowners and capitalists stood for the same ideas and policies, though they are now, in the most advanced Societies, fused into a single class. To some extent, the ideas and policies of the old and new *petite bourgeoisie* are antagonistic; and this antagonism is capable of becoming a factor of great political importance. For, whereas the new group on the whole thrives on the further development of Capitalism, and is therefore favourable to it, the older *petite bourgeoisie* has cause to fear a further decline in its power and position as capitalist organisation becomes increasingly rationalised, and more trades are brought within the range of mass-production and mass-distribution.

This antagonism, however, has not hitherto developed far. To a far greater extent both groups, having intimate family connections and a similar social status, are disposed to unite whenever they feel their positions of petty class-privilege and economic superiority threatened by the advance of Socialism. For one thing they have in common, and will unite to protect, is that they both stand above the proletariat, and depend for their incomes and status on the maintenance of economic inequality as the basis of the social system.

In Societies as highly industrialised as Great Britain, the farmers albeit still a large economic group, can only hope to reinforce the urban sections of the *petite bourgeoisie,* or to exact favours from the *grande bourgeoisie* as the price of their support. They cannot play an independent leading part. But in countries where, despite industrialisation, agriculture is still the occupation of a large proportion of the people—as it is in France, Germany, or the United States—the farmers, or upper peasants, form a far more important group. For there is, even to-day, no sign of the extensive introduction of large-scale capitalist farming in the advanced industrial countries, while in many of the less developed countries the tendency has been strongly towards the breaking-up of the great estates, and the multiplication of small and middle-sized peasant holdings. Farmers and peasants are, indeed, even to-day, notable in most countries for their incapacity for effective organisation or the foundation of constructive policies—Denmark being, of course, a notable exception. But the farmer and peasant groups are capable of bringing a most powerful reinforcement to the other groups and classes hostile to Socialism, and of being made the instruments either of large-scale Capitalism in its struggle against Socialism, or perhaps of the urban *petite bourgeoisie,* if it is capable of formulating and uniting upon a policy of its own. The question is whether it can effectively formulate such a policy.

As we have seen, the new *petite bourgeoisie,* despite its great and growing importance in the conduct of modern industries and services, has at present very little influence over economic policy. For, while it is the chief repository of technical and administrative competence and of inventive power, and thus plays the leading part in shaping the evolution of the powers and processes of production, it can act at present only under the orders of the great capitalist masters, who are interested in its achievements only as means to the extraction of profit, rent and interest. Large-scale Capitalism pays the piper, even if it gets the money largely from small investors; and large-scale Capitalism accordingly calls the tune. The present economic power of the rising *petite bourgeoisie* is therefore very limited indeed. But can the same be said of its political power?

I am aware that it is often argued that "economic power precedes and dominates political power," which is only a reflection of it, and that accordingly the *petite bourgeoisie* cannot call in its political authority to redress its economic subservience. But at this point we must beware of an ambiguity in the use of phrases. The "economic power" which the new *petite bourgeoisie* lacks is the present power to control economic policy. But it possesses economic power in another more vital and fundamental sense. It has the power to organise and carry on industry itself, without the aid of the *grande bourgeoisie,* if it can ensure the co-operation or the subservience of the proletariat. It and the proletariat, and not the *grande bourgeoisie,* are the classes which today perform the functions indispensable for the carrying on of industry and the further development of production, to which indeed the hierarchs of banking, investment and financial manipulation constitute a serious obstacle. There is, accordingly, no barrier to the creation of a successful political movement by the *petite bourgeoisie* in the lack of the form of economic power which they do not possess; and there is a positive foundation for such a movement in the form of economic power which is already theirs.

The unity and strength of the *petite bourgeoisie* of the twentieth century is certain, if it is manifested at all, to take shape primarily in a political movement. Economically, they cannot act together as a class, but only in sections, often with conflicting aims and policies, because they lack a common relation to industry such as binds the wage-earners together, and are too unclearly marked off from the class above them. But politically they can act together, and do, for the protection of the rights and privileged inequalities of the recipients of intermediate incomes, sometimes against the rich, but more often against the enactment of expensive social legislation or the improvement of municipal services. They are found banded together against high taxation on middle incomes, against high local rates, and against Trade Unions which threaten the maintenance of the essential services, as in the British General Strike of 1926.

These forms of combination are, however, merely negative and unconstructive; and they are, in any advanced industrial Society in which the peasants and farmers do not form a group powerful enough to determine the issue, likely to be ineffective in the long run. They may succeed in France in preventing the growth of social services and keeping the proletariat well under, and at the same time in checking the political influence of large-scale Capitalism; for in France peasants and urban *petite bourgeoisie* are still, despite the high finance of Paris and the growth of the proletariat, the economically preponderant groups. But neither in Germany nor in Great Britain can a purely negative policy suffice for the *petite bourgeoisie:* nor can it hope to manage much longer on such a policy in the United States. For in highly industrialised Societies, among which France still barely counts, in the long run the pressure of the proletariat for improved conditions is bound to overbear a purely negative policy of resistance, if the affairs of State continue to be conducted on a basis of universal suffrage and reasonable freedom of elections and political organisation.

Accordingly, the *petite bourgeoisie,* if it desires to preserve its cherished inequality, is compelled either to devise a constructive policy of its own, or to adopt as its own, on terms, the policy of the class above it. Hitherto, it has usually preferred the latter of these alternatives, and has acted politically as well as economically as the faithful servant of large-scale Capitalism, getting in return an increasing supply of crumbs from the rich man's table. Acting as the servant of large-scale Capitalism, it has been strong enough to help the capitalist interest to prevail in elections, even under adult suffrage. But this success has been bought only at the price of concessions to the proletariat, which have of late increased in scale and cost, and been paid for to a large extent by heavier taxation of the middle classes. The growing difficulties of Capitalism have at the same time increased the need for these services, by swelling the numbers of the unemployed, and added to the awkwardness of paying for them. The proletariat, in face of these difficulties, has become more clamant for some form of Socialism, which threatens the privileges of the *petite bourgeoisie* as well as of the class above it. The *petite bourgeoisie* has responded to a small extent, by blaming the financiers and the financial machine for its troubles, but to a much greater extent by banding itself together to resist the proletariat, of which it stands in far more fundamental fear. For it would sooner remain in subordination to the capitalist system than lose its unequal privileges under Socialism. This is the ultimate rationale of the recent growth of Fascism, which naturally develops first and furthest in those countries in which Capitalism has been most in difficulties, and the demand for Socialism become most insistent.

THE RISE OF FASCISM

If, however, the *petite bourgeoisie* is to aid the capitalists to defeat the proletariat, it needs some stronger weapon than its mere voting strength. For, in the countries hardest pressed by the growing difficulties of Capitalism, this weapon has already proved its inadequacy as a means of resisting the gradual encroachment of democratic social reform. The *petite bourgeoisie* in these circumstances goes Fascist, with the aid of the parallel elements in the countryside. It repudiates Parliamentarism, and clamours for authoritative government. But this cry for a form of dictatorship to keep the proletariat in its place cannot be effective if it is put forward as an open defence of the vested interests in present-day Society; for the proletariat is too strong, and has too many allies scattered among the other classes, and the middle-class prejudice in favour of Parliamentarism is too strong for a naked appeal to privileged self-interest to be successful in overbearing them. Fascism has therefore to assume the outward form of an alternative ideal to that of Socialism, appealing to sentiments as strong as that of democracy, and capable of attracting not only the middle classes, but also a section of the proletariat itself.

This appeal is found in Nationalism, reinforced according to local conditions by any form of anti-foreigner complex likely to be widespread in the country affected. All right-minded citizens are called upon, in the name of national honour and manhood, to take arms against the insidious propaganda of pacifism and the open cosmopolitanism of the Socialist ideal. The sense of class-struggle is countered with an appeal to the sense of national solidarity against the rest of the world; and a specious ideal of national service and self-sacrifice is held up against the allegedly materialist objectives of Socialism. These ideologies, which would be powerless by themselves, can become great powers when they are made the allies of class-interest; and a section of the worst off part of the proletariat, the unemployed, which has been ground down to despair by the attrition of economic distress, and sees little prospect of early relief in face of the deadlock reached between the capitalist and Socialist forces, is won over by large, vague hopes and promises of the rewards certain to accrue from a Fascist victory, not unaccompanied by advance bribes, to go over to the Fascist side.

If, when this happens, the working-class forces are themselves divided, the path is made easy towards a Fascist victory. For the power of the proletariat depends essentially upon substantial unity among its leading elements. But, in the circumstances here described, disunity is very likely to arise among the leaders of the proletariat. In face of the growing difficulties of Capitalism there will be some who will urge an immediate advance towards Socialism, by revolutionary means if no other way is immediately open; while others will hold that it is necessary to wait until a majority has been won over to the

Socialist cause by constitutional methods of propaganda and electioneering. Such a majority is by no means easy to secure, in face of the combined voting strength and monetary resources of the *grande* and *petite bourgeoisie,* reinforced by the agricultural interests; and it is likely that, in times of serious economic adversity, enough of the proletariat will become disillusioned at the slow progress of Socialism, especially if the Socialist cause be poorly led, to lead to a disastrous division in the proletarian ranks. This will provide the Fascists with their opportunity to jettison the substance of Parliamentarism, though they may prefer to keep its shadow, and to institute a dictatorship in the name of the "national spirit."

This consummation will not easily be reached, in any advanced industrial country, except in a time of extreme economic difficulty and dislocation; for nothing short of this is likely either to create the necessary division in the proletariat, or sufficiently to unite the *petite bourgeoisie* under the nationalist banner. Where economic difficulties are less pressing, parliamentary forms and methods are likely to be preserved, and nothing worse to happen than a setback to social reform, and perhaps a period of "economy" and reaction under the aegis of a "national" Government that will only nibble at the existing provision for the poor. It needs severe strain on the economic system to bring Fascism to boiling point, and to secure the necessary support for a forcible overthrow of the parliamentary system in the interests of the propertied classes. But, if Marx was right in predicting a period of increasing difficulty for Capitalism, the sort of situation that is capable of breeding Fascism is very likely to arise; and the events of recent years in both Germany and Italy have shown that a divided working-class movement is under such circumstances quite unable to put up an effective resistance.

Now Fascism, where it has arisen, has climbed to power only with the help of the *grande bourgeoisie*. Neither in Italy nor in Germany could the forces which destroyed the parliamentary State have been brought to the required strength without the financial support of a sufficient number of the great capitalists. For the creation of a revolutionary force based mainly on the *petite bourgeoisie* and the most hopeless section of the proletariat requires a large amount of money, which can in practice be supplied only from the resources of large-scale Capitalism. The great capitalists, however, will not finance a movement unless they consider that it is calculated to serve their ends. The *petite bourgeoisie* has therefore to give to the *grande bourgeoisie* pledges of good behaviour, and to guarantee to turn its weapons upon the proletariat and not upon "Big Business." In Fascist movements the *petite bourgeoisie* fights the proletariat definitely as the ally and upholder of Capitalism, which it represents under the guise of social solidarity as an integral element in the greatness of the National State.

This endorsement of large-scale Capitalism is by no means welcome to all the members of the *petite bourgeoisie*. The older elements in this class have a fear of high finance and rationalised enterprise which is only second to their dread of a proletarian victory. The farmers and peasants share this attitude, and want to fight for their own interests, and not for large-scale Capitalism. Fascist programmes therefore usually contain many projects designed to appeal to *petit bourgeois* sentiment, and have often an anti-capitalist seasoning, even where Capitalism is in effect giving them its support. The support is given none the less, because the capitalists believe that, if once the proletariat can be thoroughly defeated, there will be no real difficulty in keeping the *petite bourgeoisie* in proper subjection.

There are, indeed, in the advanced countries, *petit bourgeois* groups which, unwilling to become the instruments of large-scale Capitalism in the fight against Socialism, attempt to devise a constructive programme of their own. From the days when Marx, at the outset of his career, arraigned Proudhon as a *petit bourgeois* reformer—indeed, from even earlier—this has always meant the formulation of projects of monetary reform. But these projects have to some extent changed their nature with the changes in the character of the *petite bourgeoisie*. In the time of Proudhon they were predominantly schemes for securing to the small-scale producer and trader a sufficient supply of credit to enable them to stand up to the competition of large-scale business. They retain this character to a great extent even to-day in the agricultural areas of Canada and the United States; but among industrial communities the emphasis has shifted in modern times from the small-scale producer to the consumer, and the projects are now designed for the securing of low prices for consumers' goods, or of an issue of free credit to consumers to enable them to buy the greatly increased product of which modern industry is technically capable. Currency and credit cranks are now, as a century ago, foremost among those *petit bourgeois* reformers who want their class to put forward a programme of its own, instead of fighting Socialism in the interests of the great capitalists.

Side by side with the monetary reformers go the technocrats, emphasising the creative rôle of scientist, inventor and technician in the increase of material wealth, and urging the claims of the *petite bourgeoisie* to govern and reform Society by virtue of its technical competence. Both the monetary reformers and the technocrats have usually the merit of popular sympathies, and of a desire to raise the general standard of life by setting free the vast forces of productivity at present chained up by the capitalist system. But they mostly aim at reconciling the advent of the new age of plenty with the main-tenance of the privileges and economic superiority of the technical and administrative groups in Society over the manual workers, and repudiate the conception of a class-struggle be-cause it seems to threaten this superiority.

This attitude condemns these "radical" movements among the *petite bourgeoisie* to failure. For they effectively antagonise the greater capitalists, without offering the proletariat anything in which it is prepared to put its trust. Intellectually, their theories are too difficult to convert the proletariat, unless they can be combined with an appeal to its class-sentiment; but this appeal is ruled out by the desire of the *petite bourgeoisie* to hold on to its own superior status. Accordingly, while techno-crats and monetary reformers may temporarily command large followings, there is no chance of their rallying behind them, at any rate in developed industrial countries, a sufficient fol-lowing to enable them to put their ideas to the test of practice. Possibly the monetary reformers may have a better chance in a predominantly agricultural State, such as Canada, where the farmers' movement is in a position, if it can become united, to dominate the political situation. But in the industrial coun-tries such creeds as technocracy and credit reform can but create diversions: they cannot win power.

In these countries the *petite bourgeoisie,* when it makes its appearance as a serious political force, becomes the ally of large-scale Capitalism in the fight against Socialism. It cannot win without the support of the *grande bourgeoisie.* But, if these

two classes unite in the struggle against Socialism, it remains
to be determined which of them will carry off the victory in
the struggle between them which is certain to follow the rout
of the Socialist forces. Large-scale Capitalism starts with the
great advantage of being in possession of the field, and of being
able to claim that any attempt to disturb its vested interest will
result in economic dislocation and menace the consolidation
of the victory over Socialism. But the main body of the victorious forces will necessarily belong to the *petite bourgeoisie*
and the sections of peasants who have rallied to its side; and
these groups will claim the fulfilment of the promises made to
them in the course of the struggle, while the section of the
proletariat which was won over will also clamour for the
reward of its apostasy. In face of the difficulties of Capitalism,
these claims will not be easy to satisfy; and the centralised, authoritarian State set up for the purpose of destroying Socialism
will be an instrument which can readily be applied to the issuing of positive orders, in the name of the awakened Nation,
to the capitalists themselves. In these circumstances, a considerable measure of State control of industry is likely to be
instituted, so that the State, even if it tries to respect the interests
of the big capitalists as a class, will not scruple to lay rough
hands on the individual capitalist who refuses to work in
with its National Plan of economic development. There will
arise a State-controlled Capitalism designed to safeguard the
interests of property-owners, both large and small, against the
proletariat; and there will be a struggle for the control of the
new State which exerts this authority over industry.

Who will win in this struggle will depend mainly on the
coherence displayed by the *petit bourgeois* forces in the hour
of victory. There is, in the nature of things, no reason why they

should not win, and bend the great capitalists to their will, substituting for the concentrated control of large-scale Capitalism the control of an authoritarian State speaking in the name of the wider body of property-owners and industrial administrators and technicians. But the likelihood of their doing this depends on their ability to formulate a policy responsive to *petit bourgeois* and peasant needs; for, though they possess as a class the technical and administrative competence needed for the running of industry with the aid of a subjected proletariat, they can succeed only if they can maintain their unity after success, and slough off the prejudices which their desire to preserve the superiority of their class over the proletariat has engendered in their minds.

For the rule of the *petite bourgeoisie* under a system of State control is compatible only with a policy which will make plenty, instead of scarcity, its object, and aim, by raising wages as well as salaries as fast as productivity can be increased, at affording an outlet for all that a State-controlled form of Capitalism is able to provide. If this is not done, the new form of Capitalism will come to shipwreck for the same reason as the older form—its inability to avoid industrial crises, to keep its proletariat employed, and even to ensure the incomes of its own dominant class of small capitalists and salary-earners. Failing to achieve prosperity, it will engender in due course new forces of discontent; and the proletariat will find among the dissatisfied elements in other classes sufficient reinforcements to help it in sweeping the system away.

This consummation might, however, be considerably delayed, especially in a country of relatively undeveloped economic resources, where the peasants form a large element in the population, and the proletariat is relatively weak. For,

in such a country, the "market" may not be of the same overwhelming importance as in more highly industrialised countries; and the lack of purchasing power among the proletariat
may be compensated by a rising standard of subsistence among
the peasants. Fascism stands most chance of lasting long in
countries where the peasants are numerous, and the agriculture of a diversified type, producing goods mainly for domestic consumption and not for bulk export.

In an industrialised country, on the other hand, it is difficult for Fascism to establish itself as a durable system. It will
have a large proletariat to hold under, without the support of
a large peasant class; and its power to keep this proletariat at
work will depend on its success in maintaining a large and
expanding export trade in the markets of the world. This need,
under the prevailing conditions of international competition,
will induce it to keep down wages in order to reduce costs
in rivalry with other exporting countries. But its success
in achieving this will depress its own home market, and
thus create distress as well as discontent. For the day has gone
by when any country can hope, by superior efficiency alone,
to capture the lion's share of the world market. Modern methods of production are available to all the competing countries;
and while one may exceed another in efficiency in a particular
branch of production, it can hardly hope to secure a long
enough lead over its rivals to capture most of the trade unless
it is also able to keep wages low. But low wages will mean,
in such a country, low domestic demand for the chief products
of large-scale industry. The more exports are expanded, the
more the domestic market will tend to contract—a situation
quite unlike that of the nineteenth century, when the bulk of
the export trade went, not to the countries which paid the low-

est wages, but to those which had the longest lead in productive efficiency and conceded to the workers the highest standards of life.

FASCIST STATE-CAPITALISM

The form of State-Capitalism which may be expected to follow upon a victory of the *petite bourgeoisie* and its allies is therefore most unlikely to be stable, though it may have a fairly long run in a country such as Italy, where industrialism has not yet reached a high stage of development. It is far less likely to be durable in Germany, where the economic contradictions which it perpetuates can be kept from causing its collapse only as long as it can be sustained with the aid of powerful non-economic sentiments in men's minds. The Nazis could never have won power in Germany, even in face of the mistaken policy of the Social Democratic and Communist Parties, had they not been able to call to their aid the sense of frustration and resentment caused by the Peace Treaty, and to cover up with an aggressive appeal to Nationalist sentiment the bareness of their economic ideas. But, powerful as Nationalism can be when it is frustrated in its legitimate expression, it is a force which depends for its political effect on the sense of wrong and insecurity. It cannot live without an enemy ever before its eyes; and when once the enemy ceases to look dangerous its appeal is lost. In an atmosphere of constant threat of war, or in face of actual foreign rule or dictation, it may live and thrive. But it affords no foundation for a durable State-system, unless it becomes the ally of forces able to find satisfying answers to the basic economic problems of Society.

There remains, of course, the theoretical possibility of a

form of Fascist dictatorship that would really set out to serve, and not merely pretend to serve, the interests of the entire people. It is theoretically possible for the *petite bourgeoisie,* having aided the great capitalists to defeat the proletariat, first to turn upon its late allies and subdue them, and then, realising the inherent contradictions of a policy of low wages, to institute a system of widely diffused purchasing power up to the limits of the national capacity to produce. But is such a system compatible with the retention either of private property or of the class-inequalities which the *petite bourgeoisie* took power in order to defend? Surely not. A policy of plenty involves, in any advanced industrial Society, the increasing supersession of small-scale producers and traders, including the peasants, a great advance in the economic independence and collective strength of the proletariat, and a planned economic order which will steadily aggregate more power in the hands of the State. Such a policy will necessarily split the *petite bourgeoisie* into contending factions, one favourable to the concentration of capital and the development of large-scale production, and the other bitterly hostile. The first of these sections will have to court the alliance of the proletariat in order to coerce its rival; but it will be able to win this support only by altering the basis of Society from the Capitalism which it set out to defend to some form of Socialism.

If this is to be the end of the process, why not arrive at it by a shorter road—that of an alliance, here and now, of proletariat and new *petite bourgeoisie* against the large capitalists and reactionary *petit bourgeois* groups? An alliance of this sort is the only possible way of achieving Socialism by peaceful and constitutional means, and probably the only way of averting the spread of Fascist dictatorships. For the proletariat by itself is not strong enough in any country to win and hold a parliamentary majority, or to carry through the construction of the new system by constitutional means. If it has to fight alone, it can win only by violence, accompanied by a forcible destruction of all the opposing forces. Such a victory can be achieved only by the accident of a highly favourable conjuncture; and the winning of it will leave the constructive task of building Socialism far harder than it need be, because of the immense destruction that will have taken place, and because of the proletariat's inevitable lack of adequate resources of trained knowledge and administrative experience. Socialism may be successfully built in spite of these handicaps; but the building of it, under such conditions, is bound to involve a tremendous amount of suffering and, in all probability, a serious temporary fall in the standard of life.

On the other hand, if the proletariat could be reinforced by the adhesion of even a minority of the technicians, administrators, and professional men and women who form the active section of the new *petite bourgeoisie,* it could be strong enough both to resist Fascism and to build Socialism against the united hostility of the *grande bourgeoisie* and the more reactionary *petit bourgeois* groups, and even, with good fortune, to do these things by peaceful and constitutional means. That this should come about is by far the best hope for Western civilisation in its present plight.

But will it come about? There is no indication at present that a sufficient section among the new *petite bourgeoisie* to make it possible is prepared to rally to the Socialist side. Moreover, the condition of its coming about is not only that a sufficient section of the *petite bourgeoisie* should be won over, but also and above all that this should be done without any dilution of the Socialist policy. For if the proletarian Socialists, in their efforts to win middle-class support, water down their policy to one of mere social reform, and abandon their frontal attack upon the capitalist system, they will merely fall headlong into the contradictions from which Socialism provides the way of escape. In trying to find money for social reforms without destroying the capitalist control of industry, they will dislocate the capitalist machine without replacing it, and will both fail to find means of satisfying their own followers and create the conditions most favourable to the growth of Fascism. The proletariat needs *bourgeois* support in order to win Socialism; but that support is worse than useless unless it is won upon decisively Socialist terms.

In this analysis of economic classes in the twentieth century, the proletariat has been left until last; for, while the winning of Socialism may be held to require the collaboration of other elements, it is evidently upon the proletariat that the main burden of the struggle is bound to fall. What, then, is the proletariat in the advanced Societies of modern Capitalism, and of what groups and sections is it made up? How far can it be clearly marked off from other classes, and how far has it a distinct interest and point of view which hold it together as a coherent class? The attempt to answer these questions demands a chapter to itself.

CHAPTER V

THE PROLETARIAT

THE PROLETARIAT, or working class, is essentially that class in Society which gets its living by the sale of its labour-power, and does not possess resources which enable it to command the means of living except by this sale. It consists primarily of those wage-earners who, having sold their labour to an employer for a contractual payment, work under the employer's orders, and take part in creating a product which becomes the property of the purchaser of their labour-power. This characteristic of employability at a wage is the distinguishing feature of the proletariat, just as the act of employing labour, directly or indirectly, is the distinguishing mark of the capitalist class.

Obviously, it is not possible, in terms of this definition, to say precisely who is a member of the proletariat, and who is not. For, in the first place, there is clearly no essential economic difference between a wage and a salary. They are both incomes obtained under contract by the sale of labour-power. It would be absurd to exclude all salary-earners from the ranks of the proletariat, especially as both wage-earners and salary-earners may be employed by the same employer, with no fundamental difference of income or status. But it would be equally absurd to include in the proletariat all salary-earners, up to the most highly-placed Civil Servants or the managing directors of great capitalist concerns; for the richer salary-earners clearly belong to a quite different economic class from the main body of wage-earners. No clear line can be drawn between those who do belong to the proletariat and those who do not. In this case, as in those discussed in the last chapter, class-divisions become blurred at the margin, and the doubtful group at the margin is here very large.

This difficulty of exact denotation does not in the least invalidate the conception of a proletarian class. For, if the outer limits of this class are vague, its central nucleus is evident enough. It may be disputable how large a proportion of the salariat are to be regarded as proletarians, or how far down the scale the margin of employability is reached; but there is no doubt that the central mass of the proletariat consists of the manual-working wage-earners in industry, and especially of that section which has become organised in the Trade Union Movement. Larger or smaller elements of the salariat, or of the submerged groups below the regular working-class, may gather round the central mass, and think and feel themselves part of the proletariat. The central mass itself is the essential proletariat: the outlying groups belong to it only to the extent to which they attach themselves to it, and identify its interests and attitude with their own.

To a certain extent, then, proletarian is as proletarian feels. But, in general, this applies only to the outlying groups whose classification is doubtful. These have to "contract in" to the proletariat, by associating themselves with it; whereas the members of the central mass belong to the proletariat unless they definitely "contract out," and abjure allegiance to the class that is theirs by economic status. The proletariat as a whole is thus $x + y$: x being a nearly fixed, and y a highly variable magnitude.

The proletariat is often spoken of as if it were integral to the very idea that its members should possess no property of their own, but should subsist solely upon their wages, except where these are supplemented by some form of public relief. But this is not really essential. What is essential is that the proletarian should be a person who gets his chief means of living from the sale of his labour-power. Such a man or woman does not lose the proletarian status by virtue of possessing some small amount of property, but only if the property is considerable enough to constitute an important element in total income, outweighing the wage or salary. The proletarian can be, and in advanced Societies often is, at the same time an owner of some small capital resources, which eke out but do not replace the larger income derived from the sale of labour-power.

It is, of course, true that any ownership of capital, in the sense of individual property yielding an income, tends to some degree to give the possessor the attitude of a property owner, and thus to align him with the class of property owners. But a man's class must be interpreted normally in relation to his major interest; for this will be likely to be decisive in determining his allegiance in economic matters when a conflict of allegiances arises. It is by no means irrelevant to a study of the modern proletariat to observe that, in the more advanced countries, it includes a large number of members who also own some property, from money in the Savings Bank or shares in a Co-operative Society to the ownership of a house or even of industrial shares or Government Stock. Nor is it irrelevant that working-class bodies, from Friendly and Co-operative

Societies to Trade Unions, are considerable collective holders of property. For these facts do affect the economic attitude both of individual workers and of working-class organisations. But that conflicts of interest and loyalty may spring from this source is no reason for denying to the individual or collective holders of property the status of proletarians, if they do depend primarily on their labour-power for the means of life.

A further difficulty which is sometimes raised is that a section of the class which lives by selling its labour-power is definitely parasitic, in the sense that the type of employment which it follows depends essentially on the existence of a rich class. To this group belong certain types of domestic servants and workers in luxury trades providing exclusively for a wealthy clientèle. It is sometimes suggested that all such workers ought to be excluded from the idea of the proletariat as a class. This, however, is quite impossible. These workers, provided they comply with the definition already given, must be regarded as proletarians, even if many of them are likely, when a conflict arises, to fight against the rest of the proletariat rather than on its side. For it is no less possible for a proletarian than for a capitalist to take sides against his class. The proletariat is a class, and not an army: it is not necessarily all-obedient to a common discipline of its own.

The proletariat, then, consists of what ordinary people ordinarily mean when they speak of the working class. Its boundaries are ill-defined, but its central mass is always easily recognised. No class can be defined in terms of its marginal members, but only of its central mass. But this definition is fully adequate for purposes of both practice and theory.

The proletariat, as a class, emerges gradually with the rise of Capitalism. There were, of course, wage-workers, and a rudimentary proletariat, before Capitalism became the dominant system, just as there were capitalists, and a rudimentary capitalist class. But both proletariat and capitalist class reach full stature only under a developed form of capitalist system in which contractual wage-employment by a capitalist, or group of capitalists, becomes the prevailing mode of organising production.

At all stages, there are marked differentiations within the proletariat. In the earlier phases of Capitalism, when the great capitalist is still predominantly a merchant and only secondarily an employer, the number of small master-craftsmen is still relatively very great, and there is no sharp line of social or economic division between these small masters and the upper strata of skilled artisans working for a wage, from whose ranks they are largely recruited, and to whose ranks they may easily return. The gulf is often wider between the skilled artisan and the unskilled labourer than between the artisan and his master; and it is hard to distinguish between the independent small master and the piece-working sub-contractor who is virtually a wage-earner. At this stage the proletarian class is not yet fully differentiated or developed, any more than the capitalist class. But the further advance of Capitalism alters this situation, though many relics of it remain in the industries of to-day, wherever small-scale production persists. The rise of larger-scale production both drives out many of the small masters and greatly alters the relation between the artisan and his employer, impelling the skilled artisan towards a closer unity with the less skilled workers below him. The technical development of machine-industry also blurs the old distinctions between artisans and labourers, undermining the institution of apprenticeship, which kept them apart, and creating infinite gradations of semi-skilled labour intermediate between the two extremes. These two factors work together to solidify the wage-earners as a class; and the growth of compulsory State education, required by the demands of the industrial system as well as in the name of democracy, narrows the cultural gap. The working class becomes far more recognisably one, and recognises itself far more as one, than under the earlier conditions. Moreover, as the capitalists come to have large resources locked up directly in the instruments of production, that is, as Merchant Capitalism gives place to Industrial Capitalism, the class employed upon these instruments of production comes to be more clearly marked off in terms of economic status from the employing class.

But this does not mean that differentiation disappears, or is even diminished. It reappears within the now solidified class but in different forms. There is at this stage not a sharp contrast between skilled and unskilled workers, but a much greater diversity of skill and status in which one grade merges into another to an increasing extent, but new grades are also constantly appearing as the technique of industry changes. To some extent the workers in the more skilled occupations, who have built up Trade Union monopolies of labour, struggle against technical changes, and still more against the attempts of employers to invade their monopolies by the use of less skilled types of labour; and antagonisms exist on this score between skilled and less skilled workers. But as mechanisation grows, and the scale of production becomes larger, in spite of these antagonisms skilled and less skilled are increasingly driven to recognise their common interests and to join forces in collective bargaining. Technical changes weaken the old craft monopolies; and new ones equally strong seldom arrive in their place. Diversity increases; but comes to be of a sort more easily compatible with united class-action among the manual workers.

THE "BLACK-COATED PROLETARIAT"

There is, however, another process of differentiation at work. As mechanisation advances, a smaller proportion of the entire labour force is employed upon directly productive operations, and a larger proportion in clerical, technical, administrative and supervisory work, and in the distribution of goods and the rendering of personal services. This process, as we have seen, is an important factor in creating a new *petite bourgeoisie* in place of the small masters supplanted by the growth of large-scale Capitalism. But it also creates, corresponding in some degree to the upper strata of craftsmen under the old system, an upper proletariat of "black-coats," closely akin in income and way of living to the lower strata of the *petite bourgeoisie* as well as to the upper strata of the manual workers. We have seen that, among this group, it is impossible to say where the proletariat ends and the middle class begins; for at the doubtful margin the question is largely one of feeling rather than of economic condition. In any event, this upper proletariat, fading into the *petite bourgeoisie*, is of far more doubtful allegiance to the central mass of the proletariat, as a class-nucleus, than any important section of the manual workers.

Marx sometimes argued as if the subjection of this group to the same experience as the manual workers, in the cutting down of salaries, the increased speeding-up of work, and the danger of unemployment, would in due course drive it helter-skelter into conscious allegiance to the proletarian cause.

As long as this group can improve its economic position, within an advancing capitalist system, it is more likely to look away from the proletariat, out of which it is striving to emerge, than to act solidly with the rest of the proletarian class. But it is argued that when this process slows down and turns to adversity as Capitalism begins to decay, the "black-coated proletariat" will be speedily converted to a clear recognition of its proletarian status, and to an alliance with the manual workers in an attempt to change it. This view, however, needs large qualifications. In the first place, the ability of the "black-coats" to form Trade Unions is greatest in economic prosperity and falls off when Capitalism gets into difficulties; for the great mass of "black-coat" labour is easily transferable from job to job, and in face of widespread popular education the "black-coats" are in the worst position for building up sectional monopolies of labour. Moreover, their desire to hold their status of social superiority to the manual workers is strongest when that superiority is most threatened. The desire to rise individually out of the proletariat weakens their power of collective action, and tends to make each play for his own hand by courting the employer's favour. "Black-coat" Trade Unions are apt to be mushroom growths, and to die out in bad times as rapidly as they arise under conditions of favourable trade. Even where they persist, as in the public services, they have nothing like the cohesion or loyalty which exists among the Unions of the manual workers. They are apt to think of strikes as beneath their dignity; and employers do everything they can to foster this feeling of superiority as a means of keeping manual and non-manual workers apart. The non-manual worker who ventures to become an active leader runs as a rule a far greater risk than the manual worker, because he has more to lose, and because his fellows are far less likely to protect him successfully against victimisation.

Secondly, if the "black-coats" feel their position to be seriously threatened, and are stirred to defensive action, it is not certain what side they will take. Too weak and with too little coherence to act alone or to lead, they have the choice of joining forces with the manual workers or of taking sides against them under whatever leadership offers to preserve their social superiority. To join with the manual workers means, in the end, sacrificing social superiority in the interests of economic defence; whereas the leaders who seek to mobilise them against the workers offer to defend both their economic interests and their superior status, by re-establishing a Capitalism that is henceforth to be controlled in the interests of the middle classes and made prosperous again by the defeat of the manual workers. Offered this choice, the "black-coats" are likely to divide, in different proportions according to the local situation, but with a strong disposition to rally chiefly to that side which seems to have the better prospect of victory.

THE CHANGE IN MANUAL LABOUR

But the "black-coats," while they can be distinguished as a large and rapidly growing group lapping over from the proletariat into the middle class, are not separated from the manual workers by any clear line of division. Indeed, in the more advanced industrial countries, a growing section among the manual workers becomes "black-coated" both in its dress and habits of living and in its mental attitude. The more recent developments of industry not only cause a transference from manual to non-manual occupations, but also, by greater mechanisation, make many types of productive labour lighter and less rough, so that, even when the pace of work is speeded up, the exhaustion to which it leads is nervous rather than physical, and many manual jobs no longer make those who labour at them dirty or uncouth in manner or appearance. This change in the quality of labour combines with the spread of popular education to make the manner and appearance, and also the mind, of a growing proportion of the manual workers more like that of the non-manual workers, who have been hitherto regarded as their superiors in culture and education. Despite the persistence of slums and over-crowding in the towns of to-day, the conditions of housing in the new estates and suburbs assist in this process of making a large part of the better-off members of the manual-working section of the proletariat more *bourgeois* in its habits and ways of living. The manual and non-manual workers often cannot be told apart nowadays, when they are off duty. They dress alike, talk alike, live alike, think alike, to an ever-increasing extent. Of course, this change affects some sections of manual labour much less than others. It has touched the miners least of all, both because of the nature of their work, and because they live largely isolated in mining villages apart from other sections of the population. But among them too a change is coming about; and cheap motor transport, bringing the towns within their reach, helps towards their assimilation to the new type, as it does towards that of the agricultural labourers.

This change in the manual-working class cuts both ways. On the one hand, the assimilation between manual and non-manual workers makes co-operation between them easier within a common movement, as appears plainly in the Labour Party and other political organisations. But, on the other hand, fighting spirit tends to be weakened, and the sense of solidarity is often less strong in the newer industries than in the old. The worker who has come to live more like a *bourgeois*, at any rate in externals, has more consciousness of what he has to lose by kicking against the pricks, and is inclined to be more cautious in action. Mechanisation, in making labour more readily transferable, diminishes craft-consciousness and solidarity; and in many cases there is really nothing more manual in operating an automatic machine than a typewriter or a calculating instrument in an up-to-date office. The decrease in the dirtiness of industrial occupations makes heavy, distinctive clothing less necessary than it was; and this too diminishes the sense of belonging to a separate social class.

In these circumstances, it becomes easier to organise the proletariat politically, but harder to maintain the strength and vigour of its industrial organisation. Up to a point, this aids the growth of class-consciousness; but beyond this point it makes class-consciousness less militant and less intense. It leads most easily to the growth of a vague, half-Socialist sentiment, which finds expression in a mild desire for reforms rather than in a revolutionary determination to change the basis of Society. Class-consciousness becomes more prevalent, but also more diluted and less determined in action.

These, however, are to a great extent the effects upon the proletariat of a Capitalism advancing in wealth and prosperity, and therefore able without endangering its solvency to grant progressive improvements in the standard of life. If Capitalism is already passing out of this phase into one of declension and increasing embarrassment, is this situation likely to continue? Will the conversion of proletarians into marginal members of the new *petite bourgeoisie* still go on; or will the tendency of the past generation be sharply reversed?

It is a familiar theory among certain Marxists that it will be reversed, as Capitalism in its decline sets about cutting down wages and flinging the "black-coats" down into the growing mass of the impoverished. But is this theory correct? However Capitalism as a system may decline, the process of transferring workers from heavy to lighter mechanical operations and from direct productive jobs to distributive and clerical occupations is certain to continue. Moreover, on the evidence of the past few years capitalist depression is likely to impinge very unevenly upon the standard of living. It is more likely to create "pockets" of misery and destitution in declining industries, and to widen the gulf between the employed and the chronically unemployed, than to oppress the entire working class with a common oppression. If it does act in this way, it will make some members of the proletariat more, and others less, amenable to forthright Socialist propaganda, or to any alternative form of "extremism" that promises redress. It will make Communists at one extreme, and Fascists at the other, out of those upon whom the new conditions press hardest; but it will also hinder the acceptance of either extreme by those sections of the workers upon whom the scourge of unemployment and depression does not seriously fall. Extremism of both types will make headway among those who suffer extreme experiences; but there will be left many who, relatively undisturbed in their own lives, will remain sceptical of extreme courses.

Of course, if the disintegration of capitalist Society goes far enough, this will cease to be true. For economic adversity, if it becomes deep enough, is bound at some point to spread throughout the entire working class, in such a way as to drive all sections together in resistance to a common misery. The whole proletariat, including the "black-coated" section, may have its standard of living so beaten down as to drive most of it into revolt. But, even if this were to happen, it would not follow that all sections would revolt in the same way. To assume this is to assume that Capitalism, threatened with utter destruction, will passively await its doom, and allow the entire proletariat to concentrate for the attack upon it without resorting to any fresh expedients of defence. It is to assume, further, that the onset of "increasing misery," accompanied by more and more insistent claims from the proletariat for relief as well as for a change of system, will cause the middle groups to join the proletariat in its demands rather than rally to the capitalists in an attempt to break its power, and thus rebuild Capitalism on a new basis. For, if the proletariat can be thoroughly crushed, may not the middle groups as well as the capitalists, who cannot hold power without their aid, continue to live well enough even under a Capitalism that is unable to press further the development of the powers of production, or even to make full use of the powers already at its disposal? Moreover, in such a situation, may not the capitalists and the middle groups be able to suborn a section even of the undoubted proletariat, by offering it a share in the spoils of victory?

Recent events in Germany appear to show that this outcome is likely. The capitalists will not wait for the decay of Capitalism to raise all the rest of Society against them. They will lend their aid to those middle groups which, scared at the advance of Socialism, are prepared to use force to prevent its coming; and they will help any promising movement among these groups with money and influence to suborn a section of the manual workers. Of course the conflict will not appear thus nakedly in the form of a class-struggle; for in order to defeat the idea of Socialism, it will be necessary for the new movement to provide itself with a rival idea that does not openly proclaim its will to preserve Capitalism. It is already evident that Nationalism, in one or another of its many forms, is cast for this part. Whether we take Italy or Germany, or the milder rule of the "National" Government in Great Britain, or the appeals for Governments of "National Union" against Socialism in France and many other countries, it is clear that the appeal which will be made by the anti-proletarian forces will be to the spirit of national unity and solidarity against the spirit of class-conflict at home and against internationalism and pacifism in external affairs. It will be sought to unite men at home by dividing them from every one outside the nation; and, thus armed with an appeal that strikes deep down to the ancient traditions of tribal hatreds and tribal religions, the adherents of the capitalist order will trust to success in mastering the forces set in motion by the logic of economic growth.

It is true enough that in the long run this manœuvre cannot succeed, because the re-establishment of Capitalism over the prostrate body of the proletariat by an appeal to nationalist sentiment, so far from preventing the decline of Capitalism, will positively strengthen the forces making for its decay. For to beat down the proletariat is, as we have seen, to narrow the market for the products of capitalist industry, and thus to make more glaring than ever the contrast between actual and potential production; while the re-building of Capitalism on a nationalist basis will both lessen the efficiency of production, by leading to exaggerated Protectionism, and stimulate the growth of imperialist rivalries between the leading capitalist

Powers. These, with an intolerant Nationalism as their cardinal doctrine, will be more inclined than ever to fly at one another's throats over the sharing-out of world markets and sources of supply. There will be heavier and heavier armaments; and where there are heavy armaments in the long run there will be war.

THE PROSPECTS OF REVOLUTION

War, doubtless, is the proletariat's opportunity; for, however thoroughly it may be possible to crush and disorganise the proletariat in time of peace, when war is in progress nothing can arrest the growth of proletarian unrest. In war, both sides cannot win. The struggle must either be indecisive or end in someone's defeat. But an indecisive struggle discredits the ruling class that wages it, and stirs up discontent; and defeat strains the political system of the defeated country, often to breaking point. Therefore, some Socialists see the chief, if not the only, prospect of Socialist victory in another war. War begat the Russian Revolution of 1917: what fresh revolutions will not the next war bring?

To those who envisage the future in this way, the prospect of Socialist electoral victories makes little appeal. They are far less concerned with winning for some form of Socialism a wide basis of support than with the creation of a proletarian movement which, even if it be small, will have the fighting quality and the determined temper that will ensure full advantage being taken of a revolutionary opportunity when it comes. They are not even much disturbed when the fear of Socialism leads to a successful Fascist revolution, which celebrates its victory by breaking up the entire mass-organisation of the working class, and succeeds in sweeping a substantial section of the proletariat behind it into a mood of hysterical Nationalism. For, they say, their time will come. The Nationalists will lead the deluded multitude into war: war will beget unrest and disillusion; and then the mass will be ready to follow, in a hardly less irrational fashion if to a better end, the lead of a determined Communist minority.

It happened so in Russia, where the repressions of the years following the unsuccessful Revolution of 1905 broke up the mass organisations and drove the working-class movement underground, and where imperialist war and collapse made the way plain for the proletarian Revolution of 1917. It happened so in Russia; and therefore it is bound to happen so everywhere else. But is it? In Germany, perhaps, or even possibly in Italy; for when a Fascist Revolution has once occurred, and the mass organisation of the workers been successfully broken, there may be no alternative method left for the winning of Socialism. But does it follow that Fascist Revolution is inevitable in every country, or that everywhere the existing mass organisation of the workers is destined to be broken down? It may be so; but the conclusion is not self-evident.

For it has to be remembered that neither Russia nor Germany ever became parliamentary democracies in any real sense. In Russia the attempt to establish parliamentary democracy in 1917 was made in the face of complete economic and political collapse of the old autocracy, and never stood any real chance of success. In Germany the ill-fated Weimar Republic was similarly founded on the ruins of a defeated autocracy—for pre-war Germany was never really a parliamentary State—and the Socialists could have pushed it over quite easily at the outset if they had wished. That they did not wish is true

and important in its place; but it is not my present point, which
is that German parliamentarism, born out of defeat and presented with the impossible task of governing Germany as
a subject-Power at the orders of the victors, never had even
half a chance. Even in Italy, which was more a parliamentary
country before the war, parliamentarism was always weak and
had little hold on the mind of the population; and though Italy
emerged from the war nominally a victor, the disappointment
of her imperialist aspirations and the pressure of economic difficulties, with which her weak Governments were quite unable
to cope, smoothed the way for the victory of Fascism over the
divided Socialist and Syndicalist forces.

On the other hand in Great Britain, France, Holland, Bel-
gium and Scandinavia the parliamentary system is strongly
entrenched, and has behind it a long record of economic success. In these countries autocracy was superseded long ago,
while Capitalism was still a progressive system with most
of its victories still to come, by the rule of the *bourgeoisie* ex-
ercised through parliamentary forms. The suffrage had been
extended, working-class organisations had been allowed freedom to grow, economic pressure from below had been met
by concessions as well as by repressions, and the State had become a machine for the dispensing of social services as well as
for the maintenance of law and order and the rights of property. Parliamentarism got the credit of these achievements, as
well as of the rising standard of life characteristic of an advancing capitalist system. And, though there is in these countries now a growing reaction against Parliament, as the difficulties of Capitalism increase, Parliamentarism remains strongly
entrenched in the minds of all classes, including the workers.

Nor are Great Britain and France, the two leading parliamentary countries, in any danger of military defeat in the near future, provided that they stand together. If another war came soon, they would win it, as they won the last; for they are superior in arms and resources to any likely combination of antagonists. War might shake, even in these countries, the very foundations of Capitalism; but, if it came soon, it would be more likely to bring parliamentary Socialism than revolutionary Communism to power. It is also relevant that these countries do not want war, though it may be forced upon them, and though they could rely on winning it in a military sense. Their Governments want peace, both because they know that their populations want peace, and because war would very likely mean the end of Capitalism and the establishment of a Socialist system.

In these circumstances, there is at present nothing either to drive the general mass of the proletariat in these countries over to revolutionary Communism, or to incite the middle groups to unite with Capitalism in violent counter-revolution. Both the capitalists and most of the middle-class groups that stand in fear of Socialism see far more hope in forming a "National" parliamentary alliance against Socialism than in attempting to repress it by force. They are impelled to this attitude by at least three main considerations. In the first place, the mass of the working class, as well as of other classes, is still not nearly uncomfortable enough to feel in a revolutionary mood. It would strongly resent and resist the action of any section that attempted by violence to establish a form of dictatorship. Trade Unionists may often sympathise with Communists, and Conservatives with Fascist agitators; but neither the proletariat nor the capitalist class is in the least disposed to let the extremists have their head. The British and French populations are still mostly pacific at home, as well as mildly pacifist in external affairs.

Secondly, neither British nor French Socialism yet looks quite menacing enough to stir the antagonism of the upper and middle elements in Society to the depths. France has experienced Radical Governments ruling with Socialist support. Great Britain has had two Labour Governments. Nothing very terrible has happened; and there are still plenty of people who doubt if anything very terrible would really happen even if the Socialists came back to power with a majority behind them. For clearly it will take much more than a mere parliamentary majority to establish Socialism.

Thirdly, both the British and the French working classes, but especially the British, have been greatly influenced by *bourgeois* ideas and are not sharply enough marked off from the *bourgeoisie* to arouse easily the same fears as were aroused in the governing classes of England by the "starvelings" of the Industrial Revolution. The upper strata of the working class are not inaccessible to appeals that could have exerted no influence at all on the proletariat of Russia. Who would have tried to stem the Russian Revolution by telling the proletariat that its savings bank deposits were in danger? Yet this appeal has been made in Great Britain, and might be made no less effectively in France. True, it could also have been used in Germany, had the occasion arisen; for in Germany too the proletariat had largely acquired *bourgeois* characteristics. It was in fact made in Germany by the Nazis. But this does not invalidate the point. It only shows that the presence of *bourgeois* qualities in the proletariat will not avert the appeal to violence, if it stands alone. It will indeed make the appeal succeed more easily against the proletariat, when it is made. But it will also cause other methods to be used in preference to violence, as long as the two preceding conditions continue to exist; and it will help to make these methods more effective.

In effect, then, the Communist strategy of propaganda based on the inevitability of violent revolution, when it is pursued in countries still working with relative stability and prosperity under the parliamentary system, stands no chance of rallying the main body of the upper and middle elements in Society. As long as this situation remains in being, the predominant struggle will be between parties still employing parliamentary methods, and endeavouring to gain their ends by lawful propaganda. The chief immediate effect of the growth of Communism under these conditions, can only be to weaken the chances of a constitutional Socialist victory, just as Fascism can only lessen those of the successful constitutional defence of Capitalism. Hence the established parties will excommunicate the rival extremists and do all they can to prevent the spread of their doctrines. Messrs. Baldwin and MacDonald will not love Sir Oswald Mosley any better than Mr. Arthur Henderson loves Mr. Harry Pollitt.

To this ostracism the extremists on both sides will reply that they are being excommunicated because the older parties are selling the pass. The capitalist parties will be told that their weakness is leaving the door wide open for the Socialists to come in; and the Socialist Parties will be accused of being traitors to the proletarian cause. But in fact on both sides the leadership expresses with fair accuracy the minds of most of those to whom it is seeking to appeal. For, in parliamentary countries, men do not want to fight until they have lost hope of gaining their point by peaceful means.

To this extremists will answer that, even if most people do

still hold these views, they are demonstrably mistaken. The capitalist extremists will point to the gradual increase of Socialist legislation, and explain that Socialism is the inevitable outcome of parliamentary "democracy"; while the Communists will demonstrate that Capitalism in its decline must increasingly grind down the proletariat, and will certainly resort to force on the model of Italy and Germany, as soon as the proletariat refuses to be ground down. Up to a point, both these views are correct. Socialism is the natural outcome of a democratic franchise in an advanced industrial country; and Capitalism, if it relies on parliamentary methods, is bound most of the time to be fighting a rearguard action, because it must find means of keeping a majority of the electors on its side. And, on the other hand, a declining Capitalism must oppose the claims of the proletariat with increasing vigour if it is to survive at all.

Nevertheless, the conclusions drawn by the extremists do not follow; for a premature attempt at Fascism may be the surest means of bringing about a Socialist victory, and the growth of Communism may be the means of preventing the Socialists from placing themselves constitutionally in a position to render impossible a successful capitalist appeal to force. For even if the making of Socialism involves far more than the winning of a parliamentary majority, possession of the machinery of State is a most powerful instrument for the suppression of counter-revolutionary activities.

The case against the Communist policy is not that it misinterprets the attitude of the proletariat, but that it is likely, in the existing circumstances, to divide the forces of the proletariat at a crucial juncture, and so prevent a parliamentary Socialist victory and perhaps, in the measure of its own success in attracting adherents, open the door to a real growth of

Fascism. This does not deter the Communists, because they have no belief in the value of a parliamentary victory, and are intent only on building up a revolutionary movement capable of assuming the leadership when its opportunity arises. But how is this opportunity to arise?

It could come, first, as a result of the progressive decline of Capitalism even in the absence of war. But this is to contemplate an indefinite postponement of victory; for there is no evidence that, save as an outcome of renewed war, Capitalism in either Great Britain or France is likely to break up for a long time to come. The history of the past few years has very plainly illustrated the toughness and resisting power of Capitalism in these countries even in face of prolonged world depression; and who is bold enough to say that the present depression, deep and long as it has been, will not pass, and be succeeded by a phase of Capitalist revival? Capitalism may be doomed to be pulled down by its own inherent "contradictions"; but unless war intervenes to hasten the process, it is likely to take a long time for this destruction to be completed, save as the result of a victory of Socialism won by parliamentary methods.

But it may be argued that Capitalism in decline will inevitably plunge into another war. I am sceptical of inevitabilities; but let us grant it probable. Will even another war necessarily so dislocate British and French Capitalism, even if France and Britain are on the winning side, as to clear the road for a Communist revolution? It may; I see no reason to be sure that it will. Indeed, it seems to be more likely that it would smooth the way for a parliamentary Socialist victory.

It may be argued, then, that the Communists' chance will come only after parliamentary Socialism has been tried, and has failed. But, if that is so, should not the Communists help the Socialists to power, rather than do their best to destroy their chances? Moreover, is the failure of parliamentary methods really so unavoidable as the Communists would have us believe?

The main discussion of this issue must be reserved for a later chapter, in which we shall be dealing with the Marxist attitude to the State and to parliamentary action. For we must first complete our picture of the modern proletariat, upon which the victory of Socialism by *any* method must be mainly based, whatever other forces may come to the aid of the victors in the course of the struggle. What the proletariat is, and what it can become, are the vital questions which must be answered before any attempt can be made to work out a sound and practical Socialist strategy.

THE MIND OF THE PROLETARIAT

What the modern proletariat is, in the advanced parliamentary countries of Western Europe, we have seen in outline already. It consists of a central mass of manual workers and their families, shading off at one end into the unemployables and at the other into the "black-coats" of the middle class. It is greatly differentiated within itself, into many grades of labour and levels of income and education, without anywhere a sharp break between one grade or section and another. A large number of its members, while depending on wages or salaries for the means of life, are small owners of property, and its collective organisations are holders of property to a considerable extent. Its better-off groups, which have a standard of life permitting of some modest comfort, certainly do not echo the sentiment that they have nothing to lose but their chains. They are very conscious of having also their jobs, their houses and gardens, their small savings, and their share in social services provided by the State, Local Authorities, Trade Unions, Friendly Societies, and numerous other bodies. They value these things, and are prepared to defend them if they are attacked; and they want more of them with an appetite that grows with experience. They are therefore mostly "progressives" in their political attitude, and ready to support parties which promise to defend what they have gained and to improve upon it by further reforms. Many of them, but not perhaps most, are Socialists of a sort; but Socialism means to them mainly the cause that stands for giving them more of what they want, and does not mean any clear idea of an alternative kind of Society—much less a kind to be won by violent revolution. They are, in fact, at the "Lib-Lab" stage typified by the Labour Governments which have actually held office.

These people are, for the most part, capable of becoming Socialists only if and when they realise that continual progress along the familiar lines is impossible within the capitalist system, and that they can only secure a further rise in the standard of living, or indeed protect the standard which they have already, by changing the basis of economic organisation. Even so, they will need to be convinced that the Socialists, in calling upon them to deliver a frontal attack on Capitalism, do mean and also know how to create a Socialist system that will give them what they want. The Socialism to which they will listen must be a "bread and butter" Socialism, offering tangible benefits and appearing competent to make its premises good. If Socialists can appeal to them on these lines, they will follow; but they will insist that the change be brought about with the minimum of dislocation and violence, and that the attempt be made on constitutional lines if the road remains open for attempting it in this way. This applies to a great majority of the better-off wage-earners and of their allies among the "blackcoats" and in other social groups.

There is, indeed, a substantial section of the proletariat to which this diagnosis does not apply. This section consists primarily of those who have suffered prolonged unemployment and had their accustomed standards of living badly beaten down, as well as to a minority of the younger people who have grown to manhood during the years of depression. These elements in the proletariat have far less to lose, and are far more conscious of what they have already lost. They are far readier to listen to extreme policies—to become Communists, and perhaps thereafter in some cases to turn Fascist when they lose faith in a Communist victory. From having less roots in the present order, they are far more unstable in their allegiance. They are good revolutionary material; but they are also favourable recruiting ground, as we have seen in Germany, for the counter-revolution.

This section of the proletariat is, under present conditions, utterly incapable either of making a Socialist revolution by itself, or of gaining the leadership of the general body of the proletariat in countries such as France or Great Britain. It is, in these countries, still only a small fraction of the whole proletariat; and even in Germany, where it came to be a very large fraction, those who became its leaders never succeeded in winning over the great majority of the workers to their point of view. A movement based upon it alone cannot be a class-movement, but only a fractional movement within a class. It can destroy the solidarity of a class, but it is impotent to build up any new solidarity in its stead. Only national defeat in war, or the utter decay of Capitalism, which would plunge the majority of the workers down to its economic level, could avail to make such a movement the representative of a united working class.

In the parliamentary "democracies" of Western Europe, any advance towards Socialism has to be made by means of a strategy that will unite rather than divide the proletariat. This means not only the use of parliamentary methods of agitation and an attempt to capture the machinery of State, as long as these methods remain open, but also a building upon the existing mass-organisations which the proletariat has created for itself. It means using the Trade Union and the Co-operative Society, as well as the Labour Party, as instruments both of working-class defence and of the furtherance of Socialist policy. It means preserving the unity of these movements, and preventing them if possible from being torn asunder, as Trade Unionism has been in France and Spain, by doctrinal differences. For, in the industrial field, disunity is even more fatal than in political action. Rival Trade Unions, fighting one another and pursuing opposite policies, are plainly impotent to protect the workers' standard of life—much less to further the coming of Socialism. If there is a conflict of industrial policies, as there will be, it must be pursued within a united organisation, unless the workers are to court disaster.

THE PROSPECTS OF TRADE UNIONISM

This is the more important to-day because the forces of the time are in many respects inimical to Trade Unions. In times of depression the Trade Unions are inevitably set on the defensive, and compelled to hold fast to existing positions rather than seek new fields to conquer. But defence requires unity even more imperatively than attack; for it is harder, and calls for far greater patience and persistence as well as loyalty. It is, however, when Trade Unionism is forced on the defensive that unity is most difficult to maintain. Many workers, unemployed and impoverished, fail to maintain their Union contributions and drop away. There can be no easy and spectacular victories to attract members and inspire ready confidence in the value of the Union; for it looks far more successful to secure a rise in wages than to prevent a reduction, though the latter may be by far the greater accomplishment. Moreover, leaders who have always to be preaching caution cannot easily sound inspiring, and may easily have their own spirit worn away; and members, finding their Union dull, may discover more exciting things to do than to maintain the steady round of necessary work for keeping the machine efficiently in order. Trade Unionism, far more than political Labour, has to trim its sails according to the winds of trade; for in bad times it dare neither excite its own followers nor provoke the employers. As long as Capitalism is there, it has to live on terms with Capitalism; and in bad times this compels it to make the best terms it can.

It is, however, when Trade Unionism looks least inspiring that it is most important to keep it alive, both for the immediate protection of working-class standards and because it can be relied on to come alive again when the conditions change, and is at all times indispensable as a means of organising working-class solidarity in a primary way. Where there are no Trade Unions, the working class is reduced to a merely atomistic mass, incapable of concerted action in politics as well as in industry, or of being rallied effectively behind a Socialist policy. Trade Unionism may be incapable of supplying the positive driving-force towards Socialism; but without it there could be no working-class army to be led. No delusion is more foolish than the delusion that Socialists can do without Trade Unions, or afford to advance without their support.

It is, however, true that there are at present other forces besides trade depression that are tending to lessen the power of Trade Unionism. For this power has in the past been concentrated in a high degree in a few great industries and among certain special groups of workers possessing a valuable monopoly of technical skill. The most recent developments of industry have tended to decrease the numbers of workers employed in those older industries, and to increase employment in smaller and more scattered industries, in transport and distribution, and in the public utility and other services; and they have also, by the greater use made of automatic and semi-automatic machinery, broken down in part the established monopolies of the skilled crafts and made much harder the creation of solid blackleg-proof organisations on sectional lines.

It would have been much easier for the Trade Unions to adapt themselves to these changes in industrial technique and in the employment of labour if they had not coincided in time with a serious depression of trade, so that technological and cyclical unemployment have increased side by side. But even if there had been only the technological problem to face, the Trade Unions would have needed to revise their methods of organisation and bargaining to a considerable extent. For the new industrial conditions demand both a wider solidarity embracing all sections of workers and a greater concentration on bargaining in each separate establishment as well as on the general adjustment of wage-rates and hours of labour over a wider area. It is, however, exceptionally difficult to establish machinery for work-shop bargaining under conditions which involve the existence of a surplus of labour; for such Trade Union agents as shop stewards can be readily singled out for victimisation and dismissal, and the Unions, when trade is bad and unemployment prevalent, may not be strong enough to protect their active members against such treatment. Consequently, there has gone on, side by side with the introduction of new technical methods of production, a progressive undermining of established Trade Union customs and a worsening of conditions quite apart from the actual reduction of wage-rates; and only the most fortunately placed Trade Unions have been able to stand out against these innovations with success. There has been much speeding up, both by stricter factory supervision and by the introduction of new methods of wage-payment such as the unpopular "Bedaux" system; much use of less skilled or juvenile labour at lower rates on jobs previously reserved for skilled men; much nibbling at the privileges which the Trade Unions had managed to build up by long years of effort. All these causes have naturally produced a large amount of irritation in the factories; but this irritation is held in check by the fear of dismissal which is bound to be always present in the workers' minds at times of superabundant labour supply.

For these difficulties of the Trade Union movement no remedy can be found in terms of industrial action alone. The Trade Unions are driven irresistibly towards political action as a means of reinforcing their economic power. They want a satisfactory system of maintenance for the unemployed in order to reduce the pressure to accept jobs on any conditions which the employer chooses to offer. They want, in industries where wages are seriously pressed down by adverse trade conditions, a legal minimum wage. They want shorter hours of labour as a means of sharing out the available work. And, especially in the depressed industries, such as coal and cotton, these claims impel them towards a stronger demand for complete socialisation, or at least for the reorganisation of their industries under State control. Trade Unions thus turn to political action as a means of securing their industrial demands; and the Labour Party becomes more important in their eyes as an indispensable agent of economic policy.

This pressure of the Trade Unions upon the Labour Party is capable of taking opposite and inconsistent forms upon the surface. Sometimes, it seems to be pressing the party to promise a further squeezing of the capitalist orange, without any frontal attack upon Capitalism itself; for the Unions, with the immediate needs of their members most in mind, are apt to press for pledges that the Labour Party, when it comes back to office, shall concentrate on questions of "bread and butter," to the exclusion of more ultimate objectives. At other times, the Trade Unions—especially the miners—seem to be intent on pushing the more timid political leaders further towards Socialism than they are disposed to go, in their fear of offending other sections of the electorate. In Great Britain Trade Union votes, fully as much as the votes of constituency Labour Parties, have been responsible for the marked stiffening up of the Labour programme at recent Labour Party Conferences, despite the reluctance of the party Executive. The truth is that the Trade Unions, when they are acting as industrial bodies, have to be moderate just now because they are conscious of their weakness; but this very consciousness tends to make them

favour an advanced political programme because that alone
offers the prospect of strengthening their hands in the industrial
sphere.

Nevertheless, when the Trade Unions are presented with
such an issue as that of constitutionalism *versus* revolution, their
answer is unhesitatingly in favour of constitutional action. In
this the leadership rightly interprets the feeling of the great
majority of the members who, not being Socialists in any
thought-out theoretical sense, think in terms of possible reme-
dies for particular grievances rather than of a complete change
in the basis of Society. The Trade Unions may become, and
are gradually becoming, Socialist; but they become so only as
it is gradually forced upon them that Capitalism is unable, as
well as unwilling, to grant their demands.

The Trade Unions are indispensable to the Socialists; but in
these days Socialism cannot be founded on a Trade Union basis
only. It has to get behind it a mass organisation wide enough
to include, not only the Trade Unions, but the great mass of
people outside the Unions who are of the proletariat or capable
of acting as its allies. The Trade Union is predominantly a male
institution; but the enfranchisement of women makes indispensable an organisation wide enough to include them in its
scope, and to give them an increasing share in its conduct.
This need the Labour and Socialist Parties, with their strongly
organised Women's Sections, are now beginning satisfactorily
to supply. And the Party also affords room for the unorganised
"black-coats," and for all the miscellaneous converts from
other groups and classes whom conviction and sympathy induce to rally to the Socialist cause. The problem of uniting all
these elements in one mass organisation, so as both to preserve
the allegiance of the Trade Unions and to give the other sec-

tions a real share in the framing of policy in face of the Trade
Union "block vote," is not easy to solve. But it is on the whole
being solved with fair satisfaction in the gradual evolution
of the party machine.

For the Trade Unionists are aware that, if they stand alone,
on the basis of a purely Trade Union party, they have no
chance of conquering a majority in Parliament, or of using
political action as an effective reinforcement to their industrial
power. If the proletariat were merely the manual-working
group, it would be, not only a minority, but also a minority
incapable of leading the majority, or of acting unitedly with
itself. For, as we have seen, while the main body of manual
workers forms the central core of the proletariat, the manual
workers are not to-day marked off sharply as a single group
from the non-manual workers, but shade off into the other sections of the proletariat with which they have increasingly a
common standard of culture, income, and way of life. Political
action, even if the Trade Unions continue to play a vitally important part in its organisation, as they do and must, has to be
developed on a basis wide enough to include the whole proletariat, and not its Trade Union elements alone.

This brings us to a consideration of the place of the Co-operative movement. The Co-operative Movement has travelled far
since the days of Robert Owen; and its great success as a trad-
ing institution has caused it in the main to stand aside from the
industrial and political phases of the working-class struggle for
power. Becoming a great employer in competition with capitalist industry, it has been compelled to adopt towards its employees an attitude not differing greatly from that of Capitalism,
save that it has usually afforded securer employment. Seeking
a wider membership, it has been disposed until lately to eschew

political discussion and activity; and it would hardly have been drawn much into politics even now but for the ill-advised attacks launched on its privileges at the instigation of private traders jealous of its commercial success. It tends, by the very nature of its activities, to throw up to the top men marked out by business qualities rather than by propagandist zeal; and as long as it has been able to live and grow within a capitalist setting it has been inclined to forswear attacks on Capitalism that might bring its own rights into jeopardy. The Co-operative movement is never likely to place itself in the vanguard of the working-class advance. It is far more likely to come lumbering along behind, like the commissariat in the wake of an advancing army. But it is of high importance to the success of Socialism that it should not lag too far behind; and those who seek to frame working-class policy would be well advised to pay more attention to assuring Co-operators of a satisfying place in the coming reorganisation of Society, and to securing that Trade Unionists and Socialists who are also Co-operators shall more actively carry their Trade Union and Socialist principles into the Co-operative Store.

The proletariat, in the advanced countries of parliamentary democracy, is then a widely differentiated class, with many and increasing claims, but by no means of revolutionary temper as long as it is left room to organise freely and sees a chance of realising its claims within the existing framework of Society. Compared with the proletariat of Marx's day, it is not more, but very much less, "miserable," though it now includes a growing depressed section upon which the first brunt of the decline of Capitalism has fallen. This section may be destined, if the capitalist game is played out to the end, and constitutional Socialism fails to supplant it before the end is reached, to become co-extensive with practically the whole proletariat. But there is no sign, in France or Britain or the other relatively prosperous countries, of this happening soon, unless Capitalism is finally shattered by a further world war. In these circumstances, it appears that Socialist policy in these countries should, in accordance with Marxian principles, be based on the proletariat as it actually is, and not as it may come some day to be if a number of not certainly foreseeable contingencies occur. But this point—what the appropriate Socialist strategy should be—we can discuss best when we have considered the Marxian attitude to the State in the light of States as they actually are in the world of to-day.

CHAPTER VI

MARXISM AND THE STATE

ONE OF MARX'S most famous phrases is his characterisation of the modern State. "The executive of the modern State," he and Engels wrote in the *Communist Manifesto,* "is but a committee for managing the common affairs of the *bourgeoisie* as a whole." In these words Marx characterised the modern State as essentially an organ of class-dictatorship.

Later on in the *Communist Manifesto,* Marx and Engels set out to define the policy of the proletariat towards the *bourgeois* State. "The first step in the working-class revolution," they wrote, "is to raise the proletariat to the position of ruling class, to win the battle of democracy." They add that "the proletariat will use its political supremacy to wrest, by degrees, all capital from the *bourgeoisie,* and to centralise all instruments of production in the hands of the State, i.e. of the proletariat organised as the ruling class."

Much later, in 1875, Marx wrote in his criticism of the Gotha Programme of the German Socialists a passage which further clarifies his meaning. "Between capitalist and communist society lies a period of revolutionary transformation from the one to the other. To this also corresponds a political period of transition during which the State can be nothing else than the revolutionary dictatorship of the proletariat."

There are two important points to notice in these passages. First, in the contrast which they draw between the two types of State, *bourgeois* and proletarian, each is regarded as embodying the rule, or dictatorship, of a particular class which is the holder of political power. There is not, in Marx's idea, any such thing as a classless State, or any State which is not the embodiment of the ruling authority of a particular class. This is made abundantly plain in Marx's criticism of the Gotha Programme, and also in his manifesto, drafted for the First International, on the Paris Commune, and published under the name of the *The Civil War in France*.

Secondly, Marx clearly envisages a period of transition from Capitalism to Socialism or Communism, during which there will exist a new form of State, based on the authority of the proletariat. This State will be, not the *bourgeois* State simply "captured" by the proletariat and applied to the ends of the proletarian Revolution, but an essentially new State made by the proletariat to serve its own revolutionary purpose. But the proletarian State will not be lasting; for the object of the proletarian Revolution is to abolish classes and institute a classless Society. When this has been done there can be no room for any State at all. The State, which is by Marx's definition an organ of class-domination, obviously cannot remain in being in a Society wherein all class-distinctions have ceased to exist. In such a Society there will be no need or room for a State, in Marx's sense of the word. For no organ will be needed to keep one class in subjection to another. Government will endure no longer: there will be left only the problem of administration. In a familiar phrase, "the government of men will give place to the administration of things."

It is, of course, above all on this part of Marxist doctrine that modern Communism has been built up. Lenin's *The State and Revolution* is in essence a simple amplification of this view. At this point the divergence between the Social Democratic and Communist interpretations of Marxism is widest; and round it centred the bitter controversy between Lenin and Kautsky as the outstanding theorists of the rival schools. In this controversy, there can be not the smallest doubt which side can rightly claim to be "orthodox," in the sense of basing itself firmly upon the writings of the master. Marx's conception of the State and of the transition is utterly plain and unequivocal. There is not the smallest question about his own view. Lenin, and not Kautsky, says what Marx said. Kautsky was only continuing to say what the German Social Democrats so angered Marx by saying in the Gotha Programme of 1875. For Kautsky, and the Social Democrats as a party, had come to think in terms of the capture and democratisation of the capitalist State and not, like Marx, in terms of its overthrow and destruction.

This, of course, does not settle the question whether Marx was right or wrong; for we are not accepting the view that anything Marx said or held must of necessity be right. But it is well to be clear before we approach the discussion of the merits of the case that, despite all the casuistry that has been used in trying to represent Marx as holding a different view, there is no uncertainty at all about his own words, either in 1848 or, much later, in 1875. On this issue, Marx was unquestionably a Communist, and not a Social Democrat.

With this in mind, we can go on to examine rather more clearly the implications of Marx's view. Whereas other schools of social theorists usually define the State in terms of political right, or obligation, Marx defines it in terms of force. It is, in his view, the political embodiment of a certain form of class-domination, corresponding to a certain set of economic relationships, which in turn arises out of a certain stage in the development of the powers of production. Accordingly, the State is, in Marx's theory, not an association of citizens bound together in pursuance of a common purpose, but essentially coercive, standing for the power of the ruling class to punish all offences which threaten the established system of class-relationships. Any State has, of course, other functions besides these; but the other functions are, in Marx's view, secondary. The fundamental purpose of the State, in terms of which alone it can be correctly defined, is class-coercion.

It follows from this that the forms of State organisation upon which Marxists chiefly concentrate their attention are those which most clearly embody this coercive character. Whereas other thinkers dwell mainly upon the existence of representative institutions, the extent of the franchise, the growth of the modern State as an instrument for the provision of common services, the Marxists think of it chiefly as a set of institutions for the maintenance of the capitalist system of property-holding, the punishment of subverters of the established order, and the coercion of the proletariat to labour in the service of the capitalist class. The law courts, the police, and the armed forces loom as large as the legislative body in this conception of the State; and the legislative body itself—King, Lords and Commons, or whatever it may be—is thought of less as an authority for the passing of fresh legislation than as the authority under whose auspices the existing body of legislation has been enacted, to serve as the instrument of the existing dominant class. Emphasis is therefore laid rather on those features of the legislative machine which check or prevent radical legislation—the powers of the Second Chamber, and the Royal Prerogative—than on those which make possible the introduction of changes into the existing system of law.

This does not mean that Marx or his followers deny the possibility of securing progressive legislation from the capitalist State. On the contrary, Marx was well aware of the growth of such legislation; and all the programmes of the bodies which he led or inspired were full of demands for more. He believed it to be entirely possible to bring pressure to bear upon the capitalist State, and to secure social legislation by this method, at any rate at the stage of a Capitalism still advancing in wealth and prosperity. He believed, further, that the struggle for such measures of social amelioration formed, at that stage, a vital part of the training of the proletariat in solidarity and class-consciousness. But he did not believe that the cumulative effect of measures of this sort could be a change of system, or that such methods could be employed for the attainment of Socialism, or to any extent inconsistent with the maintenance of Capitalism as a working system. For such ends as the establishment of a new social order he believed an utterly different method to be required.

PROLETARIAN DICTATORSHIP

This method was revolution, involving the complete destruction of the capitalist State, and the substitution for it of a quite different type of State made by the workers in the image

of their own needs, as the instrument of a proletarian dictatorship. The establishment of this new State would involve not
only the setting up of a totally new legislative authority, rest-
ing directly on the organised economic power of the working
class, but also the establishment of a new proletarian judiciary
and code of law, a new proletarian police and military force,
a new proletarian Civil Service, both national and local—all
under the authority of a proletarian party organised as a new
governing class. It was equally inconceivable to Marx that the
Socialists should attempt to govern, after their victory, through
a Parliament of the *bourgeois* type, and that they should leave
the old judiciary in possession, or the armed forces and the
police under their old leaders. He envisaged, at the very outset of the Revolution, the complete smashing and putting out
of action of all the coercive machinery of the capitalist State,
and the setting up in its place of a wholly new organisation, conceived throughout in accordance with the needs and interests
of the proletariat organised as a ruling class.

The Civil War in France, in which Marx passes in review
the successive phases of the Paris Commune of 1871, clearly
brings out this point of view. When Marx praises the Commune, it is for destroying the institutions of the *bourgeois* State
and establishing instead new institutions of its own on a definitely proletarian basis. When he blames, it is for not going
far enough or ruthlessly enough towards the immediate goal
of proletarian dictatorship.

Obviously, this view runs directly counter to the policy actually followed by the modern Social Democratic parties. These
parties, in the more advanced countries, set themselves not
only to work for meliorative legislation, as Marx himself desired, but also to use the capitalist State as an instrument for

the gradual establishment of Socialism by evolutionary means. That this was to be the method of Social Democracy was already plain enough in the Gotha Programme endorsed by both sections of German Socialists—Marxists and followers of Lassalle—in 1875; and that it was so was the gravamen of Marx's sweeping condemnation of the programme. For to his mind to think of the existing State as a politically democratic body and a possible instrument of Socialist construction was in itself a complete betrayal of the Socialist cause.

The Social Democrats, for their part, were looking at the State in a quite different way. They thought they saw it in process of being transformed gradually from an engine of class-coercion into an institution for social service—a grand Co-operative Society of all its citizens. They thought of the widening of the franchise, up to the final establishment of universal suffrage, as making the State an essentially democratic body, within which the anti-democratic powers of Crown and Second Chamber would not be able to stand out long against the popular will, and law courts, police, and armed forces would become, by a process of evolution, the loyal servants of a triumphant democracy. The first step was to give the people the vote; the second was to educate the people to use the vote aright; the third was to institute Socialism by a series of evolutionary changes under the sanction of the popular will.

Marx utterly rejected this conception. To his mind, there was, and could be under Capitalism, no such thing as "the people," which he regarded as a mere figment of the *petit bourgeois* imagination. There were classes, contending for power, exploiting and exploited; but there could be no "people," because social solidarity could not exist within the framework of a capitalist society. If the Socialists came to believe in the figment of "the people," and to base their electoral policy on an appeal to "the people," that would be the end of their chance of getting Socialism; for it would cause them to dilute their programme in order to win this mythical "people" to their side, instead of coming out plainly in support of a revolutionary attempt to substitute working class for capitalist dictatorship. It would cause them to try to use the capitalist State as an instrument of Socialist construction, instead of setting out to smash it and build on its ruins a new proletarian State of their own.

The "people," Marx held, can come into being only within the framework of a classless Society; for, as long as States exist, classes exist, and social solidarity does not. The entire conception of evolutionary Socialism, to be achieved by progressive modification of institutions under the auspices of a democratised parliamentary State, is therefore thoroughly un-Marxian, in the sense that it is in sharp opposition to what Marx said and thought. Socialism, Marx thought, would indeed come gradually; but Socialism, as distinct from mere social reform, could not begin to come until after the working-class Revolution had been successful in establishing the proletarian State. The Marxian conception of "gradualism" was that of a gradual development of Socialism under the authority of a proletarian dictatorship.

MARXISM AND SOCIAL DEMOCRACY

There have been many followers of Marx who, admitting that this was Marx's opinion, have argued that he would not have held to it if he had lived on into the age of Social Democracy's parliamentary advance. The master, they have said, formulated his essential doctrines before the modern democratic State had come into being, or even into view, before the great growth of social legislation and re-distribution of wealth through taxation, and before the advent of manhood or universal suffrage and popular education had created the possibility of a truly democratic electorate. They contend that, if he had lived on, he would have changed his views, and realised that the State was merely a piece of machinery capable of being used for the most diverse purposes, according to the ideas and class-affiliations of the persons placed in command of it by a democratic vote. Surely, they say, it is undeniably possible to convert a majority of the electorate to support the Socialist Party, and for a Government thus returned to power to make what use it pleases of the machinery of State, so as to effect the Socialist Revolution by strictly constitutional means, and avoid all the dislocations and dangers which are involved in revolution and the smashing of the existing State. What waste, to smash a perfectly good instrument, which has gone wrong only because it has been hitherto controlled by the wrong people!

This is, of course, the Fabian conception of the transition to Socialism, which profoundly influenced not only the German "Revisionists" at the opening of the twentieth century, but also their opponents who professed to remain true to the orthodox Marxian doctrines. It rests on a denial, not necessarily of the class-struggle—though it often comes to that—but of the idea that the State is to be regarded as essentially a class-institution, adapted to a particular sort of class-domination, and not adaptable for use in the interests of a different class or of a classless Society.

As we have seen, this evolutionary conception is always

defended by stressing the parliamentary nature of the State as a representative institution capable of becoming completely democratised. It is assumed that, in the existing state, the representative and democratic elements are in process of triumphing over the other elements, and will be strong enough, with the popular will behind them, to complete the extermination or subjection of these other elements—to destroy or democratise the Crown, the Second Chamber, and the judiciary and magistracy, and to exact in the name of democracy loyal obedience from the armed forces and the police. This, however, is precisely what Marx believed to be out of the question. He held that these other institutions of the capitalist State would be strong enough to resist the process of democratisation, and at need to destroy the democratic elements, as they had done in the course of the counter-revolutions which followed the "Year of Revolutions," 1848.

Moreover, Marx held that, if the Socialists attempted to conduct their political action on the basis of an appeal to the "people," rather than to the working class, and of an evolutionary instead of a revolutionary programme, they would inevitably fail to create among the proletariat the will and driving force requisite for the winning of Socialism. For Marx, though he has often been wrongly accused of preaching a fatalist doctrine, laid in fact overwhelming stress on the need for creating among the workers a vigorous revolutionary consciousness, and believed profoundly in the educative influence of the day-to-day class-struggle in bringing this consciousness to maturity. A policy of social peace seemed to him to stand in open contradiction to the revolutionary aim of Socialism, and to be therefore inadmissible as a Socialist technique. It might be necessary at times to step back, and it might be exceedingly foolish to promote a revolutionary outbreak that could, in the circumstances, be nothing more than an abortive *émeute,* because it lacked the support of the working class as a whole; but Marx held as firmly as he held any of his doctrines that the basic policy of Socialists must be to develop the class-consciousness of the workers into a revolutionary opposition to the capitalist State, and to make no compromise with the forces of Capitalism or with the *petite bourgeoisie* that might stand in the way of this consciousness.

In effect, Marx held that the capitalist State, while it might make compromises with the claims of the workers and admit real social reforms as long as it continued to rest upon an advancing and prosperous capitalist system in the economic field, would be bound in the end to turn upon the workers, and seek to intensify exploitation, as Capitalism passed into a phase of decline and was no longer able to reconcile the encroaching claims of the workers with its own need for an expanding volume of rent, interest and profits. He did not believe that Capitalism would be successfully superseded until it had arrived at this impasse; but he held that it was the task of the Socialists to prepare the working class for the advent of this final phase of Capitalism, and in the meantime to keep clear of all forms of entanglement with the responsibility for the successful working of Capitalism. For if, at the final hour of Capitalism, the workers should find themselves lacking the requisite Socialist leadership, the means for achieving the transition to a Socialist economy would be fatally wanting.

The Social Democrats, on the other hand, were apt to assume that their sole task was to take advantage of the opportunities for the promotion of democratic methods presented by the parliamentary system, and that the governing class would

permit itself to be constitutionally superseded by the political
party representing the workers, without any attempt either to
invoke against the advance of Socialism the non-democratic
elements in the capitalist State, or to seduce a sufficient part of
the popular electorate to render a Socialist majority unobtain-
able. They ignored the fact that the capitalist State possesses
large authoritarian elements, and that these can be so used as to
divide as well as forcibly resist the Socialist forces. They tended
to leave too much out of account the need of their working-
class followers for intermediate material victories as an earnest
of the coming change of system, and to rely far too exclusively
on an appeal to common humanity and reason rather than to an
organised following consisting primarily of proletarians. Moreover, in pursuit of this policy of social reform leading gradually
towards Socialism, they tended inevitably to find themselves
committed by implication to keeping Capitalism as prosperous
as possible pending their readiness to advance towards a Socialist system. This desire to keep capitalist industry successful was,
however, in sharp conflict with the task of building up a revolutionary consciousness among the workers; for it involved
damping down industrial unrest, and resisting working-class
demands whenever they were liable to interfere with the successful operation of the capitalist system. A Socialist movement
of this type found itself reluctant to make any rapid advance
towards Socialism, because of the dislocation of capitalist enterprise which continuous frontal attacks upon it were bound
to involve.

Thus, in face of Marx's clear-cut revolutionary doctrine, the
orthodox Social Democrats were. apt to find themselves engaged, not in attacking Capitalism, but in deliberately bolstering it up until they were ready to make a real advance in

the direction of Socialism. Nor is this policy, as an electoral method, without its advantages; for, on the whole, a larger fraction of the electorate is likely under ordinary conditions to vote Socialist in times of prosperity than in adverse times. Under the conditions of adversity, the majority of the organised workers may be as ready as ever to support the Socialist cause through thick and thin. But such support is likely to be weakened in times of bad trade by defections from the Trade Union ranks; and Trade Unionism itself inevitably tends to be less aggressive and more disposed to social peace, in times of adversity than when trade is good and employment plentiful and relatively secure. It is natural for the Trade Unions to long in bad times for the return of capitalist prosperity, which would enable them again to gain concessions and to increase their following by the winning of economic advances; and it is natural for a party dominated by Trade Union influence to be more concerned over restoring the conditions necessary for effective Trade Union bargaining than over building up proletarian consciousness even at the cost of aggravating the difficulties of Capitalism, and therewith multiplying its own difficulties as well.

When, however, a Socialist party definitely devotes itself to an attempt to make Capitalism prosperous, in order to increase the bargaining strength of its own supporters, it is hard for it to avoid placing itself in the power of the capitalist class. For the conditions requisite for the restoration of capitalist prosperity are likely to be quite irreconcilable with the simultaneous pursuit of a constructive Socialist policy. This contradiction arises chiefly because capitalist prosperity is largely a matter of capitalist "confidence"—confidence, that is, in the prospect of sustained profit-making. But a Socialist Government, if it pursues a Socialist policy, is committed to destroying as soon as it can the very foundations on which the opportunities for capitalist profit-making rest. It can therefore only secure capitalist confidence to the extent to which it is prepared to forswear Socialism, and can only press on with Socialist measures to the extent to which it is prepared to forswear capitalist confidence.

In this dilemma a Socialist party which is trying to rest on a wide basis of "popular" support rather than on a determined working-class following is readily driven to prefer the confidence of the capitalists to an attempt to advance towards Socialism in the teeth of their opposition, and at the cost of a depression resulting from their lack of confidence in its measures. It hopes by this method not only to reassure the more timid of its supporters among the middle classes, but also to command the assent of the Trade Union leaders by improving the conditions under which collective bargaining has to be carried on.

Where the circumstances are favourable to a revival of capitalist prosperity, there is no reason why a professedly Socialist Government which follows this policy should not govern a capitalist country quite as successfully in the capitalist interest as a capitalist Government could; for the less degree of confidence it is likely to inspire among the more stupid capitalists will be offset by its greater success in keeping the working class in order. But when the conditions are not favourable to a capitalist revival, a Government of this sort is bound to find itself in an impossible position. It cannot create capitalist confidence in the absence of favourable objective conditions: it dare not attempt Socialist measures for fear of provoking a crisis and estranging its own more timid followers: it cannot create favourable conditions for Trade Union bargaining, and so

expiate its failure to make a constructive advance towards
Socialism. It can, in effect, only dither, as the German Social
Democrats dithered after the war, and as the British Labour
Government dithered from 1929 to 1931.

Such a Government is lucky if it does nothing worse than
dither. For, if the economic circumstances are sufficiently adverse, it is likely to be faced by a revolt among its own working-
class followers, and to be compelled to choose, in the last resort,
between acting as the policeman of Capitalism against its own
adherents, and convicting itself of a sheer failure to govern—
unless, indeed, it is able and willing to revise its entire strategy
and come out boldly with a constructive Socialist programme.
Even in that event its lot is likely to be hard. For it will be
certain to forfeit a proportion of the "popular" support with
the aid of which it rose to power; and it will not have prepared
the workers for backing it up in an attempt to maintain its
authority on a definitely proletarian basis. It is, in fact, unlikely
to make the attempt: it is far more likely to break up in the
course of an internal quarrel about the right course to pursue,
and to be compelled ignominiously to resign and hand over
the task of bolstering up Capitalism to more appropriate defenders of the capitalist regime.

THE ESSENTIALS OF SOCIALIST POLICY

If this diagnosis is correct, it follows that Marx was correct,
at any rate in one part of his contention—that is, in holding
that no Socialist Party can make a firm advance towards Socialism unless it bases its authority, not on the "people," but on
a class-conscious and politically educated working class. It follows also that a Socialist Government which seeks to govern

by gaining the confidence of the capitalists is doomed to the complete stultification of its efforts. For how can the capitalists be expected to feel confidence in a Government of which the avowed and explicit intention is to supersede and dispossess them as rapidly as it can organise production upon an alternative basis? A Socialist Government in possession of the confidence of the capitalists is nothing less than a monstrosity. Either it does not really possess that confidence, or it is not really a Socialist Government.

This, however, does not mean that it is unimportant for a Socialist Government to keep capitalist institutions at work in every sphere which it is not prepared at once to take under its own operating control. Manifestly, it is important; for the collapse of capitalist industry before the Socialists were ready to take it over would result in a dislocation of economic life that might easily bring the Government down, on whatever foundations it might have attempted to rest its authority. But it is out of the question to keep capitalist industry running by winning the confidence of the capitalists. It must therefore be kept somehow running without that confidence—that is to say, by making the conditions even more unfavourable to the capitalist who closes his business down, or contracts its operations owing to his loss of confidence, than to the capitalist who maintains employment and output despite his dislike and distrust of the Socialist Government. This can be secured only if the Government is prepared to take over, confiscate and operate any useful businesses which their owners elect to close or to contract, and if, further, a strong control is promptly established over all businesses which are to be left in private hands during the earlier stages of the transition to Socialism.

The pursuit of such a policy implies strong and authoritative

Government, amenable to pressure from a working class demanding more wages and more employment rather than from a "popular" electorate which will certainly fall into conflicting factions at the first serious sign of trouble. It involves that the Government shall feel secure of solid backing from the greater part of the proletariat for its advanced policy; and this in turn involves that the proletariat shall have been educated in advance to expect a Government of this forthright type, and shall have consciously helped to place such a Government in power. For the Government will be impotent to govern on these terms unless the greater part of the proletariat is prepared to see it through.

So far, Marx was clearly right. But was he right in holding that this sort of Government would have to begin by revolutionary measures designed to smash entirely the *bourgeois* State, and then at once to build up a new proletarian State of its own, before it could even begin upon its constructive Socialist policy? The answer to this question is not so clear; for it raises at once two further questions. First, is it possible to win a parliamentary majority, and so capture the existing State machine, on the basis of a policy appealing directly to the proletariat rather than to the "people" as a whole? And secondly, even if this is possible, can such a Government successfully carry on its task without being compelled first to attack and overthrow those elements of the *bourgeois* State which are not directly amenable to conquest by means of a majority vote for the election of Members of Parliament?

Both these questions raise highly interesting and important points. On the first, it is clearly out of the question for the Socialists to secure a working majority in the "popular" Chamber by the votes of the manual workers alone. They must, if they are to climb to office by constitutional means, with a majority clearly behind them, attract a substantial number of voters from the black-coated proletariat and from various sections of the middle class, including if possible, the farmers. This, however, cannot be done if their appeal is limited to the Trade Unions, or to the manual workers as a whole. They must find issues wide enough to enlist the support of other elements as well, and do this without abandoning or diluting their essential working-class appeal.

This is by no means impossible, if the problem is tackled in the right way. For the appeal of a constructive Socialist policy does extend far beyond the manual workers, especially among technical, administrative and professional workers who can be made to see in Socialism expanding opportunities for the carrying on of their own types of service. It does appeal to the technician to see a chance of getting his industry rationalised, not for the purpose of contracting its output, but in order to enable it to pour out needed commodities in greater abundance. It does appeal to the administrator to see a prospect of straightening out the confusions and anomalies of the system within which Capitalism compels him to work. And it does appeal to the doctor to offer him the hope of a great crusade for the improvement of the health and living conditions of the entire population. Nor are the members of any of these callings deaf to the appeal of economic equality and of a classless Society, though this appeal has to wage war in their minds with the more familiar counter-appeals of snobbery and of the desire to retain a superior economic status.

In these circumstances, everything depends on how the case is put. But it is a great mistake to suppose that the more moderately Socialists state their case the more convincing they are.

For the moderate, or "gradualist," Socialist case is exceedingly apt to look like an advance confession of defeat, and to promise not Socialism, but only socialistic measures which are likely to hamper Capitalism without setting anything else in its place. The more clearly constructive the Socialist programme is, and the further it promises to go with rapidity towards the positive construction of a Socialist system that will work, the more likely is it to appeal to the sections of the population which are most capable of becoming the efficient allies of the manual workers in putting Socialism into effect.

There is, then, a real possibility of capturing the State machine, as far as it can be captured as the result of a parliamentary election, on the basis of a policy that is not mainly social reform, but constructive Socialism. But what is the prospect that the capture of a part of the legislative and executive machine in this way will suffice to equip the Socialists with an adequate instrument for carrying this policy into effect? Clearly, the House of Commons, or "popular" Chamber, is not the State; and there are narrow limits, even in the most democratic parliamentary system, to the power of the "popular" House to govern in opposition to the remaining elements in the State.

In this matter, conditions differ widely from country to country. In the United States, the first obstacle to be encountered would probably be the Supreme Court interpreting a written Constitution, on the assumption that the Presidency and both parts of the Legislature had already fallen into Socialist hands. In Great Britain, on the other hand, a Socialist majority in the House of Commons would have no written Constitution to deal with, but would come immediately up against the powers of the House of Lords and the still extensive prerogative of the Crown. In France, it would be necessary to control the Senate as well as the Chamber before any effective advance could be made; and the President, though he could probably be overridden if both Chambers were agreed, would have a considerable power to make himself "nasty" if he so desired. Everywhere the path of Socialism to political power involves far more than the simple conquest of a majority in the "popular" Chamber. It is bound to mean serious clashes with the elements in the State which are less susceptible to conquest by constitutional means.

Something, of course, depends on the strength of sentiment and opinion at the back of an incoming Socialist Government. Were this to be evidently strong enough to threaten serious trouble, the hostile elements in the State would doubtless be disposed to hold their hand, and to await a convenient opportunity before taking action. But if they were left in possession of their authority their opportunity would be certain to come; for, as omelettes cannot be made without breaking eggs, Socialism certainly cannot be introduced, either as a whole or by stages, without large dislocations of the social mechanism or without serious mistakes being made by the Socialists themselves. These dislocations and mistakes will afford the hostile elements in the State their chance; and unless the Socialists are prompt to meet the challenge, or even to anticipate it by taking the offensive, there are likely to be large masses of disgruntlement and discontent on which the forces inimical to Socialism will be able to call.

That this is so is the substance of Marx's case. He holds, in effect, that the Socialist Party, on assuming power, ought to proceed at once to the complete disarmament of all State forces likely to be able to offer effective opposition to its policy, from Crown and Second Chamber to judiciary and police, and to the armed forces. This does not necessarily imply any complete change of personnel in these branches of the State; but it does involve the drastic purging of their leadership, and the positive elimination of any elements which cannot be successfully purged by this method. The German Republic, though it did something to alter the leadership and personnel of the Prussian police, paid dearly for its mistake in leaving the judiciary in reactionary hands, and for allowing the *Reichswehr* to be officered for the most part by extreme reactionaries, and developed in the heart of the Republic as a potentially counter-revolutionary force, on which no Government of the Left could ever depend. On the other hand, both the Bolsheviks in Russia and the Nazis in Germany at once followed up their accession to power by a drastic purging and reorganisation of all the elements in the State that were suspect of hostility to their point of view. This process of *Gleichschaltung,* as it is called by the German Nazis, was pushed to the extreme limit in every branch of the public services, and was also extended by them into industry, the professions, the Churches, and every form of private association which seemed to them important for the secure establishment of their political and economic power. More slowly, and by less sensational methods, the Fascists carried through in Italy a similar process of political purgation.

In its more extreme forms, this method is evidently possible only under revolutionary conditions, and not for a Government endeavouring to govern on democratic lines. For in most parliamentary countries, there is a powerful tradition hostile to what is known as the "spoils system," or at any rate definite limits are set by tradition to its use. As the name implies, this tradition is designed primarily to prevent corruption and jobbery within an established parliamentary regime in which rival parties govern alternately. It has no real relevance to a situation in which the change of Government involves a change of system that is meant to be permanent and to exclude finally the return of the displaced tendency to power. But the tradition, once established, becomes powerful enough to present serious obstacles to a new party which comes to power by constitutional means, and thereafter endeavours to carry through what is in effect a social revolution by parliamentary procedure. For it is of the very essence of the parliamentary system to leave open the return to office of the opposite party, and therefore to assume that the rival parties are not divided by any fundamental difference of opinion about the proper constitution of the State. As long as this assumption can rightly be made, the "spoils system" is evidently an abuse; for it means the displacing of one group of persons by another on grounds not mainly of divergent policy but rather of sheer job-finding. But when the contending parties are fundamentally divided about the entire basis of government, it becomes impossible for either side to contemplate with equanimity the possible return of its opponent to office, or to carry through its policy with the aid of the same instruments as its opponent would be content to use. Under these circumstances, changes in the controlling personnel of the vital State services become indispensable to the carrying out of the Government's policy, and something analogous to the "spoils system" becomes inevitable.

It does not of course follow that this process of displacement has to be extended over the entire field. For example, it may be true that the British Civil Service as a whole has developed so high a degree of impartiality in carrying out the policies laid down for it by Ministers as to be capable of serving adequately a Socialist Government, subject only to a few changes in the occupancy of the leading positions in the various departments. This is, however, a wholly exceptional situation; and it is more than doubtful if the same can be said either of the judiciary and the local magistracy or of the armed forces or the leading persons in the police. A Socialist Government, if it intended to carry through a really extensive Socialist policy, would have to find executants who believed in such a policy for the key positions, and would have to safeguard itself against the risks of sabotage in high places and of possible counter-revolutionary action. But it would not find the taking of these steps at all easy, in face of the powerful parliamentary tradition against them; and in practice the attempt to establish Socialism by constitutional methods would almost certainly lead to a compromise upon these vital points.

The whole question goes, indeed, much deeper than appears at first sight. As we have seen, the assumption underlying the parliamentary system is that there exists always an "Opposition," which is capable of supplying an alternative Government should need arise, and that this "Opposition" has enough in common with the views of the Government to make the party game of the "ins" and the "outs" a workable affair. This is, however, quite impracticable when the rival policies differ in fundamentals. Under such circumstances, the aim of each side is bound to be the permanent exclusion from power of its opponents—and this is, in relation to the parliamentary system, an essentially revolutionary aim, which involves using power, however secured, to bring about such changes as will render the restoration of the displaced policy as difficult as possible, if not wholly impracticable. Such changes involve a drastic revision of the controlling personnel of every vital service.

It is on this ground that Marx rests his theory of the State, and his rejection of ordinary parliamentary action as the means of effecting the transition from Capitalism to Socialism. For such a change is so far-reaching in its effects that, however it begins, it is bound to develop into a revolution if it continues at all.

THE QUESTION OF REVOLUTION

The question then is whether a movement of this sort must begin as a revolution, or can begin as a constitutional assumption of political power, and then take on a revolutionary character in the actual process of carrying it into effect. The Communist view is that it must begin as well as develop, as a revolutionary movement, and that it is bound to be accompanied by violence because of the violent opposition which the present governing classes are certain to offer to its advance. The opposing "left wing" Socialist view is that, in the countries equipped with powerful parliamentary institutions, it can and should begin as a constitutional movement, and thereafter develop into a revolution under the aegis of its constitutional authority. It is noteworthy that both Mussolini and Hitler made considerable use of constitutional forms in carrying through their several revolutions. Mussolini, indeed, began with the revolutionary action of the "March on Rome"; but thereafter he was careful to execute his policy as far as possible in formal consistency with the law of the constitution. Hitler actually came to power under the guise of a constitutional

Prime Minister, at the head of a Coalition Government. Both
used the Constitution, wherever it was usable, to give formal sanction to what were in essence clearly revolutionary
acts and policies.

Both Hitler and Mussolini, equally with Lenin, were prompt,
having assumed power, both to purge the State machine of all
actually or potentially hostile elements, and, by their methods
of government, to render as nearly impossible as they could
the subsequent return of their opponents to power. Lenin,
indeed, simply destroyed the old State and built up, in accordance with Marx's precept, a totally new proletarian State in
its place; whereas both Mussolini and Hitler, aiming at far
less fundamental changes, preserved much more of the structure of the old State, and sought rather to make themselves
completely its masters than to tear it up by the roots. But even
in Germany and Italy the changes in State structure have
already gone very far, and are clearly destined to go much
further, involving, for example, the complete destruction of
the old parliamentary institutions, and the establishment of
a quite different form of government based on a decisive re-
pudiation of representative democracy. In this sphere the Fascists have been more drastic than the Russians, who claim to
be making democracy real and effective for the first time,
by giving it an economic basis. But the claim of the Fascists and
Nazis was that representative parliamentary institutions were
not of the State's essence, but a mere excrescence upon it. They
sought to recall the State from its declension into parliamentary
democracy to its historic character as an instrument of authority wielded from above; and they were able to build upon their
existing States more largely than Lenin precisely because this

coercive and authoritarian character did exist in the *bour-geois* State, even where it had been to some extent overlaid by the growth of parliamentarism.

We must conclude, then, that the extent to which a revolution needs to destroy the State, or even build upon it by a process of transformation rather than destruction, depends on the relation of the aims of the revolution to the essential character of the State in which it conquers power. Lenin could not use the Czarist State, because its essential character was that of a military and aristocratic autocracy with aims utterly inconsistent with his own. Hitler could use the German State, because there was much in it, inherited from the pre-war Empire, that could be adapted to serve his needs.

Can, then, European Socialists hope to use the States which now exist in their countries as instruments for the attainment of Socialism? The question is not easy to answer. Clearly the German Social Democrats failed to use the German State for this purpose, and were constantly checkmated in such attempts as they did make to advance towards Socialism by the resistances generated within the State structure. Still more clearly, they cannot use the Nazi State for this purpose, even if many of the controls which it has established over private groups and corporations are fully capable of being turned to Socialist ends. For the Nazi State is essentially a one-part State, which would be broken by the defeat of its ruling party. German Socialism or Communism, if it could come to power, might hereafter make a new State resembling the Nazi State in many vital respects. But it would have to be a new State, built on the ruins of the rival State which it would have to destroy in order to gain power.

The case is different in the parliamentary countries—as long as they remain parliamentary. For these States, while they retain their essentially *bourgeois* character, do embody considerable elements of democratic service as well as of coercive capitalist authority, and have been "liberalised" to such an extent as to accord, for the present, considerable rights to the Opposition. If they can be seized and controlled, there are forces in operation within them that are fully consistent with the purposes Socialists have in view. As long as these States continue to afford to the workers both certain positive services and a freedom of constitutional agitation, it is most unlikely that any frontal attack upon them will command general proletarian support. Only when the constitutional State, spurred on by the difficulties of capitalist profit-making in bad times, seeks to withdraw these real benefits, and meets the protests against their withdrawal by curtailing the freedom of agitation, is the main body of the workers at all likely to join in a frontal attack on the capitalist State, and to demand its suppression. Until that happens, they are likely to rally round a party which presents itself to them in constitutional guise, rather than one that preaches the necessity for a thorough destruction of the existing State as the prerequisite of all Socialist construction. For they are likely to hope for a continuity that will preserve without interruption those elements in the State as it is which they have learnt to value, while making away with those which are inconsistent with the changes they desire.

A new French or English Revolution would therefore, if parliamentarism holds in these countries, be most likely to begin in a strictly constitutional way, and to endeavour to amend, rather than end, the parliamentary State, using it meanwhile as an instrument in the positive work of Socialist construction. But this would be hard enough to carry through even if these States maintained their existing character unchanged up to the moment of the Socialist success in conquering power; and it might at any time be made impossible if the anti-Socialist parties, fearing the advent of Socialism by constitutional means, were themselves so to alter the structure of the State as to strengthen in it the authoritarian and anti-democratic elements, and so to make it less usable as an instrument of Socialist policy. In Great Britain, for example, a Conservative reform of the House of Lords might easily render quite impossible the execution of a Socialist policy within the limits of the Constitution; and in France a strengthening of the powers of President and Senate might have a similar effect.

If the structure of the State is, or becomes, such as to exclude an advance towards Socialism by constitutional means, there remains for the Socialists no recourse save a resort to unconstitutional action. For this reason, many opponents of Socialism are unwilling to see such questions as the reform of the House of Lords tackled at all. They have hopes of side-tracking a purely constitutional Socialist Government, and they fear that the taking away of the chance of constitutional action from the Socialists might lead to the development of a far more dangerous Socialist movement. But how long will such moderate counsels be listened to if the threat of Socialism is once felt to be imminent? In both Italy and Germany Fascism has provided the answer to the question by taking full power into its own hands, and using this power both to render the State proof against constitutional Socialism and to crush out remorselessly every form of organised opposition. Where this has been done, Marx's analysis unquestionably holds good, as it does wherever the State is of such a sort as to be beyond the reach of working-class or Socialist pressure. For there is under these conditions no alternative to a revolutionary method as well as a revolutionary objective, and no means of carrying out a Socialist policy without first destroying the old State, and seting up a new proletarian State in its stead.

CHAPTER VII

THE THEORY OF VALUE

EVERY THEORY of value I have ever heard of, with the single exception of the Marxian theory, has for its object the explanation of prices. But Marx's theory of value is so little a theory of prices that it is hard in the end to say whether it has any point of contact at all with prices. For it explains, or tries to explain, neither why prices are what they are, nor why they fluctuate; and such elucidation of these questions as Marx does attempt comes in quite a different part of his book from his account of value. In face of this fundamental difference of object, it is not surprising that economists who persist in criticising the Marxian theory of value on the assumption that it is a theory of prices succeed in demonstrating, to their own complete satisfaction, that as a theory of prices it makes sheer nonsense.

But, if the Marxian theory of value is not a theory of prices, what is it? If it does not seek to explain prices, what does it seek to explain? The answer is easy. It is an attempt to explain how labour is exploited under the capitalist system. It is a theory, not of prices, but of capitalist exploitation.

It follows that the Marxian theory of value is applicable only to capitalist societies, and does not apply to the process of value-creation under Socialism. Indeed, Marx holds, as we have seen earlier, that all social and economic theories are valid only in relation to the actual objective conditions which they are called into being to explain, and need re-making if they are to be invoked for the explanation of different social systems. Not only does the Marxian theory of value not explain prices at all: it seeks to explain value itself only within a certain limiting set of conditions.

But what is value, apart from prices? Up to a point, all economists recognise a distinction. But again the Marxian distinction differs from all the rest. To most modern economists value and price differ only in that price is value expressed in the dimensions of a particular currency—value in money form—whereas value is the quantitative exchange relationship between commodities as distinct from its monetary expression. x tons of coal $= y$ pounds of rubber $= z$ ounces of gold expresses the values of certain commodities in equivalent form, whereas x tons of coal $= £z$ expresses the value of one of these commodities in the form of a price.

Many of the earlier economists saw a good deal more than this in the distinction between value and price. For they thought of the prices of commodities as moving continually up and down in the market under the fluctuating influence of supply and demand, and yet as having a constant tendency to return to a particular price which was regarded as more "natural" or "normal" than any other, and as being the price that would exist if the forces of supply and demand were in perfect balance. To this "natural price," or rather to the exchange relationship underlying it, many of the earlier economists gave the name of "value," denying the name to the constantly fluctuating exchange relationships expressed in actual market prices. Of course, "values," in this more restricted sense, were not fixed, and were subject at any time to change; but they were thought of as changing far less often than ordinary market prices, and for quite different reasons—though changes in them would affect market prices by their influence on the balance of supply and demand.

Economists who defined value in this way all held that the "values," and the normal prices, of commodities were determined by the conditions of supply. They gave, from Adam Smith to John Stuart Mill, many varying explanations of the manner of this determination—from the simple view which represented values, and normal prices, as depending exclusively on the "amount of labour" expended in the production of a commodity to J. S. Mill's more complex "price of production" theory. With the soundness, or unsoundness, of these various views we are not at present concerned: all that concerns us now is that they were one and all advanced primarily with the object of explaining prices.

Value, then, in non-Marxian economic writings, means either market price stripped of its specific monetary expression, or normal price, similarly stripped, and regarded as depending on the conditions of supply. Since all non-Marxian economists have in modern times dropped the conception of a normal price so determined—though vestiges of the ancient doctrine are often to be found in their writings—we can say that in modern non-Marxian economics value = the exchange relationship expressed in market prices.

Marx, however, began writing at a time when the earlier conception of the nature of value was still dominant among orthodox economists, and was indeed practically unchallenged.

In 1867, when the first volume of *Das Kapital* was published, with its formal exposition of Marx's own theory of value, the position in this respect was not vitally changed. If Ricardo no longer dominated economic thinking, John Stuart Mill did; and Mill's theory of value was fundamentally only a modification of Ricardo's. Jevons, Wicksell and Menger had yet to propound their radically different theories: it was still generally assumed that values had to be equated to "normal" and not to "market" prices, and that normal prices were somehow determined by the conditions of supply, whereas market prices depended on the interaction of supply and demand.

Marx built his theory of value upon a critique of the orthodox theory of his own day. But, when he came to discuss prices, so far from seeking to show that there was any tendency for market prices to return to the level of natural or normal prices determined by the conditions of supply, he set out to demonstrate exactly the opposite—a point which his critics have almost unanimously ignored, and often bluntly denied in the face of Marx's explicit statements. Yet Marx's view of the forces determining prices is, in its essentials, nearer to the view held by modern economists than to that of the classical school. He holds that prices are determined by the interaction of supply and demand, and that there is and can be under Capitalism no tendency for commodities to return to a level of prices corresponding to their "values."

VALUES AND PRICES

This, however, has nothing directly to do with Marx's theory of value. For prices are, in the Marxian system, merely the methods of distributing value, which comes into being quite apart from them as a consequence of the labour process. The orthodox economists of the Ricardian school had contended that the values, by which they meant the normal prices, of commodities were determined by the amounts of labour incorporated in them. Ricardo did not hold this doctrine in an unqualified form —for he modified it in order to find room for interest on capital —but he did make it the basis of his general theory of value. Marx took the doctrine over from the Ricardians, as he took the dialectic over from Hegel, in order to apply it to a quite different purpose and endow it with an utterly different meaning. For in Marx's writings "value" came to mean what commodities were really worth in consequence of the amounts of labour incorporated in them, as something quite distinct from the prices which they actually fetched, or tended to fetch, in the market.

The Marxian theory of value begins in fact with a dogma— that, whatever may be the measure of prices, one thing alone— human labour—is capable of creating value. The productive powers of Society consist of two elements only—men, and the things which are at men's disposal. These things consist in part of natural objects, existing independently of men's minds and wills, and in part of things which men have created by changing the form of natural objects. No productive power exists at all without being embodied either in a man or in a thing which men can use. But the things men use, as far as they are not mere natural objects, are products of men's activity in the past. They are products of men's labour, acting upon natural objects. Capital, then, except to the extent to which it consists of natural objects, is a product of human labour, is simply human labour in a stored or accumulated form. But natural objects, merely as natural objects, have no value. They acquire value only by being mingled with men's labour upon them. Ricardo had, indeed, admitted that certain natural objects might possess a value, by which he meant a price, by virtue of their natural scarcity. But Marx, who does not mean "price" when he says "value," is under no necessity to admit this exception. Value consists, in his definition, of that which man adds by his efforts to what is conferred upon him by nature. Defined in this way, value is clearly neither more nor less than a product of human labour; for no commodity can be more than a mingling of human activity with natural objects.

Of course, "labour" in this connection must be understood as including every sort of human activity in the field of production. It includes the labour of the brain-worker and the organiser as well as that of the manual worker who engages in the physical task of transforming matter from one shape to another or of moving it from place to place. There is no distinction drawn at this stage between the different types of labourers, and no claim that the manual worker is more productive than the rest. The claim is simply that nothing except human labour in some form can add value to the resources which are at man's disposal by the sheer gift of nature.

Stated in this way, and released from its entanglement with the question of prices, the proposition is one that cannot possibly be denied. But there lurks in it an ambiguity, which Marx must be held responsible for failing to remove, though it is none of his creating. The ambiguity lies in the use of the term "value." Following the tradition set by Adam Smith and observed by the whole classical school of economists prior to Jevons and the Austrians, Marx distinguishes sharply between "use-value" and "exchange-value." "Use-value," or "value in use," is simply the qualitative utility of a commodity considered as an object of human desire; whereas "exchange-value" is the measure of its quantitative relationship to other commodities. In non-Marxian economics of the classical school, "exchange-value" corresponds to price, whereas "use-value" does not. In modern economics, of the schools which regard prices as depending upon utility, the distinction between "use-value" and "exchange-value" disappears, and the qualitative difference between commodities is transformed into a quantitative difference directly by means of prices. But for the classical economists this direct transformation does not take place. Nothing can be a commodity, or have an exchange-value or a price, unless it possesses use-value to make it an object of human desire. But this use-value is never regarded in a quantitative aspect: it is something which a thing either possesses or does not possess, and the amount or degree of it which a thing has is regarded as irrelevant to the determination of exchange-value or normal price, since these are determined by the conditions of supply and not by those of demand, which affects only day-to-day market prices as distinct from values.

Now, when it is said that value can be added to natural objects only by human labour, is the reference to use-value or to exchange-value? In the sense in which the term "exchange-value" is used by Ricardo and the other members of the classical school, the statement is not true of "exchange-value"; for other things besides human labour can add to the price at which a commodity tends to sell—that is, to its value in the Ricardian sense. Monopoly, for example, can do this, whether it takes the form of cornering the supply of a particular commodity or means of production, or of a scarcity in the supply of the means of expanding productive activity. That is to say, under a system of private ownership of the means of production and private appropriation of the product of industry, the cost of capital as well as the cost of labour affects exchange-value, in the sense of normal price.

Ricardo saw this, and attempted to modify his labour theory of value in order to meet the point. According to him, the exchange-value of commodities depended primarily on the amounts of labour incorporated in them, including of course the labour indirectly incorporated *via* the materials of which they were made and the wear and tear of the machinery employed in making them. But allowance had also to be made for the requisite inducement to the capitalist to apply his resources to production instead of consuming them, or in other words for interest on the capital used in industry at a sufficient rate to induce and maintain an adequate supply.

In arguing in this way, Ricardo was guilty, on the face of the matter, of a childish illogicality; for he was attempting to measure the values of commodities by the impossible feat of adding together the *amounts* of labour directly or indirectly incorporated in them and the *cost,* in terms of interest, of the capital employed in their production. But clearly an amount of labour and a money cost are incapable of being added together. This did not seem to Ricardo to matter, because he thought of the relative amounts of labour as in fact sufficiently measured by the wages paid to the different bodies of labourers, so that in effect the cost of labour was being added to the cost of capital in order to arrive at the value. John Stuart Mill made this explicit, by expressing the entire theory in terms of costs, or prices, in his "price of production" theory of value.

If, however, things other than labour enter into the determination of "value," in the sense of normal price, what becomes of the Marxian theory? It remains totally unaffected, because "value" in the Marxian sense is not equated to normal price. Thus the decline and fall of the classical theory of value, which has often been regarded as dragging down with it the Marxian system, does not in fact affect the validity of Marxism either the one way or the other.

The ambiguity, however, remains. For the "value" which human labour adds to natural objects is surely, in its fundamental aspect, "use-value" rather than "exchange-value," and modern economists are surely right in contending that "use-value" as well as "exchange-value" has a quantitative aspect. For, however hard it may be to measure the utility of one thing against that of another, we are in fact constantly performing this miracle, not only in the demand-prices we assign to different commodities, but whenever we choose between things, whether any question of a price arises or not. It may be objected that these valuations are purely subjective, unless and until they receive objectivity in the form of market prices. But the so-called "objectivity" of market valuations can be nothing more than the resultant of a number of private estimates, and cannot therefore be different in character from them. On the other hand, a valuation is not made any the less quantitative by being subjective.

Marx and the classical economists share the desire to objectify value, so as to find in it some validity underlying the subjective valuations of the market. The classical economists seek to achieve this result by objectifying prices, as natural or normal prices underlying the actual day-to-day prices arising in market transactions. Marx, on the other hand, seeks to objectify not prices but use-values, by transforming them into expressions of the quantities of human labour incorporated in various commodities. Thus, whereas for Ricardo "exchange-value" = objective price, for Marx "exchange-value" = objective use-value. And again, for an orthodox economist of the dominant modern school, exchange-value = objective use-value = price. But for Marx there is no equation involving prices in any form.

It may be objected to this view that there is no reason for supposing that the amounts of labour applied to the production of different commodities correspond in any way to the amounts of use-value which they possess. But there is. The rational object of all production is to produce use-values. If a certain amount of labour can be used in different ways so as to produce either a larger or a smaller amount of use-value, obviously the preferable use is that which will lead to the former result. Unless, then, the system of production is at this point wholly irrational, it will tend to prefer the creation of a larger to that of a smaller amount of use-value, and therefore to distribute productive resources in such a way as to achieve this result. The classical economists obscured this truth by treating normal prices as depending exclusively on conditions of supply; for the influence of demand is in fact the means whereby the tendency to prefer the creation of a greater amount of use-value is made effective. But this criticism of the classical school does not apply to Marx, whose notion of "socially necessary labour" includes an explicit reference to the importance of the demand-factor in achieving this result.

Marx's "value," or "exchange-value," is, then, neither the "exchange-value" of the classical economists nor that of the modern orthodox schools, but purely and simply objectified use-value. It is the real amount of objective utility which a commodity possesses as a result of the labour bestowed upon it under a system which tends to distribute the available resources of production so as to maximise the amount of use-value.

Again it may be objected that, whereas this might be the tendency of a socialised system of production, it is emphatically not the tendency inherent in the capitalist order. But this too is a misapprehension; for Capitalism, as far as it functions successfully as Capitalism, does tend to maximise the creation of use-values. The misapprehension arises from thinking of objective use-values in an absolute, or ideal, instead of a relative and concrete sense. Objective use-values are relative to the objective situation in which they are being created, that is, to the valuations of the social system in which they exist. If the capitalist system appears, from an absolute or ideal point of view, to fall far short, even when it is functioning most successfully, of creating the maximum amount of use-values for the satisfaction of human needs, that is because the object of Capitalism is not the satisfaction of all human needs in proportion to their urgency from an ideal standpoint, but the satisfaction of some needs—of the needs of capitalists—in preference to others. Capitalism, in other words, has its own scheme and calculus of "use-values"; and its success in maximising "use-values" must be judged in relation to this calculus, and not to any ideal standard.

It is, of course, true that Capitalism often falls far short of success in living up to its own standards. It is compelled, as a condition of survival, to make concessions to standards which it does not accept—witness the growth of the social services and of industrial legislation and Trade Union bargaining. And it has its breakdowns, when it not only throws millions of workers out of work and wages, but also makes the capitalist himself go short of his anticipated profit. But that is only to say that Capitalism does not work out wholly according to capitalist desires. Assuredly it has, through all its ups and downs, a tendency so to distribute productive resources as to maximise the creation of the objective use-values appropriate to the desires and needs of a capitalist society.

We can, then, regard Capitalism as tending to maximise objective use-value in a capitalist sense: and we can equate this objectified use-value with "exchange-value" in the Marxian sense. But why does Marx choose to call it "exchange-value," at the cost of getting it confused with the quite different "exchange-value" of the classical economists?

In one sense he does not call it "exchange-value," but rather "value" which is manifested only in the exchange relationship. His point here seems to be that things of different sorts assume a quantitative and comparable character only in their exchangeability, apart from which each use-value remains a thing apart, quite without ascertainable relation to any other. This view is based on the sharp distinction drawn between use-values and exchange-values by all the classical economists from the time of Adam Smith, and discarded only by the economists of the late nineteenth century. If Marx had been able to think of use-values as quantitative, some of the most confusing parts of the opening chapters of *Das Kapital* need never have been written.

THE SOURCE OF VALUE

The truth is that Marx's "value" is not really exchange-value, but something radically different, drawn directly from a realistic analysis of the conditions of production. There is at any time at men's disposal a limited supply of energy for working upon the available non-human resources of production. The using up of any part of this energy in the making of particular goods or the rendering of particular services leaves so much the less available for all other uses. It is a transformation into particular use-values of a part of the available supply of use-value-producing energy. This energy is the source of the use-values generated by its consumption: it alone has the power to create value. But clearly it can be so used as to create either a greater or a less amount of use-value; and the object must be, within the limitations stressed earlier in this chapter, to employ it to create as much as possible. Capitalist Society uses the price-system as the means of bringing about this optimum distribution of productive resources, which in a monetary economy presents itself in the guise of the distribution that will create the greatest sum of money-values. Marx seeks to look behind the money form to the real value-creating resources of which it is necessary to arrange the distribution; and he finds these resources to be neither more nor less than the available supply of human labour. Accordingly, he proclaims that human labour is the sole source of the power to create value.

But, it may be objected, the value which is created is the result of using up, not only part of the limited supply of human labour, but also part of the no less limited supplies of available materials and instruments of production. In what sense can it be maintained that the labour which is used up creates value, whereas the materials and instruments of production do not?

It is, of course, true that animals and plants, as living beings, have the power to create. A sheep creates wool, and a tree leaves. Even the earth itself creates one thing out of another, when it gradually converts other substances to coal, or, with the air, causes crops to appear. But these acts of creation belong to nature, and are not of man's making. They are the forces which are available for man's use; for animals and plants, as well as lesser forms of organic matter, are by mankind relegated to the world of "nature," and set in contraposition to man as a creative agent. Men work upon animals and plants, as well as upon the earth itself, to make values. The values, when they are made, belong to men. The sheep creates wool, and the tree fruit; but men, in appropriating these gifts of nature to their own use, give them value.

The answer, therefore, is obvious. Materials and instruments of production and even animals and plants are, from the economic standpoint, passive things, which can create no values. They can doubtless preserve, and transfer to the commodities which they are used to make, such values as they possess for men; but they are clearly incapable of being themselves the creative agents of additional values. Mere things can never create values: that is the prerogative of human beings.

If, then, the materials and instruments of production cannot create, but can only transfer, values, it is left to inquire whence they have got the values which they are able to transfer. They get their values, Marx answers, from being themselves products of previous labour, each embodying the result of a past using up of some of the limited supply of this sole source of value. It is true that in each case we come ultimately to some element which is not a product of labour, but a part of the natural resources available for men's use. But in developed societies it is usually impossible to disentangle even in the rawest materials that which is the gift of nature from that which is the product of man's past labour upon natural objects. Marx does not deny that natural objects, even if no human labour has been spent upon them, can, where their supply is limited, have a price—an exchange-value in the classical sense. He does deny that they can possess value in his sense; for value in his sense *is* simply the character of being a product of labour.

But, non-Marxians object, the using up of a scarce[1] natural object or a scarce product of past labour is just as much a subtraction from what is left for all other uses as the using-up of a part of the available supply of labour. Surely then the owners of materials and instruments of production contribute just as much to the creation of value as the owners of labour-power; if value means exchange-value, in the sense of normal price under capitalist conditions of exchange, of course they do. For it is the entire basis of Capitalism to distribute the product of industry on precisely this assumption. But it is a very different thing to say that materials and instruments of production create value, and to say that *the owners of* these things create value. The first statement is wrong because it attributes a creative property to mere things; the second is wrong because it assumes that the fact of ownership can be in itself a source of value. Ownership is not a creative act, but a claim to share in the results of the creative acts of others. It is easy enough for a social system to exist in which the ownership of things is regarded as conferring a title to share in the product of industry, or even one in which the ownership of men confers a similar title. But no social system can make either things or the fact of ownership into positive agents of creation. The fact that ownership confers a recognised claim to appropriate value does not constitute the owner a creator, though of course he may be a creator if he works as well as owns.

There is, then, no inconsistency between the recognition that all the costs of production enter into prices, whether they arise

---

[1] "Scarce," in this context, of course means simply limited in supply.

out of the payment for labour or the claims of ownership, and the contention that human labour alone can be creative of value, because it alone is the using up of a scarce *active* agent of production. The amount of potential value in any Society is simply the amount of labour, including the surviving products of past labour, which is at that Society's disposal: the amount of actual value is that which is created by the actual expenditure of this labour. The Marxian theory of value is a theory, not of prices, but of the social distribution of the resources of production.

THE AMOUNT OF LABOUR

At this point, objection is taken on the ground that there is in fact no way of measuring the amount of labour. For labour is of many different sorts and qualities. An hour's labour of one man is not so good as an hour's labour of another, even within a single trade; and there is the greater difficulty of comparing labour of very different sorts. If we had to deal only with one sort of labour, we could doubtless express quantitatively the difference between the productivity of a good and a bad plumber, or cotton weaver, or electrician, or perhaps even bank manager or writer of books on economics—though the last two would present a problem. But how are we to compare quantitatively the labour of the plumber with that of the weaver or the bank manager? The differences are here surely qualitative, and not quantitative; and no process of reasoning can reduce them to quantitative terms.

To the orthodox economist, this problem presents no difficulties; for he solves it in exactly the same way as he has already solved the problem of quantitative comparison between different use-values. He compares the labour of the plumber and the bank-manager by comparing their remuneration, which he assumes to coincide with their productivity of value. But this method is not open to the Marxist, who is setting out to measure the productivity of labour in terms not of exchange-values in the classical sense, or of prices, but of value in the Marxian sense. Marx attempts to meet the difficulty by invoking his own form of the subsistence theory of wages, or rather a conception closely akin to it. The respective values of different kinds of labour coincide with the values which it is necessary to use up in order to produce a sufficient supply of each kind. If more values must be used up in order to produce a bank-manager, or rather a unit in a sufficient supply of bank-managers, than to produce a unit in a sufficient supply of cotton-weavers, the difference in the real unit cost of production is the measure of the difference in value.

I find this explanation unconvincing—as a complete explanation of the problem. It would be valid only if all kinds of human skill and productivity were producible at will, just as most commodities are producible, by an appropriate real expenditure of materials and means of production. It is valid, to the considerable extent to which this is true of the various kinds of technical competence—for skilled manual labour of many sorts as against unskilled labour, for example. But it ceases to be valid for any sort of skill or competence that men owe to their original endowment of mind or body, or to influences that cannot be brought within the field of commodity production, or multiplied at will. Probably Marx would have been prepared to accept this limitation, and to answer that he was speaking of labour-power only in its ordinary forms, as a commodity reproducible at will by an appropriate outlay.

Within this limit, Marx's explanation is clearly valid. For to the extent to which all labour-power is the product of an appropriate real expenditure of the means of life—as to some extent all labour-power is bound to be—the using up of any part of it is in effect the using up of the scarce use-values required for its production and maintenance. Thus, a decision to erect a power-station that calls for the labour of a thousand skilled mechanics for a year is a decision to use up more productive power than a decision to build a road with the aid of a thousand less skilled workers for the same period. The Russians, faced with an acute shortage of skilled labour, are to-day very conscious of this difference; but it is felt too in capitalist countries whenever there is a shortage of a particular kind of skilled labour. It arises, however, equally for the time being whether the form of labour of which there is a shortage is or is not capable of being reproduced by additional expenditure on training and education. Accordingly, it is not possible to contend that the "value" of all labour-power depends on the amount of the products of labour required for its production and maintenance; for clearly labour-power, when it has once been produced, has a productive quality which exists irrespective of the nature of the forces which produced it.

It would have been better, I think, if Marx had defined value not as the quality of being a product of labour, but rather as that which arises out of the expenditure of any scarce agent or instrument of production. This would not have upset his vital contention that value can be *created* only by positive human agency, and that things have the power only of transferring, and not of creating, value. But it would have enabled him to recognise that scarce natural objects can possess value apart from any contribution added to them by human labour, simply because they are scarce, and that forms of human labour-power which are not reproducible at will have a value which cannot be measured in the same terms as the value of ordinary acquired technical skill. Such a recognition would in no way have weakened Marx's argument, or have diminished the force of his contention that all values, however embodied, are ultimately social, in that they depend on the objective social situation in which they exist.

We can now come back to our question about the possibility of measuring the amount of available labour-power. The analogy of "horse-power" has often been invoked in this connection—by Robert Owen, for example, in his *Report to the County of Lanark*. We measure the power of machines in terms of this abstract unit of mechanised energy: why not employ a similar unit for measuring the power of human labour? The analogy does not hold; for the one thing that horse-power is most obviously unable to measure is the power of actual horses.

If we could assume, with the classical economists, that things tend to sell at their values and that labour-power, which is bought and sold as a commodity, tends to sell at its value, so that the wages actually paid to different workers can be taken as measuring their varying productivities, we should have in wages a common standard for measuring the amount of labour. But Marx, as we have seen, explicitly denies that commodities do tend to sell at their "values" in his sense of the term, that is, at prices corresponding to the amounts of labour incorporated in them. Are we, then, to conclude that wages are of no help in measuring one kind of labour against another, or that labour-power differs from all other commodities in that it alone does tend to sell at its "value" in the Marxian sense?

Marx, I believe, did hold that labour-power possesses this exceptional characteristic. In order to understand why, we have to inquire why he holds that other commodities do not tend to sell at prices corresponding to the amounts of labour incorporated in them. The answer is that this lack of correspondence is due to what Marx calls the different "organic composition of capitals" in different branches of production. If all commodities were produced under identical conditions, with a precisely equal mingling of labour-power, materials and instruments of production, they would all tend to sell at their values in terms of the amounts of labour incorporated in them. But in fact the conditions of production differ widely from one branch of industry to another. One industry is highly mechanised, and uses up a great quantity of machinery in proportion to the amount of labour which it employs; while another industry relies far more largely on manual labour, and requires comparatively little fixed capital. Moreover, even when two industries mingle labour-power and machinery in equal proportions, one may involve a far greater lock-up of capital than another, because it uses more, or more costly, raw materials, or involves a longer period of turn-over before the outlay can be recovered. If the prices of commodities normally coincided with the amounts of labour incorporated in them, it would always pay better to employ much labour and little machinery, because a machine can only transfer to the product a value which it already possesses, whereas labour alone has the power to create value. In that case, technical progress would never arise under Capitalism, because it would always be against the interest of the capitalist to displace labour by machinery. Which is absurd; for notoriously Capitalism has thriven upon technical progress, and has been an active agent in forwarding the mechanisation of industry.

Yet it seems at first sight as if the truth of the Marxian theory of value carried with it the implication that it should pay better to spend money on that which possesses the power to create value than on what does not. According to Marx, the entire source of capitalist profit, and also of rent and interest under Capitalism, is to be found in the exploitation of labour. Profit, rent and interest together, with certain other elements which need not concern us now, Marx calls by the collective name of "surplus value," or rather he regards "surplus value" as forming the fund from which profit, rent and interest are entirely drawn. This "surplus value" consists wholly of the difference between the value which labour has the power of creating and the value which the capitalist has to pay away to the labourer in return for his service. Why this difference exists we shall have to inquire later; at present we are concerned only with the point that, if surplus value does arise entirely from labour, and if the object of capitalists is to appropriate as much surplus value as possible, it appears as if they ought greatly to prefer employing the labour which possesses this magical property to laying out their money on machines which can only transfer to the product the value which they already possess as the outcome of earlier labour processes.

THE DISTRIBUTION OF SURPLUS VALUE

Marx's answer is that surplus value constitutes a fund, divisible among all capitalists, but not accruing directly to the particular capitalist in whose factory it is brought to birth. All capitalists are in competition one with another to secure as much surplus-value as possible; and the system of prices is the means whereby the available amount of surplus-value is shared out among them. The share which each gets, *qua* owner of capital, tends to correspond to the total amount of capital which he embarks in production, irrespective of the ways in which the capital is expended as between the purchase of labour-power or of other requisites of production. For, if this were not so, capital would obviously flow in undue measure, in relation to demand, towards those branches of industry which offered the opportunity of appropriating the largest profits. But the effect of this would be to depress, through relative over-production, the prices of the goods produced in these branches of industry, and so to reduce the profits on the capital embarked in them. Thus, the ebb and flow of capital from industry to industry in search of surplus-value tends to bring about an equalisation of the expectation of profit in all branches of production. But this process is wholly inconsistent with any tendency for commodities, except those which are produced with precisely the average organic composition of capital, to sell at their values in terms of the amounts of labour which they embody.

Commodities would tend to sell at their values if they were all produced by capitals of the same organic composition. But they are not. On the other hand the commodity, labour-power, does tend to be produced under conditions in which differences in the organic composition of capital do not affect its production to any significant extent. Accordingly, labour-power does tend to be sold at its value, though other commodities do not, and differences in the wages paid to different workers do tend to reflect real differences in the values of different kinds of labour.

This seems to be the view underlying Marx's argument. Appreciation of this point helps incidentally to clear up a problem in Marx's presentation of his case that has puzzled many Marxian students. Why does Marx, in the first volume of *Das Kapital,* so often speak as if commodities did tend to sell at their values, whereas such a view is plainly inconsistent with his case, and he makes it abundantly clear later on in his book that they do not? The answer is that, in Volume I, Marx is concerned chiefly with the conditions governing the sale of labour-power, which he does hold to take place normally at its value, and he does not want to complicate his argument at that stage by introducing considerations more appropriately to be treated when he is dealing with questions of profits and prices. He does not say that commodities do tend to sell at their values: he only implies the existence of such a tendency when differences in the organic composition of capital are left aside.

To the extent to which labour-power tends to be bought and sold at its value, in the Marxian sense, apart from day-to-day fluctuations in its price, the wage-system, as a particular manifestation of the pricing process, does serve as a valid measure of the amount of labour, and does establish a quantitative measure for labour of qualitatively different types. Wages are thus unlike all other prices under the capitalist system, in that they do tend to be a valid phenomenal expression of real values.

THE SOURCE OF PROFIT

If, however, "labour" does tend to be sold at its value, whence can capitalist profit arise? Marx is at pains to show, in opposition to certain earlier anti-capitalist writers, that profit cannot arise out of any general tendency for capitalists to sell commodities for more than they are worth. For every bargain has two sides: it involves a buyer as well as a seller. If, then, things tended to be sold for more than their values, it would follow that they tended to be bought for more than their values as well. Conceivably the producers might in this way cheat the consumers; but this would involve the capitalists tending constantly to cheat themselves. For they spend in one way or another what they get; and presumably they would tend to lose as buyers whatever they stood to gain as sellers.

Marx concludes from this that, on the average, things must tend to sell at their values—a statement which has often been misinterpreted as implying a tendency for each class of goods to sell at its value. In fact, this is not implied at all, but only that on the average of all commodities values must be expressed in prices. For as the sum of values must be equal to the sum of goods and services available for purchase, and the sum of prices must be the aggregate price of the entire supply, it is clearly out of the question for the two to be different magnitudes. In the aggregate, things must sell at a total price expressing their total value; for, whatever the total of prices is, it can express nothing except this total value. It is, and must be, the money-name of the total value that is bought and sold.

Capitalist profit cannot, then, be the result of over-charging; for, if it were, the total of profit would be nil, as each gain would be balanced by an equivalent loss. It may be objected that the capitalists might still make a net profit at the expense of the wage-earners, by selling them things at too high a price. But Marx would reply that any attempt to do this would be bound to lead to a rise in money-wages, which are finally no more than the money-expression of the real values of the various forms of labour-power. The labourer's real wage is the quantity of goods and services which represents the value of his labour-power; and the capitalist has to pay him, apart from market fluctuation, enough money to buy this quantity of things. If, then, the capitalists tried to cheat the labourers by overcharging them, the effect in the end would be to raise money-wages so as to counteract the capitalists' gain.

We come back, then, to the original difficulty. If (a) the sum of commodities cannot be sold for more than its value, (b) labour-power tends to be sold at its value, (c) labour is the sole source of value, whence can capitalist profit arise? The Marxian theory of surplus value is an attempt to explain this paradox. In order to master Marx's explanation, it is necessary to understand the distinction which he draws between "labour" and "labour-power." The thing which the labourer has to sell, and is compelled to sell in order to supply himself with the means of living, is his "labour-power"—his power, by working upon things, to create value. This labour-power—and not, as under slave-systems, the labourer himself—is a commodity; and its "value" is determined in the same way as the "value" of other commodities, by the amount of "value" that is used up in its production. But "labour" itself, when it is actually being expended in the creation of value, is not a commodity; and the value of the product of labour is by no means the same thing as the value of the labour-power which is expended in making the product. The difference between these two values is surplus value.

In plainer terms, the capitalist has to pay the labourer as wages whatever is requisite in order to produce and maintain an adequate supply of the type of labour that is in question.

But the labourer sells, in return for his wage, his entire power to create value, subject only to such limitations as are involved in the terms of sale. Normally this means that the labourer produces more than is needed for his maintenance, in other words, that the value of his product exceeds the value expressed in his wage. The capitalists get their profits, and the landlords and money-lenders their rent and interest, out of this difference between the value of labour-power and the value of the product of labour. This, as we have seen, is surplus value, and the pricing process is the means by which it is distributed among the various capitalist claimants to profit, interest and rent.

This allegation that the entire capitalist system rests upon the exploitation of labour is the focal point of Marx's economic doctrine; and it therefore deserves the closest scrutiny. It appears, in the first place, to involve a strict adherence to the Subsistence Theory of Wages; for, if workers can receive wages in excess of what is needed for their maintenance, what certainty is there that Capitalism will be able to exploit them at all? May they not, by improving their bargaining strength, so raise their wages as to absorb the entire surplus value into their own remuneration?

THE SUBSISTENCE THEORY OF WAGES

Let us be clear, first of all, what the Subsistence Theory of Wages is. In the form in which it appears in Malthus, it is bound up entirely with the question of population. Wages tend to a physical subsistence level because as soon as they rise at all above this level more children are born, or survive, and the supply of labourers is before long so increased that their competition for work forces wages down again to subsistence level.

On the other hand, wages cannot fall for long below this level because, if they do fall below it, population is so reduced as to bring them up again because of the shortage of labour. In Ricardo, the substance of this doctrine remains; but its severity is modified so as to allow more room for the recognition of conventional standards of living. Population is still the chief factor in keeping wages at or about subsistence level; but this level itself can change if, in an advancing society, the growing demand for labour keeps wages above the old level long enough for the labourers to incorporate in their established expectations a higher standard of living, which will thus become the minimum needed to induce them to breed a sufficient supply of workers possessing the requisite qualities of strength and skill.

In Marx's version of the subsistence theory of wages, insistence on the conventional element in the subsistence standard becomes much stronger. The attempt to base the theory on the Malthusian dogma about population is abandoned; and so is the tendency of wages to subsistence level, in a purely physical sense. All subsistence levels are relative to a particular time and place, that is to say, to a conventional standard of living. The point to which wages tend is, then, not that which will just suffice to keep the labourer in health and physical energy, but that which, given the labourer's own state of mind and expectation of living conditions, will in fact induce him to give labour in the requisite quantity and quality to meet the capitalist's demands. If the established wage-standards are too low to induce him to do this, wages will have to rise, and the higher wages will then be incorporated in a higher subsistence standard.

Of course, it must be understood that, in Marx's sense, the

wages which tend to subsistence level are not merely those of the least skilled and worst paid labourers, but equally those of the better paid workers. For the subsistence wage is the wage needed to secure an adequate supply of any given class of labour, and the higher equally with the lower wage-rates fall within this definition. A subsistence wage, in the Marxian sense, is in fact little more than the wage fixed by the forces of supply and demand for the commodity, labour-power, in any of its specialised forms. As we have seen, Marx holds that, as labour-power tends to sell at its value, the differences between the wages of the various kinds of workers tend in fact to coincide with the differences in the real costs of producing them in the necessary quantities. But the "real cost" of production of the labourer includes a psychological element; for it depends in part on the labourer's own estimate of what he is worth.

In these circumstances, does not any wage that is paid under Capitalism, unless it is due to quite exceptional and transient circumstances, become a "subsistence wage"? The answer is that it does. The only wages that are not, for Marx, subsistence wages are those which are due to a temporary market shortage, or redundancy, of labour. But, if this is so, why should not the workers, by raising their psychological standards and refusing to supply labour-power save at a higher price, absorb the surplus value which the capitalists now appropriate?

Marx's answer is twofold. It is, first, that a rise in the demand-price of labour tends to cause less of it to be bought, unless it can be made by some other adjustment of conditions to yield as much surplus value as before. But if less is bought, this will mean unemployment, which will reduce the workers' bargaining power, and compel them to readjust their psychological valuation of the commodity which they have to sell. For the bargaining power of the workers under Capitalism depends on the state of the labour market; and the workers can raise effectively their psychological valuation of their own labour-power only in conditions which make it worth the capitalists' while to pay more for it. In other words, only an advancing Capitalism can concede rising wage-standards. For the capitalist system depends for its working on the profit-incentive offered to the capitalist, and therefore on the continued manufacture of surplus value on a sufficient scale.

In the second place, the capitalist and the labourer are not on equal bargaining terms. Economic progress under Capitalism consists of an advancing "socialisation" of the process of production, based on the fact that the combined labour of a number of men in a complex industrial unit can be made more productive than the isolated labours of the same number of separate individuals. This progressive "socialisation" of the labour process is one aspect of the growth of Capitalism. But this same development, seen from another angle, consists of the progressive expropriation of the individual and small-scale producers from the ownership and control of the instruments of production. Beaten by the superior efficiency of combined production, these smaller producers go to the wall, and are compelled to surrender their independent power to produce value. They become wage-workers within the capitalist system—"detail-labourers" who have no individual product of their own, but are contributors only to an essentially social process of production. As this happens, whoever controls the new and more efficient instruments of production is in a position to hire labour at a wage-standard set by the lower productive capacities which are being superseded, and to appropriate for himself the increased productivity which arises out of the growingly social character of the productive process. Under Capitalism, the main benefits of the growth of productive "co-operation" accrue, not to the workers, but to the capitalist owners of the means of production. No amount of collective bargaining through Trade Unions can counteract the influence of the capitalist monopoly of the means of production, so as to enable the labourer to bargain with the capitalist on equal terms.

This being so, the power of the labourers to raise the subsistence level of wages is limited by the pace of capitalist development. Wages can advance, as long as Capitalism can advance from economic triumph to triumph; but the power of the workers is only that of taking full advantage of such opportunities for raising the wage-level as the advance of Capitalism affords. They may take or miss such chances; but they cannot by mere will-power create chances which do not independently exist.

Under Capitalism, labour-power must have this property of creating values beyond the value which it possesses as a commodity; for otherwise there would be no inducement at all to buy it. But labour conditions under Capitalism can improve; and Marx fully recognised at the time when he was writing that improvements were actually coming about. These improvements had always a tendency to diminish the ease with which it was possible for the capitalists to appropriate surplus value; but there were also means at hand whereby the capitalists were able to counteract this tendency. Marx concentrated his study of the rival forces tending to the improvement of labour conditions on the one hand and the maintenance of surplus value on the other mainly round the question of the length of the working day; for it was above all upon this issue that the industrial struggles of the early nineteenth century had turned. This accounts for the form in which Marx presents his doctrine of surplus value, though the doctrine itself is independent of the particular form in which he sets it out.

According to Marx's presentation, the labourer, in selling his labour-power to the capitalist, contracts to work in his service for the normal working day of so many hours. After working a certain number of hours, he has created enough value to meet the real cost of his own subsistence, and thus to cover the wages which he receives. But his obligation does not end there; for he has still to work for the capitalist the remaining hours of the normal working day. In this form the doctrine presents the worker as working so many hours for his own subsistence—"necessary labour time," in Marx's phrase—and so many hours at the creation of surplus value—"surplus labour time." It is of course only a way of presentation thus to split the working day into hours: the point is that in the course of the day the worker produces more value than he receives.

But now the workers, aided to some extent by other elements in society, begin to struggle for a shorter working day, and succeed in getting the hours of labour reduced by legislation, or collective bargaining, or both. They could not do this at all unless Capitalism could afford it; but even so the effect of the shorter working day must be, if other things remain equal, to reduce the surplus value accruing to the capitalist. What, then, can the capitalist do? There are two resources open to him. In the first place, he can seek to increase the productivity of labour by supplying it with more efficient machinery and in other ways improving the technique of production. To the extent to which this happens, the labourer will be able to reproduce his means of subsistence in a smaller number of working hours, and thus, if this reduction in the "necessary labour time" is equal to the reduction in the working day, to work as much "surplus labour time" as before. In that case, he will continue to produce for the capitalist as much surplus value as before; and this surplus value will be embodied in a greater quantity of goods. For a given amount of "value" is not a given quantity of goods, but the product of a given labour-time, and the "value" of commodities will therefore fall as the productivity of labour increases. The labourer, on the other hand, will receive as many goods as before for his subsistence; but he will receive less "value." Actually, of course, as productivity rises and the length of the working day is reduced, the conflicting forces may not balance. Either side may make a net gain or loss in the amount of value appropriated, within limits set on the one hand by the difficulty of overcoming the workers' resistance to a fall in their subsistence standard and on the other by the necessity of continuing to afford the capitalists a sufficient incentive to maintain the employment of labour.

THE PRODUCTIVITY OF LABOUR

It is essential at this point to observe the difference between the amount of "value" and the amount of commodities obtained by capitalists and labourers. An increase in productivity increases the volume of commodities available for distribution; but it does not increase the amount of "value"—for the change in productivity does not affect the amount of labour expended, on which the value depends. Accordingly, as productivity increases, it is perfectly possible for the real wages of the workers to increase even while the "value" of labour power is falling. The "value" of labour power rises only if wages are advancing

faster than productivity. Similarly, the capitalist may appropriate more commodities, but less value, as a result of a fall
in the working day. In face of rising productivity, it is unlikely
that either real wages or the amount of commodities appropriated by the capitalists will fall; but it is quite possible that
the value of labour power will fall. On the other hand, a reduction in the working day, accompanying a rise in productivity,
may reduce the amount of surplus value without reducing the
real profits of the capitalists below their previous level.

But an advance in productivity is not the only means of
counteracting the influence of a shorter working day. Faced
with a contraction in the total of the working day, the capitalist
will also seek to keep up the surplus value by causing the workers to labour more intensively than before. Marx distinguishes
sharply between an increase in output which is due to technical
advances in the processes of production—greater "productivity" of labour—and an increase which is due to harder work—
greater "intensity" of labour. The former adds to the supply
of commodities, but not to the amount of value, whereas the
latter increases both. For more intense labour is a greater
amount of labour, and is therefore productive of a greater value.
In Marx's view, the worker who works for an hour harder
than the pre-existing standard caused him to work works in
effect for more than an hour, and therefore produces more
than an hour's value.

Accordingly, when the intensity of labour is increased, normally wages will tend to rise in compensation for the additional
labour supplied. The previous proportions between necessary
labour time and surplus labour time will be undisturbed, and
the value of labour-power and the surplus value will retain the
same proportions as before. But the amount of commodities

appropriated by the capitalist, and also the amount of value, will be greater, unless the working day is reduced. Here then is another means open to the capitalist of counteracting any tendency for surplus value to fall off as the length of the working day is reduced.

These means may avail to keep up both the rate and the amount of surplus value. But they will not normally suffice to maintain the rate of profit. For normally any steps taken to increase productivity (and some steps designed to increase intensity as well) will involve changes in the organic composition of capital. The capitalist will get as much surplus value as before, or most likely more, out of each unit of labour that he employs; but in order to get it he will have to employ a larger mass of capital, over the whole of which this surplus value will have to be spread. For capital will demand its profit or interest, whether it is used to employ labour directly or to purchase machinery and other means of production upon which the labourer is to work. Accordingly, the rate of profit on the total capital will tend to fall unless the rate of surplus value on each unit of labour employed can be made to rise so fast as to offset the change in the organic composition of capital. Marx, in common with other economists of his time, believed firmly in the existence of a tendency towards a falling rate of profit on capital; but the explanation which he offered differed from other economists' in linking the fall directly to the continual change in the organic composition of capital.

Before we discuss this question further, it will be well to restate in Marx's own phraseology the gist of the foregoing argument, using as far as possible his own technical terms. According to him, the capital used in industry can be regarded as consisting of two elements—Constant Capital and Variable

Capital. Variable Capital is that which is spent in employing labour—that is, on wages and salaries. Constant Capital is what is spent on machinery, buildings, other instruments of production, materials, fuel—in fact, on anything and everything except the employment of labour. The two names, taken together, express Marx's view of the character of the value-creating process. Constant Capital is so called because it is spent on things which cannot create, but can only transfer, value. Its value therefore remains constant throughout the productive process in which it is expended. On the other hand, Variable Capital is so called because it is spent on something—labour-power—which creates more value than it costs to buy. Accordingly the value of this kind of capital varies: it emerges from the productive process more valuable than it went in.

SURPLUS VALUE AND PROFIT

Now the capitalist, as we have seen, reckons his profit on the total capital he expends, irrespective of the method of expending it. And profits do actually tend to be equalised, through the pricing process, over the total capital. But surplus value, which is the source of profit, arises, according to Marx's contention, only out of the use of capital in its "variable" form—that is, only out of the exploitation of labour. Marx, then, draws a sharp distinction between the rate of profit, which he defines just as his predecessors defined it, as a rate per cent on the total capital, and the rate of surplus value, which he calculates on the variable capital alone. If one employer locks up £100 in his business, and has £5 gain at the end of a year, we say his profit is at the rate of 5 per cent per annum. But suppose he spent £80 out of the £100 on raw materials and wear and tear of machinery and only £20 on wages, Marx would say that the rate of surplus value was not 5, but 25 per cent; for he would reckon it on the £20 alone.

If now the degree of mechanisation increases, so that wages account for only £10 out of every hundred, and other expenses for £90, each labourer who previously produced a value 25 per cent in excess of his wage will have to produce a value 50 per cent in excess, if the profit on the total capital is not to fall. Marx believes this to explain why Capitalism, in its attempts to counteract the tendency to a falling rate of profit, is always trying to increase the productivity of labour, and so to decrease the necessary labour time in which the worker reproduces the value of his subsistence, and leave more time available for the production of "*relative* surplus value," whereas "*absolute* surplus value" proceeds from the prolongation of the total working day. Increased intensity of labour thus adds to absolute surplus value, while increased productivity adds to relative surplus value.

But the increase in productivity is accomplished only by altering still further the organic composition of capital, so as to increase the proportion of Constant to Variable Capital. It therefore continually re-creates the problem of the falling rate of profit, by calling for a larger and larger total capital in order to set any given amount of labour in motion.

In considering the validity of this doctrine, it is necessary to ask first of all whether there is in reality any tendency for the rate of profit to fall. The classical economists all thought there was, as an observed fact which needed to be explained; but their data related chiefly to the rates of interest at which money could be borrowed at different periods rather than to profits in a strict sense. But the fall in interest rates was largely due to two factors—the increased plentifulness of capital as societies became more wealthy, and the reduced risks of lending as the capitalist system became more settled. The reduction of risk would not tend to reduce profits, but rather to increase them, if it stood alone. But the greater plentifulness of capital would tend to reduce the rate of profit, by driving capital into less productive uses than would be worth while if it were scarcer. Thus the increase in the wealth of Society, especially if the accumulation passes mainly into the hands of the rich, does tend, by making capital more abundant, to lower the rate of profit. But on the other hand this abundant supply of capital also tends, by making labour more productive, to reduce necessary labour time, to increase the production of surplus value, and thus to expand the opportunities for the profitable employment of capital. There seems so far to be no necessary reason for the one tendency to outweigh the other.

There is, indeed, no reason to suppose that, throughout the past century, the rate of profit has continued to fall, though it has tended to be higher in less than in more developed societies. But it is undeniable that the chief factor in preventing the fall in profits has been the expansive power of Capitalism, which has enabled it to find markets for its rapidly growing output in the less developed countries. For, without this power to expand, Capitalism must soon have encountered the difficulty that its ambition to maintain profits and opportunities for accumulation must conflict with its desire to find a market for a rapidly increasing output of goods and services. In the last resort, the size of the market for ultimate products must determine that of the market for capital; for capital is finally required only for the production of ultimate products. But, to a great extent, the capitalist wants not to spend his money on such products, but to accumulate it by investing it in additional instruments of production. His desire to get profits by keeping down wages is therefore in constant conflict with his desire to sell the growing product of industry. Marx saw in this most fundamental of the inherent contradictions of capitalist production the root cause of the final breakdown of the system, when once its power to overcome the difficulty for the time by finding markets and spheres of investment abroad began to wane.

This part of the Marxian doctrine, however, belongs rather to the theory of capitalist crises than to the theory of the normal working of the system. Normally, in Marx's view, the development of capitalist enterprise sets up a tendency for the rate of profit to fall, because as mechanisation increases larger and larger amounts of capital are used in setting a given amount of labour in motion, so that the surplus value derived entirely from the labour has to be spread thinner over these growing accumulations of capital. This does not mean that the total amount of profit tends to fall: on the contrary it grows steadily both as a quantity of commodities and as an amount of value. Increasing population provides a growing supply of labour-power, and thus swells the sum-total of value. Growing intensity of labour has the same effect, even if the working population is stationary. Increasing productivity reduces the necessary labour time, and thus adds to the amount and proportion of surplus value; and all these factors together increase the total real wealth of commodities and services. Against these forces is arrayed the demand for a shorter working day, which will decrease the sum-total of value, save to the extent to which it is counteracted by an increase in the working population or by a greater intensity of labour. And there is also arrayed against them the pressure of the labourers for a higher level of subsistence, which will have the effect of increasing the necessary labour time and decreasing the surplus labour time available for the creation of surplus value.

Marx thinks that the normal resultant of these forces is a falling rate of profit, but a rising rate of surplus value. In other words, he thinks that the effects of a shorter working day in reducing the rate of surplus value will normally be outweighed by the reduction in necessary labour time due to increasing productivity, and that the labourers will not normally be able so to raise their subsistence level as to redress the balance. But he also holds that the increase in the rate of surplus value will not normally be enough to prevent a fall in the rate of profit as the total mass of capital increases and a far larger amount is used in proportion to the amount of labour. Both these judgments are evidently not logical necessities, applying to Capitalism at every phase of its development, but probable conclusions based on an attempt to measure the relative strength of conflicting forces. It is quite possible to reach a different judgment on either point in relation to a particular phase of capitalist growth, without questioning any fundamental doctrine of Marxism. In fact, either or both may be true of Capitalism at one phase of development, such as the phase of British Capitalism in the early nineteenth century, which Marx was chiefly observing, and not be true of it at another phase, owing to a change in the exact balance of the opposing forces.

It may, however, be contended that Marx's two conclusions are valid, not for Capitalism at every phase, but as statements of what is absolutely bound to happen to it in the long run. For, in the first place, the bargaining strength of the labourers clearly depends on the demand for labour in relation to the supply, and the growth of mechanisation is continually reducing the quantity of labour needed for the production of a given quantity of goods. If the demand for goods expands fast enough to offset this influence, there need be no decrease in the labourers' bargaining strength. But this condition requires a very rapid expansion indeed; and whence is this expansion to come? It cannot come from the capitalists; for the limits to their consumption of mass-produced goods are soon reached, and their desire is to find means for the creation of further surplus values through investment rather than to consume. It can come from the workers only if wages rise so as not merely to represent as much value as before, despite the fall in the value required for keeping up the established level of subsistence, but also to encroach on the surplus value previously appropriated by the capitalists. But is this possible? The individual capitalist cannot pay higher wages, except for more intense labour, without suffering defeat at the hands of his competitors; and accordingly capitalists always tend to keep wages as low as possible, even where the need is to raise them in order to expand consumption. As soon as Capitalism develops on an international scale, this condition applies through international competition to the capitalists of each country regarded as a combined group; for no national group of capitalists can afford to pay wages higher than those which exist in other countries save to the extent to which the national productivity is greater. But the demand for commodities cannot expand on a sufficient scale until wages have risen, and the labourers cannot be strong enough to enforce a sufficient rise in wages until the demand for commodities has expanded. Accordingly, in the long run Capitalism is bound to get caught in a vicious circle of low wages and inadequate demand.

CAPITALIST CONTRADICTIONS

This inherent contradiction of Capitalism need, however, manifest itself only in the long run. It will indeed appear speedily in the working of any capitalist system which is confined to a single country, and depends exclusively on the home market. But for a capitalist system which has scope for foreign trade and investment the nemesis may be long postponed. For the capitalists in such a country may create a demand for their goods abroad by successfully destroying the less developed industries of pre-capitalist or semi-capitalist countries, and by the investment of surplus resources in the development of such countries. This was on the whole the position of Great Britain in the latter half of the nineteenth century; and Marx has much to say about it in the third volume of *Das Kapital*.

Any such situation, however, is inherently unstable. For the more other countries develop economically, the more widely the same conditions are reproduced. Other countries come in their turn to depend for the maintenance of their Capitalisms on finding markets and spheres of investment abroad; and competition to exploit and develop the still undeveloped areas becomes more intense. This competition, as we saw, reacts on the home market; for it leads to competitive pressure to keep down the wage-level, and thus limits the growth of domestic demand. But at the same time it intensifies the efforts to make industry more productive, and thus increases the quantity of goods that can be produced. Greater productivity, however, in face of limited demand means decreased employment; and this further limits demand, and causes wages to be actually reduced by the competition of the labourers for jobs.

Critics of Marx have sometimes written as if he supposed that this state of affairs, plainly manifesting the inherent contradiction of Capitalism—its tendency at once to increase productivity and to restrict demand—would arise only when the whole world had become industrialised, so that there were no longer any backward areas to develop and exploit. But this is not Marx's view. The difficulty begins as soon as the competition among capitalists to secure a share of the market becomes severe; and it becomes critical as soon as the extent of economic development in the advanced countries makes it impossible to press forward the exploitation of the less advanced countries fast enough to meet all their needs. For at this point the conflict between rival Capitalisms becomes intense; and the Economic Imperialisms which have already grown up through the inner need of each developed country to expand come into conflict seriously one with another, and so lead on to wars which become world struggles endangering the very foundations of the capitalist system.

This question, in its relation to the historical tendency of Capitalism as a whole, is discussed in another chapter of this book. It has been introduced here only to the extent to which some mention of it arises necessarily out of the consideration of Marx's theory of value. That theory could not be adequately discussed without raising this question at all, because Marx's view of the inherent contradictions of capitalist production is bound up with his theory of profit, which in turn has to be understood in relation to his theory of surplus value. The reader is referred back to earlier chapters both for a fuller treatment of this problem of capitalist contradiction and for the consideration of the closely connected doctrines of the "concentration of capital" and the "increasing misery" of the working class.

The object of the present chapter has been only to get at what Marx really meant by his theory of value, and to reveal its intimate connection with the previous economic theories as a criticism of which Marx built it up. This has involved some passing of judgments upon the soundness of the theory at certain particular points; but the main object of this chapter has been expository rather than critical or constructive. In general, however, the conclusion is that the Marxian theory of value remains untouched by the criticisms which have been levelled against its fundamental validity, though there is much in its expression and in its secondary doctrines that is either invalid or of no importance to-day, sometimes because Marx never escaped from invalid assumptions which he took over from his predecessors, partly because circumstances have so changed that provisionally valid criticisms of an earlier phase of Capitalism have lost their meaning now, and partly because Marx never completely straightened out his own thinking, or escaped from ambiguities and uncertainties in his own mind. We cannot, however, be content to leave matters there; for if the Marxian theory of value has a living virtue in relation to our time, we must attempt to restate in terms appropriate to our own problems whatever of it we believe to be still valid and important, with such modifications and additions as are called for both by changes in the objective situation and by further development of economic thought. That this is difficult, and that the attempt will fall short of complete success, goes without saying. Nevertheless, the attempt has to be made.

CHAPTER VIII

THE THEORY OF VALUE
(continued)

VALUE, in the fundamental economic sense of the term, is scarcity. Valuable things are things which are scarce in relation to the quantities of them men would use if they could be had without effort. Anything that is capable of being scarce in this sense is capable of having a value. It follows that nothing has a value in itself, without reference to men's need or desire for it. All values are social; and no such thing as the "intrinsic value" of any commodity exists.

If no one needs or wants a thing, even if it can be had for nothing, that thing has no value, however much effort its production may have required. If humanity finally gave up war, the instruments of war could have no value, unless they were capable of being applied to other uses. Thus, the mere fact that a thing is a product of human labour does not suffice to give it value.[1]

But clearly no one in his senses will intentionally expend

[1] Marx recognises this when he says that only "socially necessary" labour is productive of value.

labour in making things that nobody wants, unless he does it either as part of a technical process of training, or because he takes pleasure in the activity itself, apart from its product. Bad water-colour paintings that nobody wants have no value, but the painting of them may give the artist pleasure. An uneatable pudding has no value, but its making may be part of the necessary expense of producing a cook. Apart from these special cases, the aim of all human labour is to produce things that are wanted, and cannot be had without effort. In other words, the general object of human labour is to produce values.

Human labour, in the wide sense which includes all human effort directed to the production of values, is scarce. There is not enough of it to produce all the things men would use if no effort were involved in their production. Accordingly, the production of any particular thing always involves the non-production of something else that could have been produced. The cost of producing a thing can therefore be reckoned in two ways—either as the actual expenditure of effort which its production involves, or as the forgoing of the alternative things that might have been produced with the same expenditure of effort.

Things whose production involves the same expenditure of effort have accordingly, subject to the reservation stated below, the same real cost; for their real cost is measured by the amount of effort, or productive power, that they use up. This is the truth underlying the contention that labour is the measure of value.

We cannot, however, conclude that things whose production has involved the same expenditure of effort have the same value. For, in the first place, the effort may have been well or ill applied to meeting the needs and desires of mankind, and secondly men's needs or desires may change between the time when the production of the thing is undertaken and the time when it passes into use. In either of these cases, its value depends on man's need or desire for it; and not on the cost of producing it.

All production is based on an estimate of future needs, nearer or more remote according to the nature of the economic system and of the commodity produced. The purpose of the economic system is always to select for production those things which are more needed, in preference to those which are needed less. But the conception of "need" is not absolute or ideal. It is always relative to the particular economic system in which the production is being undertaken. Under the capitalist system, need is equated to "effective demand," by which is meant the willingness and ability to expend money on the acquisition of a commodity. Capitalism thus recognises the possession of more money as carrying with it the existence of greater need. Capitalism takes no account of "needs" which cannot somehow find expression as effective demands.

Capitalist Economics is therefore based on the conception that effective demand is the sole measure of value. It equates value with market price, as determined by effective demand. Modern capitalist economists often go so far as to insist that the expenditure of effort involved in producing a commodity is wholly irrelevant to its value, which is derived exclusively from the effective demand for it. The nature of the effective demand will influence the amount of effort that will be put into making the commodity, and thus decide the amount of it that will be produced. But the cost of producing a thing will never determine how much people will be prepared to give for it; for that must depend on the intensity of their desire for it as against other things.

This was not the view of the earlier capitalist economists, who held that the value of things—meaning the exchange relationship with other things expressed in their "natural" or "normal" prices—depended on the conditions of their production. This view, however, was incapable of explaining why one thing was produced in preference to another; for, if value depended on the conditions of production and not on demand, the same value would be created by the same expenditure of effort, no matter what might be produced. This is of course plainly nonsensical. If all human effort were directed to producing fire-grates, and none to producing fuel to burn in them, the same value would not be created as if fire-grates and fuel were produced in balanced quantities. The term value has no meaning except in relation to some sort of need or desire.

But capitalist economics picks out one sort of need or desire —effective demand—and makes this alone the arbiter of value. Other economic systems, corresponding to other forms of economic society, could select other criteria instead, and thus give the term "value" a radically different meaning. Thus a purely Communistic Society might make its criterion its collective view of what was really most useful to men, and not what they were willing and able to pay for.

The criterion of effective demand has the obvious attraction that it enables every commodity to be measured against every other in terms of its price. The money offers which the possessors of money are willing to make for goods become the determinants of their relative values. In capitalist Societies goods always sell at their values, because their values are simply the non-monetary forms of the prices at which they sell. This way of measuring values is valid for capitalist Societies; for it measures them appropriately according to the capitalist standard.

The basis of this method of measuring values is the taking for granted of the money-incomes available for the buying of commodities. These incomes are assumed absolutely; for apart from them there could be no effective demand, and no values could come into existence. This is a legitimate assumption for capitalist economics; for capitalist economics is based on the existing system, and within that system money-incomes do actually exist.

Nevertheless, this assumption involves a contradiction; for actually these incomes come into existence only as a result of the productive processes which they are invoked to explain. Incomes are prices, are values in the capitalist sense: they are the prices set upon the factors of capitalist production. Or, where they are not this directly, they are derived from incomes which possess this character. No incomes can exist apart from production.

Capitalist economics recognises this fact at a second stage, when it goes on to explain incomes—as the prices of the factors of production—in the same terms as it has already employed in explaining prices in general. Wages, salaries, rent, interest and profits are all explained as prices derived from the prices which the possessors of effective demand are prepared to pay for goods and services. Thus incomes are derived from incomes, at the end of a fallaciously circular process of reasoning. In the end the incomes which have been taken for granted at first are explained; but the explanation is that they are derived from themselves.

This vicious circle of capitalist economics does not destroy its validity as an analysis of capitalist production. But it does reveal that the economics of capitalism is valid only for Capitalism and upon capitalist assumptions. Capitalist economics is a theoretical system built up within the assumptions of an existing capitalist world.

THE CRITIQUE OF CAPITALIST ECONOMICS

In order to make a critique of Capitalism, or of capitalist economic theories, it is necessary to go outside the assumptions of Capitalism. This involves going outside the assumption that effective demand, as it arises out of the distribution of incomes under Capitalism, can be regarded as a satisfactory measure of value. But if we reject this standard, what alternative standard can we adopt?

The quest for an absolute standard is vain; for any standard of value must be relative to a particular social system. We can criticise capitalist standards only by some other standard which is no less relative in its nature. For there can be no absolute standard of human needs or desires. Conceptions of what men need arise out of the social conditions in which they live; and what men actually desire is also relative to their social environment.

On this basis, certain alternative standards suggest themselves as relevant to the conditions of the modern world. With alternatives that are not relevant we need not concern ourselves here; for any useful critique of Capitalism must be in terms of real and practicable alternatives to it.

The first alternative is one that discards effective demand altogether as the measure of values, and accepts instead a collective estimate of human needs as its basis. Such a standard could be appropriate only to a Society in which the entire mechanism of production and distribution was under collective control, so that the Society itself decided collectively what to produce and how to distribute the product in accordance with its collective view of men's needs. Such a Society might institute unlimited free supply of certain kinds of goods; but for all other goods it would have to work by means of a rationing system. Its economic system would express the principle "To each according to the collective idea of his needs."

The second alternative is one that continues to accept effective demand as the means of distributing goods and services, but discards it as an independent and self-sufficient measure of values, and undertakes to control effective demand itself by collective regulation of the distribution of incomes. Such a standard would be appropriate only to a community in which the collective control of the incomes of the members was undertaken in accordance with a collective estimation of human needs. The Society itself would determine the distribution of incomes, leaving the business of deciding what to produce— whether actual production were collectively undertaken or not —to depend upon the preferences of the possessors of incomes, as it does under Capitalism. Such a Society would, by regulating incomes, dictate the general character of effective demand, but it would leave demand for particular commodities free to fluctuate within the general conditions so dictated. It would not involve either free distribution of some commodities, or rationing of others; and it would involve the continuance of a monetary economy.

Both these alternative standards differ essentially from the capitalist standard in refusing to take the existing distribution of incomes as a basis for the determination of values, and in setting up instead a standard based ultimately on collective control. They both discard the underlying assumptions of *laissez-faire*—the assumption of a fundamental economic harmony which exists in the absence of collective regulation. They both appeal from men as self-interested individuals to man as a social being. In this sense, they are both Socialist.

The difference between them is indeed at bottom a difference of mechanism, and not of principle. This can be seen from the obvious fact that a society might exist embodying both of them in part, without any friction or contradiction arising from their coexistence within a single system. There would be no inconsistency in a society deciding collectively to distribute certain goods freely without limit; and to ration others, while leaving yet others to be bought at a price within a system of incomes collectively settled and distributed. Indeed, it is plausible to suggest that any actual Socialist system is likely to rest on a combination of our two alternative standards.

But both these alternative standards are in sharp opposition to the standard of capitalist Society, because they both rest on a collectively determined conception of human needs. Now, it is formally possible that men might collectively decide that Capitalism is the best of all possible systems and the distribution of incomes under Capitalism the best possible distribution. In that case, the substitution of the Socialist for the capitalist standard would make no practical difference. Socialism and Capitalism, as opposites, would meet at the extreme. But this is possible only in a purely formal sense. Practically, it is quite impossible.

For, if once the appeal is made to a collective standard of valuation, or away from the standard which actually exists to any other, the existing distribution of incomes at once becomes irrelevant. It is no longer merely a question of taking an existing set of facts as a basis for economic analysis, but of deciding, within the practical opportunities which the situation presents, what alternative set of facts to substitute for them. Economics, as it can never establish universal truths beyond the merest truisms, inevitably becomes normative, and ceases to be primarily descriptive, as soon as it begins to question the standards accepted in the existing economic system. It prefers one standard to another, on grounds which are never purely economic, even if its preference has to conform to the economic requirements of the time. Accordingly, the critique of capitalist economics and of capitalist standards must rest on a belief in the practical desirability of an alternative economic system. For the alternative standard on which the critique is based can have no real content unless it is capable of being embodied in an alternative system.

Systems, however, come into being not of themselves, but as the result of active forces operating upon the objective situation. To any alternative standard of valuation that is to be historically valid there must therefore correspond a set of forces capable of bringing it to realisation. Any valid critique of capitalist economics must base itself not only upon an alternative theoretical doctrine, but also, and more fundamentally, upon a movement powerful enough to act as the agent in replacing Capitalism. But, in the economic situation of to-day, the only self-consistent alternative to Capitalism is some sort of Socialism—the substitution of social for individual and private control of the powers of production and distribution. The force corresponding to this alternative system, and capable of bringing it into being, is the working-class movement. The workers may indeed find allies in the struggle; but the working-class movement is the only possible point of focus for the forces capable of becoming the active agents in the supersession of the capitalist system. Any valid critique of capitalist economics must therefore be in terms appropriate to the aspirations of the working-class movement. In other words, it must logically be in essence a Socialist criticism. The standard by which it criticises capitalist economics must be that which Socialists are seeking to establish in place of the capitalist standard.

Now, the aspiration of the working-class is to cease to be a working-class. This does not mean that it wants to cease working, but that its aspiration is to lose the stigma of social and economic inferiority which at present attaches to it because of its work. The fundamental aim of all working-class movements, whether it be explicit or not, is to abolish class-distinctions, and to reorganise Society upon a classless foundation.

AN ALTERNATIVE STANDARD OF VALUE

The valid standard whereby to criticise capitalist economics must therefore be a standard appropriate to a classless Society. But a classless Society means, in the modern world, a Society in which the distribution of income is collectively controlled, as a political function of Society itself. It means further that this controlled distribution of incomes must be made on such a basis as to allow no room for the growth of class-differences. This does not necessarily involve absolute equality of incomes among all the members of Society; for it may allow scope for differences corresponding to recognised differences of social service. But it does involve that these differences shall not be so great, or so permanent, as to form a basis for the survival or reintroduction of a class system. To that extent at any rate, the appropriate system of distribution must be equalitarian, as to a great extent it already is in the Soviet Union.

An equalitarian system of distribution, even in this sense, is clearly out of the question unless the processes of production are brought decisively under collective control. For either incomes will continue to be distributed, as they are now, in connection with the productive processes, or they will not. If they do continue, the control of incomes will involve the control of production. If they do not, production will have to be carried on collectively, because the entire basis for its conduct in any other way will have been destroyed. The controlled distribution of incomes therefore carries with it the socialised control of production.

If, however, production and distribution are to be controlled in accordance with the requirements of a classless Society, the only possible standard of value for a Society organised upon this basis will be one of the collective estimation of human needs. Value will belong to things because Society holds them to be valuable. Value will become completely a socialised conception.

Under these conditions, the social conception of value will be embodied directly in the collective decisions about what is to be produced, and indirectly in the collective decisions about the distribution of income. Many things will be produced directly for collective use, or for free distribution among the members of the community. Every decision to produce such things will be a decision that it is worth while to produce them, in a double sense. It will mean both that they are worth the effort which their production involves, and that they are better worth this effort than any other products which could be pro-

duced by the same expenditure of effort. Society will have constantly to make such collective judgments of value, weighing
the value of things against the claims of leisure and against
the hypothetical value of other things which it decides not to
produce.

This is easily seen; but it is equally true that, when goods
continue to be produced for sale at a price, so that consumers
are left free to guide the course of production by deciding what
to buy and what to refrain from buying, collective judgments
of value will be involved, again in a double sense. For, first,
the distribution of income collectively established will of itself
profoundly influence the character of demand, so as to make
the relative demand for different products radically different
from that which exists to-day; and, secondly, Society, since
it controls production, will also control prices, and be in position to influence the direction of demand to any extent it may
desire by its policy in fixing the relative prices of different
goods. Thus, "individual effective demand," to the extent to
which it survives, will be itself a result of the controlled social
forces of the new collective system.

Under these conditions, on what will the collective estimates
of value be based? Clearly not, in any primary sense, on the
prices things will actually fetch in the market; for these will be
largely the controlled results of social decisions previously made.
Society will think of value as existing in commodities or products of any consumable sort only in a secondary sense, and
purely by virtue of the scarce factors of production which have
had to be used up in their manufacture. Value will be regarded
as belonging primarily to the means of production rather than
to the product, and above all as existing in human beings as
sources of productive energy. The value which will be pre-

dominant in the new Society will be the value of human labour. And human labour will have value, as it has now, because it is a scarce factor of production.

Ultimately, scarcity is of two kinds. Some things are scarce in the sense that the quantity of them that *can* be made available on any terms falls short of what men would demand if they could be had freely in unlimited supply. But the great majority of things are scarce only in the sense that their production involves an expenditure of human effort, which is itself scarce in the other sense. Thus the scarcity of things is in the great majority of cases only a manifestation of the scarcity of human labour. This, as we saw, is the fundamental truth behind the assertion that labour is the source and measure of value.

It is sometimes objected that the production of useful things involves an expenditure, not only of human effort, but also of raw materials and instruments of production, which must be equally a source of value. But these things are, as we saw, in the great majority of cases, themselves the results of a previous expenditure of human effort. The value which they represent is ultimately the value of the human effort which produced them, though the value of the things may no longer be equal to that of the effort which was applied to their production.

It is, however, true that in the last resort the processes of production go back to things provided by nature, which are not the products of human labour. Such natural goods can embody a value, if they are scarce in the first sense in relation to the quantities of them which men desire to use. Their value, being like all value social, in that it depends upon men's needs and desires, is created by Society itself, and exists in natural objects only by virtue of the entire activity of the Society in which they exist. For they are scarce, not absolutely, but only in relation to social demand. Above all, their value cannot be due to their ownership by any particular person or class of persons, though it may be appropriated by such persons or classes under a particular social system, and their prices may be enhanced as a result of monopolistic ownership. But, by the standard of a socialised system, their value is purely the expression of their scarcity in relation to social need. Thus if in a socialised system a choice has to be made between two possible acts of production, it will be a relevant consideration that one involves using up more of an inevitably scarce means of production than the other.

In any developed Society, it is often difficult to distinguish the value which belongs to natural objects from that which is the product of past human effort. The Ricardian theory of rent slipped up on this difficulty. For land, as it exists in any developed country, has incorporated in it the results of the labour of past generations. There is no possible means of distinguishing its original properties from those given to it by the expenditure of human labour.

Fortunately, it is not of the smallest importance to achieve this feat. For, if a thing exists, it does not matter in the least how it came into existence, from the standpoint of determining its value. The conception of value is of importance only in relation to things that are to be made in the future, and not to things that have been made in the past, save to the extent to which things that have been made serve as the means of making other things. The conception of price may be of a great importance in relation to consumable goods: that of value is of none at all, except within the assumptions of capitalist economics, in which value is equated to price. Value, as distinct from price, is an important conception only in relation to the using up of scarce real factors of production.

A socialised economy is necessarily a planned economy. It involves collective decision about what is to be produced. This collective decision is in fact a decision about the use of the scarce real factors of production, including both the available man-power and the raw materials, and the machines and other instruments of production already in being. Value, which is the power to create useful things, exists in all these factors of production. The magnitude of the value in any one thing depends on that of the utility which it can be used to create. But as the utility of a consumable thing can never be known until that thing actually reaches the stage of consumption, the actual utility that will result from the expenditure of a factor of production can never be accurately known. It can only be imputed, by anticipation, on the basis of a collective estimate of what Society is going to need. The value of the factors of production is thus always the outcome of a process of imputing the power to produce utilities.

In this process of imputation, the value of a factor of production must always be estimated on the basis of its use as a whole, to create the largest possible sum of utility—utility being measured, of course, by the collective standard of social need. Thus the value of a factor of production corresponds not to the utility which it actually produces, but to that which Society deems it to be capable of producing. This explains the divergence between the values used up in producing a thing and the value of the thing when it has been produced.

We have, then, a conception of value as existing primarily in the scarce factors of production, and only secondarily, and in a practically unimportant sense, in consumable goods. We have, further, the conception of Society as determining collectively the use of the values available to it, so as to produce the largest total of utilities in accordance with its collective estimation of human needs. Values, in this sense, are the scarce things which are used up in producing utilities.

But, it will be objected, if we once depart from the use of prices as a standard for the measurement of values, shall we be left with any standard that we can practically apply? Under Capitalism, all capitalist values are commensurable by means of prices; and this commensurability is the very basis on which capitalist economics rests. If we take this away, what is left? For the capitalist price-system enables us to measure, not merely one kind of labour against another, and one kind of goods against another, but also labour against goods, and both goods and labour against capital itself. Is not this commensurability essential to any sound judgment in economic matters? And, if so, is not this the final vindication of capitalist economics, and even of Capitalism itself?

Be it admitted at once that the capitalist system of prices, whereby all things are reduced to a money measure, possesses very great conveniences, and that it is so rooted in men's way of living in the modern world that in any change of system they are certain to retain much of its form, even if they alter its meaning. But while it is convenient to measure all things by a common standard, such measurement may be appropriate to one situation, but wholly inappropriate to another. Capitalism is able to measure men and things by the same standard, because it is based—though not in the same crude way as the slave system—on treating men as things. It can measure labour as a commodity, because it treats labour as a commodity. But if labour emancipates itself from this commodity status, it be-

comes by virtue of its emancipation incapable of being measured in commodity terms. A new standard of measurement
comes to be needed for measuring that which is being regarded
in an utterly different way.

In effect, under the changed conditions the value of labour-
power ceases to be a money-cost of production. As a consumer,
the labourer has now become a claimant to share, according
to his need, in the social dividend which comes out of production. His claim as a consumer has been divorced from his contribution as a producer, to the extent that his remuneration is
now determined socially, and not by the higgling of the labour
market. The value of his labour cannot therefore be measured
any longer by the wages which he receives; for the two magnitudes are now independent of each other. How then is the value
of his labour to be determined at all, in comparison with that
of other labourers? Or again, how is the value of his labour
to be made commensurable with that of the materials and instruments of production which he uses for the creation of
utilities?

THE PROBLEM OF SOCIALIST ACCOUNTANCY

This is the fundamental problem of the accountancy of a
socialised system; and it is no more possible to solve it fully
in advance than it was for pre-capitalist thinkers to anticipate
how the money-system would develop under Capitalism. For
theory follows facts, and cannot march ahead of facts into the
future. Humanity solves its social problems only when they
have been presented to it in a practical form. Consequently,
all we can hope to do at present is to decipher such partial
anticipations of the solution of this problem as are already

being offered by actual experience of socialisation. Obviously Russian experience is likely to offer the most significant suggestions.

The Russian experience is of special value for this purpose because the Soviet leaders have been faced so dramatically with the problem of scarcity. This scarcity is indeed neither of sheer human labour power nor of natural resources; for they have both these in plenty. The Russian scarcity has been above all of skilled labour and technical competence, and of a sufficient inheritance of means of production derived from past labour. The problem of production has therefore presented itself to them very plainly. It has made them realise that crude labour-power, as well as crude productive resources still undeveloped, has no present value. It has been brought home to them that inherited means of production, as well as skilled labour, have a very great present value. This has caused them to visualise their problem as above all that of using the presently valuable resources at their command in such a way as to realise as rapidly and fully as possible the potential value which exists in at present valueless labour and productive resources.

In seeking this end, the Russians have necessarily been concerned above all else with making the best possible distribution and use of their limited supplies of skilled labour and real capital in the form of productive resources. Their problem has been, in its fundamental character, inexpressible in money terms. Its valid units of accounting have been scarce workers and technicians and machines, and not the sums of money these factors of production are supposed to be worth. But throughout, as the heirs of a capitalist economy used to thinking in money terms, and recognising the convenience of money as a unit of account, they have been anxious to re-express in monetary language as many as possible of the judgments they have made about the use and distribution of the real factors of production.

Russian accounting, however, differs, and is bound to differ, radically from the accounting of capitalist Society. For the items of which it is made up are almost all controlled items, socially determined by one or another of the collective organs of the Soviet system. They are not prices arrived at by the higgling of a free market, but prices deliberately and to some extent arbitrarily imputed for the purpose of using them as units of account. Such prices are of vital importance in the system as "control prices," for the purpose of enabling the responsible authorities to discover how far the processes of production and distribution are actually going on according to the collective plans. But they have no independent validity, and no commensurability save as the expression of collective judgments made by the planning authorities themselves. They are in that sense arbitrary, and the responsible authority can alter or adjust them at will. Perhaps this can be put most clearly by saying that the profits or losses made by Soviet enterprises are always "accounting" profits or losses, and bear no necessary relation to the real efficiency of the enterprise. They measure its success or failure in living up to the expectations of the planning authorities which set the prices—that, and nothing else.

In other words, the commensurability in terms of money which appears to exist to a great extent in the Soviet economy is really an illusion. Things are, and must be, constantly measured one against another, and men against men, and men against things. But these measurements are actually made in terms of scarce real factors of production, and only turned into monetary expressions for convenience in accounting.

When capitalist economists discover this, they are apt to regard it as a sufficient reason for dismissing the entire Soviet experiment as economically unsound. But why? Individuals in their private lives are constantly making judgments about the use of their time which they cannot possibly translate into monetary terms. In pre-capitalist Societies, similar judgments were constantly made by peasant households (as indeed they are to-day), and by such institutions as the manor. Modern States and municipal bodies have to make the same sort of judgments whenever they are deciding what to undertake and what not to undertake in the sphere of commercially non-reproductive public works; for though such decisions involve the consideration of factors which can be expressed in terms of money they can never be based solely upon these considerations. Why cannot a whole economic system similarly rely in the last resort on judging between real things, instead of between monetary expressions which are supposed to stand in the place of real things?

Capitalist economy seeks inevitably to universalise the money-measure because it is based on private property and the individual appropriation of values under a system of exchange. Seeking to make all its means of production as well as all its products capable of exchange and of individual appropriation, it must try to make them all commensurable in money terms. But a socialised system, while it may retain the exchange of products in an amended form, will discard the exchange of the means of production. Apart from human labour, these will be socially owned, and therefore incapable of being exchanged; and there will be no need to place a money valuation upon them. For money is essentially relative to exchange. Labour itself will not be socially owned, but will be collectively the social owner of things; so that it will no more be bought and sold (save in a purely transitional stage) than the material means of production. Labour will have an income, but not a price; for the wage-system will have disappeared. There will, then, be no need to measure either labour-power or any other factor of production against consumable goods in terms of a common money standard.

But there will be a need to measure one kind of labour against another, and each kind of labour against the other factors of production. An example will make this plain. Without some standard by which this can be done, it would be impossible to decide when to introduce machinery in place of labour, or to prefer the use of one kind of labour to another, or how intensively to cultivate a particular piece of land. For this sort of measurement a socialised Society will have to discover and establish a standard; but there is no reason why its standard should be that of money. Indeed, there is every reason for using for such measurements a quite different standard from that which is employed for the pricing of exchangeable goods.

A SOCIAL STANDARD OF VALUE

This standard can be nothing else than that of productive power, or value. Society itself will establish this standard, to meet the requirements of the new system of production; and Society will sustain and work it by means of a continual process of collective decision. In correspondence with the requirements of an individualist economy, the price system under Capitalism undergoes constant adjustment under the influence of individuals exercising their power of effective demand. But in the collective economy the standard of value will be set not by individuals, but by the "collective," which will assign its appropriate value to each scarce factor of production, and constantly readjust its values in accordance with changes in the objective situation. Thus, if skilled engineers are scarce in relation to the collective need for them, a high valuation will be set upon their services in terms of the new collective standard; whereas if they become relatively abundant this valuation will be lowered by collective decision of the same authority as fixed it in the first place. Any enterprise which demands the services of highly valued workers or the use of highly valued implements or materials of production will be debited in the collective accounts with a proportionately high social cost, and expected to deliver a proportionately large sum-total of utilities. But the accounting charge on account of the scarce kinds of labour will bear no necessary relation to the incomes allowed by Society to the workers in question: nor will the prices charged for the goods produced be necessarily proportionate to the accounting costs of production, which will be expressed in terms of a totally different standard. Indeed, many of the products of industry will probably have no money prices, being produced either for collective use, or for free or rationed distribution, or for employment as means of production in further processes.

I am, of course, aware that these adumbrations of a new collective standard bear some resemblance to certain proposals put forward by various schools of currency reformers for adoption under the capitalist system. There have been proposals for an alternative currency standard, to be called the "erg," or unit of work-energy, or by some similar name; and there have been plans for a double standard, based on separating "money of account" from the "current money" supplied for use in ordinary retail transactions. This resemblance is not merely accidental. These monetary reformers are feeling, at one point, after a standard whereby to make a critique of existing economic conditions; and they are feeling after a real thing. But they make the mistake of supposing that their new standard can be grafted on to Capitalism, and used as a means of reforming Capitalism; whereas its entire validity is relative to a quite different economic system, based on the recognition of collectively estimated need, instead of effective demand, as the rationale of production. The energy unit, or unit of productive value, is a conception wholly appropriate to the accounting of a socialised economy; but it is entirely inapplicable to the practice or theory of the capitalist system.

Further than this it is, I believe, impossible to push the analysis of the new standard at the present stage. Its exact form and substance can be determined only in practice, in the course of growth of an actual socialised economy. But it is surely clear that the evolution of such a standard is fully possible, and that it can meet the need of a socialised economy for a means of estimating the real economic costs of different projects far more valid, in relation to the needs of such an economy, than any monetary standard could possibly be. For always and everywhere the root problem for a socialised economy will be that of distributing its available productive resources so as to yield the best possible return in terms of its own collective conception of social needs. In establishing its calculus of needs by a series of acts of collective judgment, it will be also inferentially setting values on all the scarce factors of production with the aid of which these needs will have to be met. Its valuation of the factors of production will thus follow from its estimates of social needs. It will of course be fully possible for the collective to go astray in making its estimates, both by estimating wrongly what men need or desire, and by misjudging the productive quality of this or that factor of production. But the possibility of such errors is inherent in the entire business of production, however it is organised. They are constantly being made and painfully corrected under Capitalism in relation not to need, but to effective demand; and they will be constantly made and corrected, it is reasonable to hope less painfully, under a collective economy. The utility of things made will inevitably diverge from the values used up in making them; but the entire collective system will be directed to making such errors as small as possible, and to eliminating them promptly when they occur. A collective system, worked on a basis of collectively estimated needs, will clearly be in a far better position both to anticipate and to correct than a capitalist system, working to meet an uncertain flow of individual effective demands, can possibly be. Nor will anything make more surely for successful planning than the severance, within a system of collective production and distribution, of the system of prices and incomes from the system of real costs involved in the using up of scarce factors of production.

THE EXPLOITATION OF LABOUR

From this point we can come back to our more immediate critique of capitalist economics and of the capitalist system. The fundamental tenet of the capitalist economists is that every factor of production does tend to be paid for at its value, in accordance with its specific productivity; and that accordingly it is nonsense to speak of the exploitation of labour. In a sense, this statement is perfectly true. Under Capitalism, the factors of production are put into competition one with another, so that each is employed and paid for up to the point at which it pays the capitalist better either to call a halt to further production or to employ some other factor of production instead. The remuneration paid for the use of the various factors does tend to be determined by their competition at the margin, in such a way as to make their marginal productivities equal; for if they were not equal, it would pay better to alter the proportions in which the various factors were employed. Of course, marginal productivity in this sense must be understood as referring entirely to productivity of money values, and not to quantity of output. It is therefore productivity in a purely capitalist sense, in relation to the capitalist standard of effective demand.

With the fact that this tendency towards equality of productiveness at the margin works out very imperfectly in practice I am not for the moment concerned. It is sufficient that it does exist as a tendency, and that its existence is vital to the working of the capitalist price-system in relation to the pricing of the factors of production. In a capitalist sense, as Marx showed long ago, labour is not exploited; for the commodity, labour-power, is paid for at its capitalist value. The exploitation of labour cannot be demonstrated within the circle of capitalist economic ideas, but only by going outside them and making a critique of capitalist economics and institutions in terms of an alternative standard.

This alternative standard we now possess, in a provisional form which suffices as the basis for a critique of Capitalism.

For the capitalist valuation of labour-power now appears to us as valid only within the assumptions of the capitalist system. It measures the productivity of labour on certain assumptions —that this productivity is to be measured in terms of money and not of physical product, and that labour, as a factor of production, is to be equated to all other factors in terms of a common money measurement.

As soon as we adopt the standpoint of a collective economy, these assumptions cease to be valid. For we are now considering the factors of production not as things privately owned and offered for sale, or used as the means of procuring private incomes, but as parts of a socially controlled supply of productive power, to be directed collectively in accordance with a collective estimate of social needs. All claims to productivity or value based upon private appropriation therefore disappear; and the production of value has to be considered from a social point of view—from the standpoint of a Society collectively attempting to make the best use of its productive resources.

Value in this sense exists in all the scarce factors of production, and not in living labour alone. For the most part these factors of production, apart from living labour, are the products of past living labour working upon things which would have no value—because they would have no scarcity—apart from the labour expended upon them. They are thus also products of labour, which has been incorporated in them. But their present value cannot be equated in any way to the amount of labour incorporated in them in the past: it depends entirely, like the value of living labour, on their anticipated potency in the creation of future utilities.

There are, however, certain natural goods which are scarce; and any natural good is capable of becoming scarce under certain objective conditions. Thus, unimproved land has no value in an undeveloped country, but it can acquire a value as it becomes scarce with the growth of population. All values belonging to natural objects by virtue of their scarcity are the creation of Society itself; for scarcity is essentially a social conception.

When a factor of production is scarce, it is irrelevant to its value whether it is a product of labour or not, or to what extent it mingles labour with purely natural resources. Its value is its scarcity: its scarcity is its value. The question of its origin does not arise in this connection.

Labour therefore is not the sole source, and still less is it the sole measure, of value, though it is by far the most important source and measure of value. Labour is, moreover, the source of value to which, in any normally working economic Society, the power actively to create new values exclusively belongs. Existing things have a value; but living labour creates new values whenever it is productively applied. It is true that the value of existing things—natural goods or instruments of production—can rise if they become scarcer with the growth of population or the development of the Society in which they exist. But to the extent to which their value is raised by positive action in the Society, it is due to the activity of living labour in creating new values. Similarly, the activity of living labour can lower or destroy the value of scarce natural objects, as when means are found of reproducing synthetically a scarce good previously available only in its natural state.

We can therefore legitimately speak of living labour—including of course all forms of human productive energy by hand or brain—as the sole *active* source of new values. It follows that labour is exploited, in the sense of receiving as the reward of its energy less value than it produces, unless the sum-total of the new values created in Society accrues to it. Capitalism, on the basis of its own standards, pays the labourer the full value of the productivity of the commodity, labour-power. But, on the basis of our collective or socialised standard of value, Capitalism definitely exploits the labourers by paying them collectively less than their collective product.

It may be answered that the labourers are constantly receiving a share, not only in the new values currently created, but also in the store of previously created values which is being used up, and that accordingly the existence of exploitation is not proved. But all previously created values, to the extent to which they are the products of past labour, were at some period new values created by labour, and labour has accordingly the same title to them as to the products of current labour. Moreover, such values as exist in natural goods by virtue of the social situation are, as we have seen, indirect products of the labour-process, and belong to labour by the same title as the rest. The exploitation of labour is therefore clear, in the light of the collective standard of value by which we have replaced the capitalist standard for the purpose of this critique.

THE SOCIAL DISTRIBUTION OF INCOMES

We are now explicitly criticising capitalist economics and the capitalist system of distribution, by the criterion of a standard which belongs not to Capitalism, but to a socialised economy. In doing this, we are *not* laying down how value ought to be distributed in such an economy, or making any claim that the labourer should have, under Socialism, a right to his entire product.

For, in the first place, we are dealing with the general exploitation of the class of labourers as a whole, and not with the wrongs of any particular labourer or group of labourers; and it is clearly impossible, under modern conditions of production, to determine in any save the capitalist sense what the value of the product of any particular labourer or group of labourers is. Value has become even under Capitalism essentially a social product; and only the capitalist method of estimating it in terms of marginal productivity serves to conceal its social character, and give a veneer of individualism to the social process of production.

Secondly, our socialised standard of value has nothing to do with the distribution of incomes. It is a standard for the right distribution of productive resources, and not for the repartition of the incomes arising out of production. Its standard of distribution, and its criterion of the worth-whileness of production, are based on collective estimates of need; and it is therefore irrelevant to its standard of distribution how much value this or that labourer is capable of producing. It would be wholly inconsistent with our collective standard to recognise any claim by the labourers to the whole produce of labour, save in the sense in which for a classless society the labourers and the community constitute an identical group. By our collective standard all value, however created, accrues to the Society as a whole, to be either consumed collectively, or distributed in accordance with the collective estimate of social needs.

The thesis that labour is exploited under Capitalism can thus be expressed in the following form. The capitalist pays the labourer the full capitalist value of his labour-power. But the capitalist value of labour-power is an utterly different thing from the social value of labour. Capitalist exploitation consists in applying to the remuneration of labour a capitalist standard, by equating the labourer to a commodity. The labourer, as soon as he repudiates this commodity valuation, sets up a claim to be judged by a different standard. Under Capitalism, this leads to a claim by the labourers to receive collectively the entire product of their labour. But such a claim arises only as an antithesis to the capitalist claim, within the class-struggles that develop in capitalist Society.

It has no relevance as a principle of distribution for a socialised economy, though the principle which serves the labourers under Capitalism as a fighting claim will find its true place in a socialised economy as a standard for the measurement of social value.

This I conceive to be correct development of the truth inherent in the Marxian theory of value. Expressed in this way, it appears stripped of the forms in which Marx set it out as a critique of the capitalist economics of the early nineteenth century, and reshaped as a critique of the capitalist economics of the twentieth century. As Marx built upon Ricardo, this post-Marxian theory builds, by way of criticism, upon the marginalist economics of the modern schools. It is twentieth-century Marxism—in any sense in which Marxism is not merely a meaningless repetition by rote of the phrases rather than the essential meanings of its founder.

THE INSTITUTIONAL BASIS OF CAPITALISM

This fact of capitalist exploitation can also be expressed in another way, not as critique of capitalist economics but as an historical interpretation of Capitalism itself. Obviously, the antithesis between the capitalist standard and the collective standard of value, which have been analysed in this chapter, rests upon the antithetical institutional shapes of capitalist and socialised economic systems. A socialised economy is an economy that rests upon the principle of social owner-ship and control of all the factors of production; whereas a capitalist economy is one that rests upon the rival prin-ciple of private ownership and control. For the socialised economy, there is but a single owner and controller of all the resources of production—the classless community itself. Ac-cordingly, there can be for this single owner only one standard of value and principle of production, the key to which is to be found in the single conception of social need. On the other hand, for the capitalist economy there is no such self-evident standard; for there are many owners and controllers each exert-ing his private claim and pull upon the forces of production. Capitalism has therefore to use the money system as a means of reducing to commensurability all the discrepant claims that exist within it; and, as a result of this reduction, its standard becomes one of effective monetary demand. Human claims are reduced to money claims; and the creative power of human labour is reduced to the commodity claims of vendible labour-power possessing a certain amount of marginal productivity, not of goods, but of money.

Private ownership is thus the institutional basis of Capi-talism, and is recognised under Capitalism as the only title to appropriate a share in the social product. The non-human means of production are privately owned and controlled; and the labourer has his claim only because he is regarded as the private owner of the commodity, labour-power.

Given this institutional basis of private ownership, in a Society subject to economic change and advancing in productive power as man's command over the forces of nature grows greater with the improvement of knowledge, it is inevitable that a large part of the economic benefits of growing productivity should accrue to the capitalist owners of the means of production. This does not mean that the owners of labour-power alone will secure no share in these benefits. They can and will; for in an advancing Society there will tend to be a growing demand for labour; and the labourers will be able to make some gains both by means of collective bargaining, when the barriers in the way of Trade Union organisation have been broken down, and, even in the absence of Trade Unions, by using their opportunities to shift from declining to expanding occupations, in which the brisk demand for workers will tend to make wages relatively high. In advancing capitalist countries, labour standards will improve; and some share in the growing wealth will pass to the exploited class.

But the class of labourers is always at a fatal disadvantage in relation to the capitalists in the struggle to appropriate a share in the benefits of advancing productivity. For the labourer must work in order to live; and his power to withhold his labour, while it can be increased by effective combination, is always and inevitably far more limited than the capitalists' power to hold out against him in the last resort. This does not prevent the labourers from gaining some victories; for on occasion the capitalists deem it more profitable and expedient to give way, if they are not pressed too far, or asked to sacrifice any vital part of their control. But it does mean that in the last resort the capitalists can always defeat the labourers, as long as the struggle remains purely economic, and is carried on upon the assumption of the continuance of Capitalism.

Moreover, the capitalist can shut his factory, not only in

consequence of a labour dispute, but whenever it suits him to do so. Whenever he does this, or curtails the number of his employees, he deprives some of the labourers of their incomes, by refusing to buy their labour-power. It follows that, if Capitalism is to afford the labourers their incomes, the capitalist must be offered a sufficient monetary incentive to keep the labourers employed. This necessity constantly sets limits to the power of the Trade Unions to secure higher wages or improved conditions of labour, and thus to lessen the degree of exploitation; and the limits become narrower when Capitalism becomes strongly competitive internationally, on a scale transcending the power of labour to organise effectively for collective bargaining or political pressure. In addition, as Capitalism develops, more and more capitalist claims upon the product of industry are converted into fixed claims to receive rent or interest, so that they become debts which the active capitalist *entrepreneur* has to meet. It then becomes necessary, if factories are to be kept open and the labourers to retain their incomes, to acquiesce in the active capitalist retaining a sufficient profit after meeting all the claims to rent and interest which fall directly upon industry, as well as his share in taxes levied on behalf of the creditors of the State.

Thus, while Trade Unionism can be a considerable force for the raising of wages at those stages of capitalist development at which there is a considerable profit-margin over and above the incentives necessary to the system, its power becomes narrowly limited, or valuable only in defence, when international competition reduces profit-margins, or for any other reason the prosperity of the active capitalist *entrepreneurs* tends to diminish. For even if the Trade Unions were in a position to enforce higher wages, they could then do so only at the cost of diminishing employment, and thus undermining their own bargaining power as well as depriving a section of the labourers of their incomes.

Even when, under systems of universal suffrage, the labourers invoke their political influence to aid their economic strength, the same limitations remain. If Capitalism is to go on providing them with incomes, they must consent to these incomes remaining low. Under Capitalism, it is always impossible for the working class to get more than a pint out of a quart pot.

Accordingly, exploitation of labour is not merely an accidental accompaniment of a particular phase of capitalist development, but always and everywhere inherent in the capitalist system. As long as the means of production are privately owned, the claims arising out of private ownership are bound to involve the exploitation of labour. For the capitalist recognition of the labourer's ownership of his labour-power is also by implication a denial of his right to the ownership of the product of his labour.

Of course, it is perfectly possible under Capitalism for a capitalist to labour and for one who labours to own property as well. Capitalists and labourers, as individuals, do not fall into perfectly distinct and isolable groups. In all capitalist Societies, many capitalists perform productive labour; and in highly developed capitalist Societies, a substantial number of labourers become small owners of property. In some capitalist Societies, there is a good deal of individual interchange between the two classes. But, from the standpoint of an analysis of Capitalism, these points are irrelevant, though they are important, as we have seen, in relation to problems of political and economic strategy. Whatever minglings and blurrings there may be, in every capitalist

Society capitalists and labourers exist as well marked and clearly distinct social classes, having different and contrasting economic functions and a radically different status. The labour class is none the less exploited as a class because some of its members, as small owners of capital, obtain some part in the fruits of the exploitation: nor is the capitalist class less an exploiting class because it includes active producers as well as passive *rentiers* and mere financial manipulators. Colours are none the less colours because they run into one another; good and bad are none the less opposites because they are often hard to disentangle. To deny the reality of economic classes under Capitalism is merely absurd; the analysis of their composition and changing detailed relationships belongs to the discussion not of the theory of value and exploitation, but of the strategy and tactics of social transformation.

CHAPTER IX

THE DIALECTIC—
CONCLUSION

FINALLY, we come to the question of Marx's method—Dialectical Materialism, as it is commonly called. There is, among professing Marxists, an extraordinary divergence of opinion about the value of this method, some regarding it as the corner-stone of the Marxian system, while others dismiss it as a tiresome fad of the master, who could never escape from the trammels of the Hegelianism of his youth. We shall have to ask which of these views is right, and to come down on the one side or the other—for in this matter there is no possibility of splitting the difference. The Dialectic is either Marx's strength, or his weakness; it cannot be a matter of no account whether it is right or wrong.

First, then, wherein does the Marxian dialectic consist? Like Hegel's Dialectic, it rests on a denial of the ultimate validity of the concepts of Formal Logic. The fundamental principle of Formal Logic is the exclusion of the contradictory. Within the categories of Formal Logic a thing cannot both be and not be, cannot be at once itself and that which it is not. Obviously, if reality is conceived as static, this standpoint of the logicians is correct. A thing incapable of change cannot both be and not be, and cannot be both itself and that which it is not. As long as we remain within the realm of the unchanging, Formal Logic holds the field.

But, as Marx and Hegel both insist, the realm of the static is not the world of reality. It is a world of abstractions, which can be static only because they are not real. The mind of man can make for itself static conceptions; but such conceptions can never adequately express real things. Every thing that is real is in constant process of change, is continually becoming something other than it was before. Reality never stands still, nor can man call a halt to it: all he can do to make it stand still is to make abstractions from it in his own mind—abstractions which he is then prone to mistake for the reality itself, or at least for a true and sufficient representation of reality.

As soon as this is admitted, the inadequacy of the categories of Formal Logic must be admitted too. For, of things that are in process of change, the exclusion of contradiction postulated by the logicians no longer holds good. A thing can be that which it is not; for it can change into something else. Indeed, it must do so, since by the very law of its being it cannot remain the same. Reality is not static but dynamic and evolutionary; and any Logic that sets out to explain the fundamental nature of things must partake of the same dynamic and evolutionary character. It cannot exclude contradiction: indeed, it must be based on admitting contradiction as a vital part of the law of development.

This the Hegelian Dialectic did, on the plane of the Idea. Hegel saw the universe as the expression of a divine Logic working itself out by a process of perpetual contradiction and conflict. All human history—and with that alone we are here concerned—spread itself out before him as a long process of ideal conflict, leading irresistibly towards the final exclusion of contradiction in the perfect self-realisation of the Universal Idea. The evolution of Societies upon the physical plane was but the derivative expression of this ideal process. What was happening in human history was not what seemed to happen, but the gradual and progressive actualisation of the reality immanent in the Absolute Idea. Everything was present in potentiality throughout the entire temporal process of development; but the potential could become actual only by means of the long struggle of the Idea towards self-realisation.

Thus, the understanding of the universe required a Logic of a different order from Formal Logic, which could fulfil the needs only of the secondary world of abstractions. Formal Logic had its due place in this world; but infinitely superior to it was the Dialectical Method which alone could give the clue to the understanding of reality. To this higher Logic the syllogism of Formal Logic, with its premisses and its conclusion based on the exclusion of contradiction, must needs be utterly inadequate. Instead of the syllogism the higher Logic required an appropriate form of its own, expressive of a dynamic process of becoming instead of a static condition of being. For major premiss, minor premiss, and conclusion Hegel accordingly substituted thesis, antithesis and synthesis, as the expressions fitted to be used in explaining the true rhythm of reality.

This is the basis of the Hegelian Dialectic of becoming and of conflict. In terms of human history, every phase of civilisation is a thesis, the embodiment of an incomplete and imperfect version of the Idea. But the incomplete necessarily suggests some part at least of what is needed to complete it. It suggests a contradictory phase, embodying a different facet or aspect of the Idea. Thus, the posing of any proposition, or the establishment of any institution, at once involves the posing of a rival proposition, or the establishment of a rival institution, based on a different conception of truth and value. Between these opposites a struggle is then bound to follow; for neither the human mind, nor human civilisation, can accept contradictions without an effort to resolve them. But out of this struggle of thesis and antithesis neither can emerge absolute victor. For the contest between them will necessarily, as they are not static but changing things, set up within themselves and within the universe in which they exist forces which will alter their character and the conditions of their conflict. In this process, reality and the institutions which reflect the advance of the Idea, will move on to a higher plane. Out of the struggle of thesis and antithesis will emerge a synthesis which is neither of the combatants, but embodies the valid elements in them both. This synthesis will thereupon become the thesis for a new conflict, evoking in turn its own antithesis, and so leading on to a new synthesis which embodies a yet higher validity. By these stages, repeated again and again, human history, reflecting the march of the Idea from potentiality to actuality, gradually approaches perfection.

Marx, of course, did not accept the Hegelian Dialectic; but he did build his own very different Dialectic upon Hegel's method. In Marx's conception, as in Hegel's, thesis, antithesis and synthesis replace and transcend the categories of Formal Logic, and reality is conceived in dynamic instead of static terms. What is, is becoming: nothing ever stands still in the real world.

Marx's real world, however, is very different from Hegel's; for it is nothing other than the phenomenal world of everyday experience. The things we experience in ordinary life are not, Marx holds, abstractions or derivative and imperfect expressions of a superior reality existing outside space and time, but ultimates beyond which we cannot and need not go—for beyond them there is nothing. They are reality—the one and only reality in which all thought, all ideas, all purely mental or spiritual constructions are built. Men can seek to understand this reality, and, what is more, to make themselves increasingly masters of its development. But they cannot go outside or beyond it; for it and nothing else is the universe in which they are. Being precedes thought; for thought can be only thought of being, and about being. There can be no perception without something to perceive; no conception without a mind to reflect upon experience of things. The external world is the external world, and not either an idea in our minds or a reflection of some ideal substance outside and beyond our experience.

But the real world of experience is not static. Nothing is static save the abstractions which men make in their own minds in their attempts to rationalise their experience. Everything changes: human history is the process of human change writ large in the common experience of mankind. In that Hegel was abundantly right; but as things are real, and not mere reflections of the Idea, the dynamic Logic which Hegel applied to the Idea must be applied directly to the things themselves, and used directly in explaining the course of historical movements. Things change. Things are continually becoming that which they were not, in the ordinary temporal process of human development. But by what law do they change? By the dialectical law of human conflict. What, then, are the nature and method of this historic law?

Since things, and not ideas, are the ultimate realities, things and not ideas must, it seems, be the ultimate motive forces of human history. But what things? Marx, as we have seen in earlier chapters, makes answer that the underlying forces of history are the changing "powers of production." As these expand with the increase in men's knowledge and opportunities, human history passes through corresponding phases of development. To each broad phase of development of the powers of production corresponds a phase of human evolution.

But where, in this presentation, are we to find the Hegelian dialectical process at work? The powers of production advance as men's knowledge and command over the forces of nature increase; but in this advance there appears so far no necessary element of conflict, save the perpetual conflict of man with the niggardliness and reluctance of natural forces. Clearly this is not Marx's conception, any more than it is Hegel's. The conflict of which Marx is thinking is a conflict between men, and not between mankind and nature. Where, then, are we to seek for the thesis, antithesis and synthesis which the Dialectic postulates?

THE BASIS OF THE MARXIAN DIALECTIC

Each stage reached by the powers of production, Marx holds, gives rise among men to a set of economic relationships designed to further their use; and to these economic relationships correspond appropriate political and social relationships which arise out of, and react upon, the economic conditions. We have been over this ground in an earlier chapter, and there is no need to go over it here again. Marx's point, as we have seen, is that these relationships necessarily range men in economic classes, and that it is between these classes that the struggles which make human history are waged. The thesis and the antithesis, according to Marx, are these classes; and the synthesis is the new class which arises out of the struggle of class against class at each turning point of history, up to the conflict which succeeds at length in establishing a classless Society, and therewith brings the dialectical process of class-conflict to an end.

We have seen already that this process cannot truly be regarded as "materialist," in the most familiar sense of that term, because the forces upon which the entire movement rests—the powers of production—are not forces of matter as opposed to mind, but embody the result of mind's action upon matter—man's command over nature, for short. For this reason Marx's Conception of History has been called in this book "Realist" rather than "Materialist." Still more clearly, the struggle by which the process of historical evolution is carried on is not one of matter with matter, in any sense in which matter can be contrasted with mind, but of men with men. It is a class-struggle, or rather a series of class-struggles which continues to its end in the total obliteration of class-distinctions and the establishment of a classless Society.

But what then becomes of the dialectical process? Clearly it cannot continue to obey the formula of class-struggle; for no classes remain in being. For the new phase of human history which then begins, and for the further phases that are to follow, a new formula is needed. "Pre-history ends," Marx writes, "and history begins." But what is to be the law of this new history of a classless world?

The Marxists' answer is that they do not know. For Marx held, as we have seen, that each age sets itself only the problems which it needs to solve, and is in a position to solve; and mankind is neither able nor in need to solve as yet the problems of the Socialist future. Clearly this need not mean that the Dialectic will no longer apply; for the law of the Dialectic admits of many different formulæ besides that of the class-struggle, and the formula may be changed without changing the dialectical character of the historical process. Struggle can proceed upon other planes than that of class, and in higher and less brutal forms. But what these forms will be the Marxist neither pretends nor even wishes to know in advance of the event. All he does pretend to know is that, whatever is to come after the winning of a classless Society, it is not in the nature of reality ever to become static and unchanging. As long as mankind exists, mankind will have a history, and that history will proceed dialectically, in some form.

Such is the Marxian theory. What, now, of its validity and of its value? It has, in the first place, the supreme merit, not always borne in mind by its professing adherents, that it absolutely excludes dogmatism. For, as it regards social ideas as the expression of class-attitudes, and classes themselves as corresponding to the continually changing powers of production, it must regard social ideas as subject to change and development as changes in the powers of production alter the class-structure of Society. If the structure of classes has changed since Marx's day, as I have tried to show that it has, the theory which Marx formulated as appropriate to the class-conditions of his day can no longer be adequate to meet the needs of the present time, at all events until it has been modified and adapted in conformity with these changes. Every Marxist is compelled by his Marxism to be a "Revisionist," though of course his Revisionism need not agree with that of Bernstein, or that of Sorel, or that of any of the other schools of thought which have in the past set out to adapt Marxism to current needs and conditions. It is, of course, easy under cover of revising Marxism really to abandon it; and this tendency has given all attempts at revision a bad odour among Marxists, and driven them towards a defensively dogmatic interpretation of Marx's doctrines. But, in fact, no Marxist can escape revisionism without denying the dialectical principle. For to lay down hard and fast dogmas is to fall back from the evolutionary Dialectic into the static categories of Formal Logic.

MARXISM AND THE CLASS-STRUGGLE

Marx's method is, indeed, fully as important as his doctrine. For it is at once an injunction to look again and again at the changing facts of the social situation, to relate them to the changing character of the powers of production, and to draw freshly at each stage of development the practical conclusions which this process of observation suggests. Some Marxists will doubtless object to this interpretation on the ground that the vital factors of social development change in essence only over long periods, corresponding to the entire span of the conflict between two rival classes, so that the essential character of the struggle between capitalists and proletariat can be expressed in a single comprehensive generalisation, which can become a dogmatic theory valid for the whole duration of the capitalist system, or at most needing only minor modifications in the province of Socialist tactics. Capitalists and proletariat, they will argue, are fixed economic classes, the denotation of which may vary from moment to moment, but not so as to affect their general character or the nature of the opposition between them. Accordingly, for the complete duration of the struggle between them the Marxian presentation holds good; and observation of changing facts can do nothing to modify any essential point, indispensable though it undoubtedly is as a guide to day-to-day strategy.

There is, of course, an element of truth in this view. The major antithetical relation of capitalists and proletariat does endure for the whole span of the capitalist system; and to this extent Marxism is and must be dogmatic. But for any correct development of Socialist strategy it is no less important to observe the variations within the general class-structure of capitalist Society than to grasp the fundamental antagonisms which it involves. In earlier chapters it has been argued that there have been in fact highly important variations in the arrangement of social classes, corresponding to the further evolution of the powers of production, since Marx formulated his doctrines; and it is a fatal error to ignore the significance of these variations, or to assume that they do not affect the correct formulation of the Marxian theory. For within the general antithetical relationship which exists in Society over a major phase of development there are many lesser relationships which possess a similar antithetical character. Nor do these result, though Marx often wrote as if they did, merely from the survival within capitalist society of obsolescent elements left over from an earlier phase. The most significant of them are, as we have seen, themselves products of an advancing Capitalism which has found the art of diffusing industrial ownership while continuing to concentrate the effective control of economic policy in fewer and fewer hands, and has created a large and influential class of salaried and fee-taking professionals who form the nucleus of a new *petite bourgeoisie* very different in character from the old, and infinitely superior in initiative, driving-force and power of resistance to the proletarians if it takes sides against them. To ignore or minimise the importance of these changes in the class-system is to be guilty of wilful blindness; and to recite in face of them an unrevised Marxian creed is to prefer a dogma to a workable policy of Socialist advance.

For it is evident that Marx was mistaken in supposing that the further advance of Capitalism would result in driving the entire intermediate element in Society down into the ranks of the proletariat, at any rate without an intervening phase in which this intermediate element would be powerful enough to make on its own behalf a bid for social and economic authority. Marx appears—very naturally—to have foreseen neither the extent to which the further advance of capitalist prosperity would, with the aid of joint stock structure and technical invention, swell the ranks both of the functionless small capitalist shareholders and of the active and functioning professional and technical groups, nor the form which their reaction to the threat of the decline and suppression of Capitalism was likely to take. If there had not been the great increase in the absolute and relative numbers of these two closely connected and overlapping groups, and the great advance in their incomes and status, which accompanied the growth of Capitalism in the half century preceding the Great War, the subsequent decline of Capitalism would doubtless have forced down more and more of the members of the intermediate groups into the proletariat, and have given them the attitude of proletarians. But in fact these groups, having achieved a great advance and become more and more conscious of their economic importance, receive the narrowing of their opportunities and incomes which the decline of Capitalism involves not with acquiescence in proletarianisation, but in a mood of revolt and determination to preserve or retrieve their economic and social superiority against the threat of Socialism. They are antagonistic to the large capitalists, and especially to high finance, which they blame for their economic adversities; but they do not become antagonistic to Capitalism itself. Indeed, they become determined to defend it at all costs against the exponents of equality, by reconstructing it on a basis which will subordinate the conduct of large-scale industry and finance to their own claims.

Marxism, as Marx expounded it, tacitly assumed that there could exist between the capitalists and the proletariat no class capable of winning power for itself, and creating a new social system in the image of its own needs. He assumed further that the scale of capitalist industry was bound to increase, and to lead to a growing concentration of capitalist power—wherein he was quite correct—and that the capitalist era would end when the great capitalists were no longer able to develop further the use of the powers of production, or to resist the claims of the advancing proletariat. This last view is, however, a far less obvious deduction to-day than it seemed in the light of the facts upon which Marx based his conclusions. For it is now indispensable to consider the possibility that the intermediate groups created and strengthened by the advance of Capitalism may be powerful enough for a time to defeat the proletariat, and to seize power for themselves.

Doubtless, they can hope to do this only if they are in a position to reconstruct Capitalism, or to construct a new type of Capitalism, upon a basis consistent with the further development of the powers of production. But it is illegitimate to exclude out of hand the possibility of this being done. It certainly cannot be done unless the new *petite bourgeoisie* is prepared to borrow, and to apply to its own ends, much of the technique and policy hitherto associated with the propaganda of Socialism. For assuredly the powers of production cannot be developed, or advantage taken of the modern possibilities for the expansion of the wealth-creating process, without a high degree of centralised control and operation of the productive and financial machine. The new Capitalism of the *petite bourgeoisie,* if it comes, will be to a great extent State Capitalism, under which industries and services will be operated on the grand scale under State influence and protection, whether they are in form nationalised or left in private hands, in the interests of the bondholding, shareholding and salaried elements in Society. Sorel, that courageous Marxian "revisionist," visualised this possibility in one of its forms, when he spoke of the possible alternative form of "State Capitalism." The Fascists and Nazis are now attempting to realise it in its other form, in which industries are left mainly in private ownership, but made subject in matters of policy to the overriding authority of the Corporative State.

It is, of course, true that this policy involves at the very outset a practical contradiction. For, if the middle groups are to be strong enough to seize power, the new *petite bourgeoisie* of *rentiers,* shareholders and salaried professionals must succeed in carrying along with it the surviving elements of the old *petite bourgeoisie* of small-scale traders and producers, including the farmers and peasant-owners engaged in small-scale agriculture. These latter groups, however, by no means desire an advance of large-scale production and State control, but still hanker after the destruction of their large-scale competitors and exploiters. Accordingly, Fascist movements present the paradox of appearing at once as the advocates of planned Capitalism, and as the enemies of centralised banking, large department and chain stores, large-scale merchanting, and even at times as the defenders of small-scale craft production against the encroachments of the machine. These reactionary elements of their programmes are, indeed, mostly window-dressing; and no serious attempt is likely to be made to carry them into effect if once the new *petite bourgeoisie* comes to power. But there is one important exception to this generalisation; for the Fascist Revolution, when it succeeds, is likely to find itself decisively committed to upholding the cause of the peasant, and therefore to maintaining the position of small-scale agriculture.

This one necessity is enough to drive Fascism in power to adopt a policy of Economic Nationalism, even apart from the fact that it has used nationalist sentiment as a means of defeating the internationalist aspirations of Socialism. Some Socialists, relying on the doctrines of orthodox Political Economy, hold that this necessity to pursue Economic Nationalism inescapably condemns the movement to failure, because it makes impossible the further development of the powers of production, which cannot be fully utilised except on a basis of expanding international exchange. This view is, however, for most large States, highly disputable. Undoubtedly, in order to secure the maximum production that is technically possible for the world as a whole, it is necessary to have a highly developed system of international exchange, based on the valid principle of comparative real costs. But in relation to the gross under-production characteristic of capitalist Society to-day it may be possible for a large country to add greatly to its output of goods and services by organising its economy to a substantial degree on a basis of national self-sufficiency and production for the domestic market. Economic Nationalism, while it is bound to be less productive from the standpoint of the world as a whole than a well organised economic internationalism, may thus offer to particular countries the prospect of greater wealth and prosperity than is possible for an unregulated Capitalism more dependent on the world market; and this possibility may suffice to give such a system a chance of establishing itself, at least for a time, on foundations sufficiently compatible with the development of the powers of production.

A new system organised on these lines in the interests of the *petite bourgeoisie* is likely to command the support, or at least the assent, of the majority of large capitalists, wherever this class finds itself to be in real danger of defeat by the forces of Socialism. For, while the acceptance of the new dictatorship involves the large capitalist in a certain loss of freedom and control, it is likely to enable him to retain for some time at least his wealth and a good deal of his power; and it offers him the compensation of destroying, what he has been quite unable to destroy, the organised power of the proletariat in those forms in which he has been most conscious of it as an employer. If he has to choose between Fascism and Socialism, there can be no shadow of doubt which he will choose; for the *petite bourgeoisie* threatens only to control him, without taking away his wealth, whereas the avowed aim of the Socialists is to do away with him altogether.

It is ludicrously unrealistic in face of possibilities such as these—already to a great extent made actual in two great countries—merely to go on reciting the Marxian *credo* about economic classes, as if Capitalism were still identical in its class-structure with the half-grown Capitalism of 1848. For matters are not so simple as to save all further thought when the fundamental antagonism between the capitalists and the proletariat has once been grasped; nor does the Dialectic serve its purpose once and for all in revealing the existence of this antagonism and pointing the way towards its resolution by means of Socialism. The picture of the class-struggle thus presented needs to be filled in; and the candid user of the dialectical method will keep his eyes wide open for changes in the class-structure of Society that may give him cause to modify his tactics and perhaps also his diagnosis of the social situation.

The real question, of course, is whether the new class of *petits bourgeois* that is now interposing itself between the *grande bourgeoisie* and the proletariat is capable of reconstructing the economic system on a broad enough foundation to give it a new lease of life without Socialism. We have seen reason to suppose that, by enlisting the spirit of Nationalism on its side, and also by coming to terms with the older type of *petit bourgeois* and with the peasants, the new intermediate class can for the time being do something to increase production and restore a limited prosperity on a basis of Economic Nationalism. But can this success, such as it is, last for long? If it can, then the road towards Socialism is likely to be far longer than Marx and his successors supposed; for in that case there can intervene between Capitalism, as we know it, and Socialism a whole new phase of social development, based on a system of State-controlled Capitalism under *petit bourgeois* influence.

What are the obstacles in the way of this reconstruction? The first is the hampering necessity of an alliance with the obsolescent elements in the *petite bourgeoisie* and with the peasants; for this is bound to check the growth of productive efficiency, and to mean that in most countries a policy of Economic Nationalism will involve high costs of living and of production. This obstacle can be overcome to the extent to which the victorious class is able, after its victory, to trample upon its late allies. But this can be done only with the support of other elements in the population, and especially of a section of the proletariat. The support of such a section, however, depends on the ability and intelligence of the victorious class to enforce the compliance of the great capitalists in a higher standard of living; for unless this is granted the main body of the proletariat is likely to remain sullen and aloof. If the victors do pursue this course, and take the side of the proletariat against the large capitalists, they will be unable to prevent the re-birth of the proletarian movement, however firmly they may have crushed it in the course of the initial struggle. But the proletariat, thus reorganised, will begin again to hanker after Socialism, for which the regime of State Capitalism will be necessarily preparing the way. The drive towards Socialism will thus be resumed in a new form; and under the changed conditions no fresh intermediate class is likely to be there to interpose itself between the combatants and turn their dissensions to its own profit. Unless Western civilisation collapses altogether, the advent of Socialism is likely under these circumstances to be only delayed and not prevented.

All this is on the assumption that the new *petite bourgeoisie* does prove powerful and alert enough to profit by the struggle between capitalists and proletariat so as to seize authority for itself. But that this will happen, over Western civilisation as a whole, is neither certain nor, perhaps, even probable. It has happened in Italy and Germany, in both cases under very special conditions; but on the other hand in Russia the proletariat has seized and held power in such a way as apparently to exclude all possibility of either a capitalist or a *petit bourgeois* counter-revolution—above all now that the Russians have carried through the collectivisation of agriculture as well as industry. In face of these two contrasted developments the outcome in other countries remains uncertain. The United States seems most likely, especially as no effective Socialist movement yet exists, to move towards a system dominated by the small middle class in alliance with the farmers, under some form of State-controlled Capitalism. France may succeed for some time yet, since she is less than most countries at the mercy of world forces, in maintaining her *petit bourgeois* Republic almost unchanged, except by the infusion of a growing element of State control. Finally, Great Britain may succeed in establishing a form of parliamentary Socialism which will leave large elements of Capitalism still in operation, and be distinguished from the systems dominated by the *petite bourgeoisie* less in its mechanism than in the nature of the forces which are in control.

THE OUTLOOK FOR SOCIALISM

This point demands elaboration. The chance of establishing Socialism by constitutional means in any country depends on the failure of all the other elements in the population to unite against the proletariat, and on the success of the proletariat in attaching some elements from other classes to its own cause. There is the best prospect of this where the economic conditions are such that the question of Socialism comes to a head while both the *petite bourgeoisie* and the proletariat are in general prosperous enough not to be driven by despair to extreme courses. For, under such conditions, both sides will be inclined to give and take. The Socialists will be prepared to ease the transition in order to prevent undue dislocation and to weaken opposition; and considerable elements in the middle groups may be prepared to tolerate the advent of Socialism provided that it comes without violence and without too much or too sudden upsetting of their accustomed ways of life. Even a considerable number of the technicians and professional men, who form the key elements in the *petite bourgeoisie,* may be ready to welcome and help Socialism if it can come in this form.

This possibility, as we have seen, makes it a vitally important matter for the Socialist appeal to be cast in such a form as to attract these doubtful elements, provided only that the attempt to do this is not made by watering down the Socialist policy. This watering down would defeat its own ends; for the Socialist policy can appeal only if it does offer a workmanlike solution consistent with the successful development of the powers of production; and this is impossible unless it is thorough-going in its methods and objectives. The Socialists can afford to do everything that is possible to minimise the hardships and dislocations of the transition; but they cannot on any account afford to demand less than plenitude of power over the entire economic system.

In Great Britain and in other countries of Western Europe the chance of a constitutional transition to Socialism still exists. But its continued existence depends on the persistence of conditions which do not drive the contending parties to the unrestrained extremism of despair. If a large part of the British proletariat were to go Communist, or a large part of the British middle class Fascist, the possibility of getting Socialism by constitutional methods would disappear; and the serious development of extremism on either side would inevitably lead to a parallel growth on the other. The reason why there has not been a large-scale growth of either Communism or Fascism as yet lies simply in the relative solidity and prosperity of the countries concerned, partly as a result of the huge accumulations on which they are able to fall back. The loss of the revenue from overseas investments, or a large further setback of British trade, might speedily alter the entire political situation in Great Britain. The hope, therefore, of a constitutional victory of Socialism in Great Britain depends on British prosperity surviving long enough for it to be won. It would be swept away in an instant if Great Britain ceased to be able to maintain her hold on the world market.

But where, it may be asked, in all this discussion of class-changes and national policies, is the Marxian Dialectic? Very much with us all the time; for, as throughout the book, the Dialectic is being explained by actually employing it. To those who cannot see this, I despair of explaining it by further words. I even refuse to make the Dialectic, any more than the rest of the Marxian system, into a dogma. I find that it helps me to think in dialectical terms, rather than in the terms of Formal Logic, about the factors of social development; and I feel that it ought to help others. But, if it does not help them, even after they have tried it, there is no more to be said; for no one can think outside his nature, and I know that the processes of thought go on very differently in different people. A man can think realistically without the Dialectic, though I am sure he cannot if his thinking is shut up within the categories of Formal Logic. With this caution, let him think in the way that suits him best; but, if he wants to understand his Marx, he will have, even though he reject the Dialectic, to make himself master enough of it to understand the form in which

Marx actually thought. Failure to do this has been responsible, as we have seen throughout this book, for much supposed refutation of Marxism that is merely beside the point, as well as for a tendency, among undialectical Marxists, to make of Marxism a dead dogma instead of a living source of fresh observation and inference. Having said that, and presented in this book my conception of what Marxism really means, I can only ask the reader, if he is in any doubt, to go and study for himself what Marx wrote, and not merely what others have written about him.

A NOTE ON BOOKS

I DO not propose to append to this book any large bibliography of Marxian writings, which are, except in Great Britain, almost coextensive with the literature of modern Socialism. It is enough to give references to the most important of Marx's own works, and to those of his collaborator, Engels, with only a very few books expository or critical of his doctrines.

Among Marx's own writings, pride of place must be given to his *magnum opus, Capital*. This consists, apart from supplementary studies, of three volumes. The first of these, *Capitalist Production,* originally published in 1867, is now available, translated by Eden and Cedar Paul, in Everyman's Library (2 volumes), with an introduction by me. There is also a larger edition of the same translation, and also an older translation, by S. Moore and E. Aveling, edited by Engels himself. This was the only volume of *Capital* published by Marx himself. The remaining volumes were edited by Engels after his death. Vol. II., *Capitalist Circulation,* is available in a translation by E. Untermann, originally issued in America. It is important for students of the details of Marx's economic theories, but far less important for most readers than Vol. III. Vol. II. was left by Marx in a fairly finished state, whereas Vol. III., *Capitalist*

Production as a Whole, was put together by Engels from many papers written at very different dates. It is less a book than a vitally important quarry for the Marxian student. Without it, Marx's theory of value cannot be fully understood—especially in relation to the connection between value and price; and it contains most of Marx's doctrines on such questions as the causes of capitalist crises and the changing class-divisions in capitalist Society. It is available in E. Untermann's translation, published only in the United States.

There have been several attempts to summarise *Capital* in a single volume. By far the best of these is Julian Borchardt's *The People's Marx,* translated by S. Trask. A useful volume of selections from *Capital* and other writings, edited by Max Eastman, has been published in the United States in the *Modern Library.*

As a pendant to *Capital,* invaluable to students of Marx's economic theories is his posthumous book, *Theorien über den Mehrwert,* also available in French as *Histoire des Doctrines Économiques.* This contains Marx's detailed studies of the theories of the classical economists, especially Ricardo, and throws indispensable light on the formation of his own economic doctrines. Of Marx's other definitely economic writings the most important is his *Critique of Political Economy,* published in 1859, eight years before Vol. I. of *Capital.* This is available in an American translation by N. I. Stone. Apart from its importance in economic theory, it contains in the preface (and also in a draft introduction found among Marx's papers after his death, and published as an appendix in the American edition) the only direct exposition he ever made of the Materialist Conception of History and his method of ar-

riving at it. These few pages are quite indispensable for anyone who wants to grasp the essential foundations of Marxism.
They should be read together with the *Communist Manifesto*
of 1848, by Marx and Engels, the earliest clear formulation of
Marxism as a system. The *Manifesto* is available in many editions. The fullest is that of D. Ryazonoff, which makes a stout
volume of over 350 pages, with elaborate notes and comments.

Students of the Materialist Conception of History and of the
philosophical basis of Marxism will also need to read *The
Poverty of Philosophy,* Marx's answer to Proudhon, published
in 1847 and available in an English translation by H. Quelch.
If they can read German, they should also read Marx's *Theses
über Feuerbach* (best text in *Marx-Engels Archives,* Vol. I.,
published by the Marx-Engels Institute at Moscow), and the
two volumes, *Aus dem literarischen Nachlass von Marx, Engels
und Lassalle,* edited by F. Mehring, Marx's biographer. For
English readers, some of Marx's early writings are available
in *Selected Essays by Karl Marx,* translated by H. J. Stenning.

For Marx's views on the State and on Socialist policy, the
best introduction is Marx's *Critique of the Gotha Programme,*
written in 1875 as an attack on the policy of his German followers in connection with the fusion of the Marxian and Las-
sallian Socialist parties in Germany, and suppressed at the
time by the German leaders. It is available in an English edition. With this should be read *The Civil War in France* (written in English), originally published as a manifesto of the
First International on the fall of the Paris Commune—a most
important book for the understanding of Marx's political attitude. His views of Socialist strategy, especially in relation to
the position of the *petite bourgeoisie,* should also be studied
in his earlier works, *The Class-Struggle in France* (not avail-

able in English, but in either German or French) and *The Eighteenth Brumaire of Napoleon Bonaparte* (translated by E. and C. Paul) and also in *Germany: Revolution and Counter-Revolution* (English translation available), which was written for Marx by Engels. These three books deal with the revolutionary and counter-revolutionary movements of 1848 and the following years.

Of Marx's other writings, two important pamphlets may be mentioned here. These are *Value, Price and Profit* (1865) and *Wage-Labour and Capital* (1849), both important for the development of his economic doctrines. For the student of Marxism there is an immense wealth of material in the volumes of his *Correspondence,* including the long series of letters which passed between him and Engels (available in German or French), and his letters to Sorge and Kugelmann. Some of Marx's other writings (*Herr Vogt,* 3 vols., *Œuvres Philosophiques,* 3 vols., *Œuvres Politiques,* 8 vols.) are available in French as well as German. A complete French edition of the writings of Marx and Engels is now in course of publication.

Of the works of Engels, the most important are his *Condition of the Working Class in England in 1844* (translated by F. K. Wischnewetzky), his *Origin of the Family, Property and the State* (available in English), his *Peasant War in Germany* (translated by M. S. Olgin), and his *Anti-Duehring,* of which a complete English translation has been announced. A part of *Anti-Duehring* is available in an American translation, under the title *Landmarks of Scientific Socialism,* translated by A. Lewis, and in another partial version, *The Development of Socialism from Utopia to Science* (various pamphlet editions). See also another pamphlet, *Historical Materialism,* and Engels' book on *Feuerbach* (not yet in English).

The standard life of Marx is by F. Mehring (not in English). In English, a useful short book is Max Beer, *The Life and Teaching of Karl Marx,* and the best life that of O. Ruhle, *Karl Marx* (translated by E. and C. Paul). See also D. Ryazonoff, *Karl Marx and Friedrich Engels.*

Of many books about Marx, I select a very few. First, small critical works include *Karl Marx,* by A. Loria (translated by E. and C. Paul), *Karl Marx's Capital,* by A. D. Lindsay, *Historical Materialism and the Economics of Karl Marx,* by Benedetto Croce (translated by C. M. Meredith). For Marxian philosophy, see G. Plekhanov, *Fundamental Principles of Marxism,* and S. Hook, *Towards the Understanding of Karl Marx.* For a criticism from the standpoint of orthodox economics, see F. Böhm-Bawerk, *Karl Marx and the Close of his System.* For a "Trotskyite" interpretation, see Max Eastman, *Marx, Lenin and the Science of Revolution.* Lenin's own writings, especially *The State and Revolution, The Proletarian Revolution,* and *Imperialism,* are all of primary importance. See also Lenin's *Materialism and Empirio-Criticism* for Marxist philosophy. N. Bucharin's *Historic Materialism* is disappointing. Of works not in English, G. Sorel's *La Décomposition du Marxisme* is exceedingly interesting from a Syndicalist standpoint, and Arturo Labriola's *Karl Marx* (in Italian or French) is one of the best critical expositions.

INDEX

i